T0192608

Think Like a UX Researcher

How to Observe Users, Influence Design, and Shape Business Strategy

Think Like a UX Researcher

How to Observe Users, Influence Design, and Shape Business Strategy

David Travis

Philip Hodgson

CRC Press
Taylor & Francis Group
Boca Raton London New York

CRC Press is an imprint of the
Taylor & Francis Group, an **Informa** business

CRC Press
Taylor & Francis Group
6000 Broken Sound Parkway NW, Suite 300
Boca Raton, FL 33487-2742

© 2019 by Taylor & Francis Group, LLC
CRC Press is an imprint of Taylor & Francis Group, an Informa business

No claim to original U.S. Government works

Printed on acid-free paper

International Standard Book Number-13: 978-1-138-36529-2 (Paperback)
International Standard Book Number-13: 978-1-138-36535-3 (Hardback)

Visit the Taylor & Francis Web site at
http://www.taylorandfrancis.com

and the CRC Press Web site at
http://www.crcpress.com

Contents

Acknowledgments

Many of our colleagues have provided insight, ideas, and comments on the essays in this volume. In alphabetical order, we would like to thank Nigel Bevan, David Hamill, Miles Hunter, Caroline Jarrett, John Knight, Beth Maddix, Rolf Mohlich, Ali Vassigh, and Todd Zazelenchuk. We are indebted to Gret Higgins and Lynne Tan for help in proof-reading and curating the essays. Any remaining errors are, of course, ours.

We are also indebted to the hundreds of UX researchers who signed up at our website, uxresearchbook.com, and helped shape decisions on everything from the book's content to the cover design. Your comments and opinions helped us improve the book, and we hope that you're as proud of the final result as we are.

Finally, we would also like to thank our many students and clients who have asked us difficult questions over the years. Those questions made us think like a UX Researcher and led directly to many of the essays in this book.

Introduction

Currently, user experience (UX) researchers are in an enviable situation. There are many more jobs than people suitably trained to fill them. Practitioners are swamped with work. This has obvious advantages—but it comes with its own share of problems.

Not least of these problems is the difficulty of maintaining one's own area of expertise by staying up to date with best practice and new ideas.

We know from the training courses we deliver to UX researchers that many are too busy (and may feel too knowledgeable) to read a comprehensive, introductory text on user experience. In fact, if you're like us, you probably have more than one UX book on your shelves that you started but couldn't finish.

That's why UX researchers turn to shorter articles and blog posts to keep their knowledge fresh. But blog posts aren't curated. It's not clear how they fit together because they lack the kind of structure imposed by a book. And they vary in quality—both in the quality of the content and the quality of the writing.

With printed books feeling overwhelming and the quality of blog posts being too variable, it's not clear what UX researchers are meant to do to stay current.

This book aims to bridge the gap by providing user experience content that is authoritative but at the same time easily digestible. It contains a series of essays on UX research. Although you could read the book from cover to cover, we have planned the book on the assumption that you will dip in and out of it, somewhat like a bedside or coffee-break reader. Think of it as a launch pad for UX research ideas. But if you prefer to read linearly, we've organized the chapters (and the sequence of essays within each chapter) to build upon each other.

This Book Is Not Just for UX Researchers

Who should read this book?

- UX researchers who want inspiration and stimulation in various aspects of their craft. If that's you, dip in anywhere—but especially Chapters 1 through 4.
- Project owners and Scrum masters who want to stimulate discussion of UX research with their development team. If that's you, turn to any essay in this book and pick a discussion question (you'll find these at the end of every essay in a section titled "Think Like a UX Researcher").
- Designers who want to get user feedback on a new product idea or a prototype. If that's you, turn to the essays in Chapter 3 to avoid many of the common bloopers in UX research.
- Business analysts and marketing managers who want to persuade development teams, senior managers and stakeholders to take action on the results of UX research. If that's you, review the essays in Chapter 5.
- Anyone who wants to build a career in user experience. We wrote the essays in Chapter 6 just for you.

In a Nutshell

The book has six chapters. The first chapter contains some introductory essays that set the stage for the later parts of the book. It covers topics such as the kinds of question you can answer with UX research, common mistakes made by practitioners, and how to apply psychology to UX research.

Chapter 2 covers the planning and preparation phase of UX research. The essays in this section will help you decide if UX research is needed on a project, and if so what kind of research to do. It will help you take the first steps with your research, for example in deciding what kinds of participants to include.

Chapter 3 focuses on conducting UX research. This is where you engage with users and observe them working in either natural or controlled environments. It is the phase of research in which you collect data. The essays in this chapter will help you gain informed consent from your research participants, run an ethnographic interview and avoid common usability testing mistakes.

Chapter 4 discusses data analysis: the process of turning raw data into a story. This is where the meaning of your findings, and the insights and "Aha!" moments, start to emerge. It's the "So what?" of a UX research study.

Chapter 5 describes how to persuade people to take action on the results of your UX research. This chapter will help you confidently stand your ground with development team members critical of UX research. The chapter covers both persuading the development team and persuading senior managers and stakeholders.

The final chapter of the book aims to help organizations build a user experience team and help you build a career in user experience. With guidance for both new UX researchers and people who have been in the field for some time, these essays will help you evaluate, improve, and present your skills.

This book has been several years in the making, since each of the essays started life as an article on the Userfocus website. One benefit of this is that while writing the book we have been able to engage with other UX researchers to discover what works, what is confusing and what content is missing from those earlier drafts. In a very real sense, the essays in this book have been through the same build-measure-learn cycle that we encourage design teams to follow.

How to Think Like a UX Researcher

In addition to re-writing the essays and curating them for this volume, we have added a section at the end of each essay titled, "Think Like a UX Researcher." This section contains five questions and its aim is to encourage you to reflect on how you can apply the thoughts, issues and ideas in the essay to your current user experience role. Some of these thinking prompts contain an outline of a workshop topic that you can run with your team to help them become more user centered.

As well as helping you reflect on the topic of the essay, you'll also find these questions helpful in preparing for competency-based job interviews.

What We Mean by "UX Research"

Perhaps because user experience is a nascent field, different practitioners use different terms to describe the same thing.

UX research is one of those terms. We are aware that some practitioners prefer the term *user research,* arguing that everyone on the development team is responsible for user experience, not just the UX researcher.

Although we agree with the philosophy that user experience is everyone's responsibility, we have still decided to use the term UX research throughout this book. User research implies a focus on users only; in contrast, UX research encourages practitioners and stakeholders to take a more strategic view and focus on what really matters: the user's experience. This term also reflects the reality of the work: The best practitioners study users but they also research their users' goals, their users' environments and the business context of the product—indeed, anything that affects a user's experience with a product or service.

1

Setting the Stage

The Seven Deadly Sins of UX Research

Most companies would claim to design products and services that are simple to use. But when you ask customers to actually use these products and services, they often find them far from simple. Why is there a disconnect between what organizations think of as "simple" and what users actually experience?

It's fashionable to blame poor usability on firms not doing enough user research. On the face of it, this seems like the obvious cause of poor usability. If firms only did the research, they would realize their product was a dud. But, like most obvious reasons, it's wrong.

In reality, there's never been a better time to be a purveyor of UX research tools. Every organization seems to want to "take the temperature" of their customers. Take a quick look in your email junk folder at the number of times you've been asked to complete a survey over the last month. If it's like ours, it will number in the double digits.

The problem isn't with the *quantity* of UX research. It's with the *quality*: organizations struggle to distinguish good UX research from bad UX research.

Here are seven examples of poor UX research practice that we've come across in our work with clients—along with some ideas on how to fix them.

- Credulity.
- Dogmatism.
- Bias.
- Obscurantism.
- Laziness.
- Vagueness.
- Hubris.

Credulity

The dictionary defines credulity as a state of willingness to believe something without proper proof. The form this takes in UX research is asking users what they want (and believing the answer).

A couple of months ago, David was attending a usability study on behalf of a client. He was there because the client thought that the usability tests they were running were not delivering much predictive value. The client was concerned they weren't recruiting the right kind of people or maybe the analysis wasn't right.

As David sat in the observation room, he watched the administrator show three alternative designs of a user interface to the participant and ask: "Which of these three do you prefer? Why?"

Asking people what they want is very tempting. It has obvious face validity. It seems to make sense.

But it's also wrong.

Here's why. Over 40 years ago,[1] psychologists Richard Nisbett and Timothy Wilson carried out some research outside a bargain store in Ann Arbor, Michigan.

The researchers set up a table outside the store with a sign that read, "Consumer Evaluation Survey—Which is the best quality?" On the table were four pairs of ladies' stockings, labelled A, B, C and D from left to right.

Most people (40%) preferred D, and fewest people (12%) preferred A.

On the face of it, this is just like the usability test David observed.

But there's a twist. All the pairs of stockings were identical. The reason most people preferred D was simply a position effect: The researchers knew that people show a marked preference for items on the right side of a display.

But when the researchers asked people why they preferred the stockings that they chose, no one pointed to the position effect. People said their chosen pair had a superior denier, or more sheerness or elasticity. The researchers even asked people if they may have been influenced by the order of the items, but of course people looked at the researchers like they were crazy. Instead, people confabulated: they made up plausible reasons for their choice.

There's an invisible thread joining the study by Nisbett and Wilson and the usability test we've just described. The reason we call the thread "invisible" is because few UX researchers seem to be aware of it—despite the fact that there's a whole sub-discipline of psychology called Prospect Theory[2] devoted to it—and that Daniel Kahneman won a Nobel prize for exploring the effect.

People don't have reliable insight into their mental processes, so there is no point asking them what they want.

This quotation from Rob Fitzpatrick[3] captures it perfectly: "Trying to learn from customer conversations is like excavating a delicate archaeological site. The truth is down there somewhere, but it's fragile. While each blow with your shovel gets you closer to the truth, you're liable to smash it into a million little pieces if you use too blunt an instrument."

How can we overcome this problem?

Our definition of a successful UX research study is one that gives us actionable and testable insights into users' needs. It's no good asking people what they like or dislike, asking them to predict what they would do in the future, or asking them to tell us what other people might do.

The best way of gaining actionable and testable insights is not to ask, but to observe. Your aim is to observe for long enough that you can make a decent guess about what's going on. Asking direct questions will encourage people to make things up, not tell you what is actually going on.

There are two ways to observe. We can observe how people solve the problem now. Or we can teleport people to a possible future and get them using our solution (a prototype) to see where the issues will arise.

The key point is: What people say is not as useful as what people do, because people are unreliable witnesses.

Dogmatism

Dogmatism is the tendency to lay down principles as undeniably true, without consideration of evidence or the opinions of others. The form this takes in UX research is believing there is one "right" way to do research.

We're sure you've worked with people who think that a survey is "the right way" to understand user needs. Perhaps because we hear about surveys every day in the news, people tend to think of them as being more reliable or useful. The notion of using an alternative method, like a field visit or a user interview, doesn't have the same face validity because the sample size is comparatively small.

But sadly, having a large number of respondents in a survey will never help you if you don't know the right questions to ask. That's where field visits and user interviews come in.

Field visits and user interviews are a great way to get insights into your users' needs, goals and behaviors. But these aren't the only solution either.

Recently, we worked with a UX researcher who seemed to think there was no room for any research method other than user interviews. To validate personas, run more user interviews. To identify your top tasks, run more user interviews. To compare two alternative landing pages, run more user interviews.

This kind of dogmatism is unhelpful.

Field visits and user interviews give you signposts, not definitive answers. It's broad-brush stuff, a bit like the weather forecast. There may be some patterns in the data, but these aren't as useful as the conversation you have with users and the things you observe them do. It's those conversations that help you identify the gap between what people say and what they do—and that is often a design opportunity.

But there comes a point when you need to validate your findings from field visits and user interviews by triangulation: the combination of methodologies in the study of the same phenomenon. Quantitative data tell us *what* people are doing. Qualitative data tell us *why* people are doing it. The best kind of research combines the two kinds of data. For example, you might choose a survey to validate personas you've developed through field visits. Or you might choose multivariate A/B testing to fine tune a landing page that you've developed by usability testing.

Triangulation is like having different camera angles in a movie. It would be hard to understand the full picture of what is going on in a movie if every frame was shot as a close-up. Similarly, it would be difficult to empathize with the characters if every image was shot as a wide angle view. Like movies, you want your research to show the close-ups but you also want to see the bigger picture.

Bias

Bias means a special influence that sways one's thinking, especially in a way considered to be unfair.

UX research is a continual fight against bias. There are a handful of different kinds of bias that matter in UX research, but it's response bias we want to discuss here. This is caused by the way in which you collect data.

Sometimes the bias is obvious. For example, if you ask poor questions you're likely to get participants to tell you what you want to hear. You can correct this bias by teaching people to ask the right questions. But there's an even more pernicious type of response bias that's much harder to correct. This happens when the development team carries out the research and find that people don't really have a need for the product or service. It's tempting to hide this from senior managers because no one wants to be the purveyor of bad news. But if there's no need for your product, there's no point trying to convince senior managers that there is—you'll be found out in the end. It's a bad idea to cherry pick the results to support what a senior manager wants to hear.

You shouldn't approach interviews with a vested interest: The UX researcher's job isn't to convince people to use a service, or to get the results management want; it's about digging for the truth. This doesn't mean you shouldn't have a point of view. You should. Your point of view should be to help the development team understand the data, not just tell the development team what they want to hear.

Obscurantism

Obscurantism is the practice of deliberately preventing the full details of something from becoming known. The form this sin takes in UX research is keeping the findings in the head of one person.

UX research is often assigned to a single person on a team. That person becomes the spokesperson for user needs, the team's "expert" on users. This approach is a poor way to do research, and not just because the UX researcher doesn't know all the answers. The reason it fails is because it encourages the development team to delegate all responsibility for understanding users to one person.

One way you can prevent this sin on your own project is to encourage everyone on the team to get their "exposure hours." Research[4] shows that the most effective development teams spend at least two hours every six weeks observing users (for example, in field visits or usability tests).

What you're aiming for here is building a user centered culture. You do that by encouraging the whole development team to engage with users. But you also need to design iteratively. And that takes us to our next sin.

Laziness

Laziness is the state of being unwilling to exert oneself. The form this takes in UX research is in recycling old research data as if it's boilerplate that can be cut and pasted into a new project.

Our favorite example of this comes from the world of personas.

We find that clients often approach the process of developing personas as a one-time activity. They will hire an outside firm to do field research with the requisite number of users. That firm will analyze the data and create a set of beautifully presented personas. Now we already know this is a bad idea because of the sin of Obscurantism. We want the development team doing the research, not an external firm.

But let's ignore that issue for a moment. The reason we're using personas as an example here is because we are often asked by a client if they can re-use their personas. They are now working on a new project, which has a passing resemblance to one on which they developed personas last year. Since their customers are basically the same, isn't it OK to recycle the existing personas?

This idea so misses the point of what UX research is about that it serves as a good example.

Here's a secret many people don't know: *you don't need to create personas to be user centered.* User centered design is not about personas. In fact, personas really don't matter. Creating personas should never be your goal—understanding users' needs, goals and motivations should be your goal. In some ways, a set of beautifully formatted personas is just proof that you met with users, in the same way that a selfie with a celebrity proves you were at the same restaurant.

The world you want to move to is one where the development team knows its users so well that personas aren't needed. You don't get to this world by recycling old research. You do it by making UX research part of the culture.

We've known for a long time now that you achieve user centered design by iteration: you build something, you measure its usability, you learn from it and you redesign. Re-using old data, whether it's in the form of personas, usability tests or field visits, is not iterating—and it's certainly not learning.

Vagueness

Vagueness means not clearly or explicitly stated or expressed. In terms of UX research, we see it when a team fails to focus on a single key research question and instead tries to answer several questions at once.

This sin is partly caused by the sin of laziness. If you do research only occasionally, you need to answer lots of questions. This means you end up learning a little about a lot. In fact, you can learn an important lesson about UX research from a dishwasher. If you cram a lot in, nothing gets very clean.

With UX research, you actually want to learn a lot about a little. That "little" question is the specific question that's keeping you up at night. To uncover this question, we ask the development team to imagine the most useful, actionable research results possible. What would they tell us? How would we use them?

Everyone on the team should agree on the questions you plan to answer and the assumptions you plan to test. These top questions should be the drivers of every research activity.

This means you need to get specific with your research questions: you should be able to articulate your research questions on a couple of small sticky notes.

In fact, that leads us to an interesting exercise you can do to discover your research question.

Sit the development team in a room. Give each person a set of sticky notes. Tell them to imagine that we have an all-knowing, insightful user outside the room who will answer truthfully any question we throw at them.

What questions would they ask?

We get the team to write one question per sticky note. After five minutes, we work as a team to affinity sort the sticky notes. Then we dot-vote on the group of questions that are most urgent to answer. This idea works well because we not only identify the high-level theme but we also have a list of the specific questions to which we need to get answers.

Hubris

Last but not least we have Hubris. Hubris means extreme pride or self-confidence.

In UX research, it takes the form of taking undue pride in your reports. All UX researchers suffer from this to some extent, but those with PhDs are the worst. And we say that as proud recipients of a PhD.[5]

UX researchers love data. And when you love something, you want to share it with people. So you create detailed reports packed with graphs and quotations and screenshots and callouts. Look at my data! Look at how beautiful it is!

Sadly, few other people are as fascinated by data as we are. Our challenge is to turn that data into information, and turn that information into insight.

There are two problems with excessive detail.

People don't read the report. They turn the page, see more data, appreciate how clever you are, get bored, move on.

Overly detailed reports delay the design process. You don't need to do extensive analyses in a spreadsheet to find the top problems. That analysis is useful later, when you want to dig into the details, but the critical findings need to be fed back quickly. This is so the design can be modified and so the build-measure-learn cycle can continue.

Instead, you need to create information radiators (like usability dashboards and one-page test plans) to get teams understanding the data so they can take action on it. Information radiators are essentially advertising billboards that gradually permeate the team's awareness of your results. As a general rule, if people need to turn the page, your report is too long. So ask yourself: how can we capture the results in a single glance?

This could be a concise visual way of presenting research data, like a user journey map, a persona, or a usability testing results dashboard.

What Does Good UX Research Look Like?

As we've reviewed these sins, you may have noticed that many of them appear to have a common cause: the root cause is an organizational culture that can't distinguish good UX research from bad UX research.

Companies say they value great design. But they assume that to do great design they need a rock star designer. But great design doesn't live inside designers. It lives inside your users' heads. You get inside your users heads by doing good UX research: research that provides actionable and testable insights into users' needs.

Great design is a symptom. It's a symptom of a culture that values user centered design. Bad design is a symptom too. It's a symptom of an organization that can't distinguish good UX research from bad UX research.

And perhaps that's the deadliest sin of them all.

THINK LIKE A UX RESEARCHER

- Think of a recent project you worked on where UX research failed to deliver the expected business benefits. Were any of the "seven sins" a likely cause? If you could return to the beginning of that project, what would you do differently?
- We introduce the notion of "information radiators" in this essay: an at-a-glance summary of UX research findings. Thinking of the last UX research you carried out, how might you present the findings on a single sheet of paper?
- We talk about the difficulty of delivering bad news to senior managers. What prevents your organization hearing bad news? How can you help your organization learn from its mistakes?
- Every UX researcher has their favorite UX research method, be it a field visit, a usability test or a survey. This becomes a problem when you use the same tool to answer every research question. Identify your favorite and least favorite UX research methods and question if this "favoritism" affects your practice. Identify two research methods you would like to learn more about.
- We define a successful UX research study as one that gives us actionable and testable insights into users' needs. What makes an insight "testable"?

Think Like a Detective

In this essay we take a close look at what UX researchers can learn from the investigative methods used by detectives. And, in the spirit of all the best whodunnits, we arrive at an important conclusion: if you want to become a better researcher you should think like a detective.

The similarities between a good researcher and a good detective are quite striking. Maybe this is not a surprise as both disciplines involve investigation, both seek to establish a trail of evidence and both use that evidence to arrive at the solution to a problem. But it goes further. The knowledge required, the skills and experience needed and the methods and techniques used also have much in common. In fact, it is not stretching things at all to say that detective work actually is research and that research actually is detective work.

So what can we learn about doing UX research from the greatest detective of them all—Sherlock Holmes?

Holmes was an investigator par excellence, but he was not a super hero (he did not have super powers). Instead, he had well-honed skills and specialist knowledge about a few things. And he was nothing if not methodical. His method comprised these five steps:

- Understand the problem to be solved.
- Collect the facts.
- Develop hypotheses to explain the facts.
- Eliminate the least likely hypotheses to arrive at the solution.
- Act on the solution.

These steps will already feel familiar to UX researchers. So, we'll alternate between wearing our deerstalker and our UX researcher's hat as we take a look at what each of Holmes' steps can teach us about doing good UX research.

Understand the Problem to Be Solved

"I never guess. It is a shocking habit—destructive to the logical faculty."
The Sign of Four (1890).

This may seem like an odd question, but bear with us: What gets you excited the most and which do you find the most interesting to think about: questions or answers?

Admittedly, we strive for answers in most walks of life and certainly as UX researchers we are expected to be able to find out things. But really, it's no contest: questions are inherently more interesting to researchers than are answers. Questions are full of mystery and possibilities and can take your thinking in new and unexpected directions. Answers have a habit of bringing everything to a halt, rather in the way that discovering how an amazing magic trick really works extinguishes interest in the subject. Answers are important but a good researcher is already wondering what the next question is. Holmes would base his decision whether to accept a case on whether the question presented a sufficiently intriguing problem.

In the world of product development, the converse often holds true as a premium is put on answers and solutions. Indeed, in the corporate world "solutions" has become such an overused buzzword that it has practically lost all meaning. Solutions should never be the starting point for an investigation. The cost of focusing too early on product solutions, as many development teams do, is that you quickly lose sight of the problem you are trying to solve. Sherlock Holmes resisted leaping to solutions, arguing[6]: "It is a capital mistake to theorize before one has data. Insensibly one begins to twist facts to suit theories, instead of theories to suit facts."

Holmes always started each case by focusing on the problem. The problem would sometimes arrive in the form of a letter, sometimes as an item in the newspaper, but most often it would announce itself by a knock at the door. The client would present a mystery to Holmes and he would probe the client for salient information. He would bring to bear his considerable knowledge on the topic, recalling prior cases and finding out all he could about the likely protagonists. Holmes never relied on guesswork or on assumptions. For Holmes, each new case was unique and what mattered were reliable and verifiable facts about the case. These gave the investigation an initial focus and direction.

Here are some things we can learn from Holmes's approach that can help our UX research thinking:

- Focus on the problem not the solution.
- Create an explicit research question (actually write it down with a question mark at the end).
- Don't start doing any research until you have this question.
- Don't assume the question has never been asked before.
- Find out what your colleagues and your company already knows.
- Do an archival search—start by reading any prior research reports.
- Interview team members and stakeholders.
- Use a checklist to collect background information in a systematic manner.
- Leave nothing to guesswork.

Collect the Facts

"I am glad of all details ... whether they seem to you to be relevant or not."
The Adventure of the Copper Beeches (1892).

For Holmes, the seemingly unimportant aspects of a crime scene and the minutiae of the case were vital. From small clues, large inferences can often be drawn.

Although Holmes made skillful use of questioning, he knew that relying on people to accurately report what they may have seen or heard, or what they know and think, is an unreliable approach to investigation. Opinions are not facts and speculation is not evidence. Instead, his primary method of collecting facts was careful observation[7]: "You know my method, Watson. It is founded upon the observation of trifles."

Observation is essential to UX research. When used in field visits it can help us understand the "messy reality" of how people work. It's how we see the minutiae of people's work and the details of workflow in a way that people often cannot see themselves. This is key to identifying unmet user needs— needs that people can't articulate because their behaviors have become habitual and automatic and because they have adapted to design limitations and because they don't know there may be another way.

A good practice during an observation session is not to worry about the relevance of the information you are capturing. Avoid applying any kind of filter based on your prior expectations, assumptions, or pet theories. Don't judge or weight information at this stage. Don't try to interpret the things you observe or fit things into a plan or a solution. All of that comes later. Reflecting on a successful case, Holmes reminds Watson[8]: "We approached the case, you remember, with an absolutely blank mind, which is always an advantage. We had formed no theories. We were simply there to observe."

Right now you just need to be sure you catch everything. You can always discard items later, but it may be impossible to revisit the site and collect information that you missed.

You may not get to wear a disguise or crawl about on the carpet with a magnifying glass, but here are some things we can learn from Holmes to improve our observation skills:

- Watch people actually doing their work—don't just get a demonstration.
- Remember that your participants are the experts, you are the "novice."
- Focus on the most typical tasks, busiest days, typical days, and critical incidents.
- Find out what activities precede and follow the task you are observing.
- Look for inconveniences, delays, and frustrations.
- Shadow people; follow them wherever they go.
- Point to things and find out what they are for.
- Get copies or photos of artifacts, samples, forms, and documents.
- Make diagrams of the workspace.
- List the tools people are using.
- Note people dynamics and interactions.
- Be alert to things happening simultaneously.
- Record anything unusual about the scene you are looking at.
- Ask yourself if anything is missing.
- Observe behavior at a low level of detail—watch what people touch and what they look at.
- Pay attention to the sequences and timing of events and actions.
- Don't get in the way.
- Pay attention to trifles.

Develop Hypotheses to Explain the Facts

"Watson, you can see everything. You fail, however, to reason from what you see. You are too timid in drawing your inferences." The Adventure of the Blue Carbuncle (1892).

Holmes formulated hypotheses by interpreting facts in light of his considerable knowledge and experience[9]: "As a rule, when I have heard of some slight indications of the course of events I am able to guide myself by the thousands of other similar cases which occur to my memory."

His knowledge was very deep but it was also very narrow. He had unparalleled understanding of chemistry, footprints, bloodstains and various poisonous flowers (though not of gardening in general), and he was an accomplished violinist. On the other hand, he was quite unaware that the Earth circles the Sun ("What the deuce is it to me? You say that we go round the sun. If we went round the moon it would not make a pennyworth of difference to me or to my work.") The narrowness of his knowledge is evidenced by his monograph on the distinction between 140 different forms of cigar, pipe and cigarette tobacco.

Our knowledge may not be so narrow or eccentric, but we must still bring to bear our knowledge of human behavior, technology advances, market trends and our company's business goals, to help us formulate hypotheses that best fit the facts we collected in UX research. Our hypotheses now help us to identify the gaps in the way people work—a gap being the opportunity that emerges when we compare the way something is currently being done, and the improved way it might be possible to do it in the future. To help our innovation and development teams spot these gaps, this stage of our work must provide detailed answers to questions about the users, the tasks and the environments of use (Who? Doing what? Under what circumstances?).

Our models, personas, scenarios and stories should include:

- The primary goals that people have.
- The workflow of tasks people carry out.
- The mental models people build.
- The tools people use.
- The environments people work in.
- The terminology people use to describe what they do.

When the analysis is completed, all of the salient facts should have been explained, and the gaps and opportunities should start to emerge, and we can—finally—begin to work on solutions.

Eliminate the Least Likely Hypotheses to Arrive at the Solution

"It is an old maxim of mine that when you have excluded the impossible, whatever remains, however improbable, must be the truth." The Adventure of the Beryl Coronet (1892).

At this point a detective is usually faced with a number of possible suspects, and, if we have done our jobs well, we will be faced with a number of hypotheses and potential design solutions, product ideas and improvements. In this step we begin eliminating those solutions and ideas least likely to succeed. The detective asks, "Does the theory fit the facts?" and we ask, "Does our hypothesized solution fit the results of our investigation?" We start by eliminating the weaker solutions—those that don't quite account for everything we observed; and we drop the solutions that only fit the data by dint of being overly complex or contrived, or that create their own problems.

Eliminating potential solutions is a high stakes game. The evidence put forward in favor of one solution versus another must be compelling. This is nothing new for detective work but "strength of evidence" seems to be rarely considered in UX research. Evidence for or against a solution must be reliable, valid, and unbiased. Not all evidence is equal in this respect (see the essay "UX research and strength of evidence" in Chapter 4).

Holmes, remember, was a student of science. He knew the importance of experimenting. One way we can test the strength of our hypotheses, ideas and solutions is to carry out experiments. As we move into the development cycle, controlled testing should continue as an iterative process, with the team prototyping its way towards success. You should not expect to get there with a one-shot approach based on little more than gut feel and hope.

Act on the Solution

"Nothing clears up a case so much as stating it to another person." Silver Blaze (1892)

Once Holmes had solved a case, he would present his results to his "audience," explaining to the client, and to Watson and the police, how he had solved the crime. Then he relied on Inspector Lestrade of Scotland Yard to make the necessary arrest and the case was closed. Holmes archived the experience in his great mental storeroom and moved on to his next adventure. Here are some recommendations that can help us ensure our development team takes action on the results of our investigation:

- Conduct a one-day UX research and design workshop to "explain what we found and how we did it" and to transition the user experience findings and solutions to the development team.
- Provide the development team with specific and actionable design recommendations.
- Agree accountability for implementing your user experience recommendations.
- Promote iterative design by arranging to test multiple versions of the prototype.
- Create and present a clear series of next user experience steps—both tactical and strategic.
- Educate the team in UX research methods.
- Don't just attend design meetings: chair them.

How to Think Like a Detective

There's just one more thing…

Much as we may admire Sherlock Holmes, he did have one characteristic that most detectives would consider to be, at the very least, an inconvenience— he didn't really exist. So, though we can learn a lot from Sherlock Holmes, let's leave the last word on detecting to a real detective.

To get a real life perspective, Philip decided to talk to a real life detective. He got in touch with Peter Stott, an old school friend, recently of the West Yorkshire Criminal Investigation Department, and asked him, "If you had just one piece of advice to give to a new researcher, what would it be?" Peter didn't hesitate for a moment: "Never, ever, ever, act on assumptions. Search out the facts and act on those."

Holmes himself could not have put it better: *Never, ever, ever, act on assumptions. Search out the facts and act on those.*

Facts and evidence, not guesswork and assumptions. That's how to think like a detective.

THINK LIKE A UX RESEARCHER

- Sir Arthur Conan Doyle wrote four novels and 56 short stories about Sherlock Holmes. Pick one of them to read and, instead of thinking of Holmes as a criminal investigator, think of him as a UX researcher. What jumps out at you? Which of his characteristics or abilities do you think would be most useful to a UX researcher?
- Do you have a favorite fictional detective? Miss Marple? Hercule Poirot? Jessica Fletcher? Precious Ramotswe? Morse? Columbo? What's unique about his or her investigative methods? What techniques can you apply to UX research?
- How good are you at "observing trifles"? Without looking, whose head is on the back of a US dime? Which way is he facing?
- Research and list three ways you can improve your observation skills—then try them out on your daily commute or in and around your office.
- Dr. Edmond Locard, a pioneer of forensic science, famously stated in his Exchange Principle[10] that criminals will always leave some trace of themselves at the crime scene and will also pick up some trace of the crime scene on themselves: "Every contact leaves a trace." Does the Locard Exchange Principle also work in UX research, for example during field research? What would be some examples of this?

The Two Questions We Answer with UX Research

Fundamentally, all UX research answers one of two questions: (a) Who are our users and what are they trying to do? (b) Can people use the thing we've designed to solve their problem? You answer the first question with a field visit and you answer the second question with a usability test.

Field Research Answers the Question, "Who Are Our Users and What Are They Trying to Do?"

A field study focuses on the big picture: how people currently solve their problem. With field research, you examine the workflow across multiple channels and observe user behaviors, needs, goals and pain points. Field research is fundamentally outward looking: your aim is to find out what's happening in the real world.

The typical research location is a participant's home or workplace. You're looking to discover how people achieve their goals right now, before your system has been built or invented. What problems do users face? What needs do they have? What are their skills and motivations?

Lean Startup[11] researchers characterize this as "getting out of the building" but getting out of the building isn't enough. A field visit is much more than a pop-up user interview in a coffee shop. To use the analogy of animal behavior, an interview is like a visit to the zoo whereas field research is like going on safari (this is an analogy we will return to in the next essay). With field research you observe real behavior: you see what people do, not just listen to what they say they do. In short, you go where the action happens.

Without field research, you're designing in the dark. With field research, it's like someone has turned on the room lights.

Again, to use the language of Lean Startup, field research helps you validate the *problem hypothesis*. Is the problem that you're trying to solve for users really a problem? This is important because development teams often experience a kind of groupthink where they believe they are solving a real user need but in fact few people are bothered by the problem.[12]

The other issue you'll uncover with your field visit is how serious a problem this is. Some problems aren't so serious for people that they are willing to spend time or money solving them. You may have discovered an itch, but a field visit will show you if your customers are happy with their current way of scratching.

Usability Testing Answers the Question, "Can People Use the Thing We've Designed to Solve Their Problem?"

A usability test focuses on how people do specific tasks and the problems they experience when using a particular system. Traditionally it takes place in a lab, but in practice it can take place anywhere (including the field). Typical research locations include:

- A participant's home or workplace.
- Public spaces, like coffee shops and libraries (so called "pop-up research").
- Research studios or labs.
- Meeting rooms.
- Your desk (using a laptop or phone for remote research).

Usability testing is fundamentally inward looking: you give your users a prototype and a set of tasks and you see if they can complete those tasks.

The key difference between a usability test and a field visit is that with a usability test you're evaluating a specific design idea with your users. If a field visit is like turning on the lights, then a usability test is like looking under the microscope. Field visits give you the big picture whereas a usability test lets you evaluate a specific solution.

To use the language of Lean Startup, a usability test helps you validate the *solution hypothesis*. Does your proposed solution work?

Should You Run a Field Visit or a Usability Test?

Field visits and usability tests are complementary research techniques so you need to do both. A field visit tells you if you're *designing the right thing*. A usability test tells you if you've *designed the thing right*. For example, your product might perform fine in a usability test but it would still fail in the market if people don't really care about the tasks you've asked them to complete.

Your choice of method depends on where you are in your development lifecycle.

If you're in the discovery phase, you should be carrying out field visits to turn on the lights. This is because you want to answer the question, "Who are our users and what are they trying to do?"

Later in the development lifecycle, it's time to get out your microscope and usability test your design solution with users. This is because you want to answer the question, "Can people use the thing we've designed to solve their problem?"

In summary, you simply need to ask two questions:

- Is there a user problem to be solved? (If unsure, carry out field research).
- Have we solved it? (If unsure, carry out usability testing.)

THINK LIKE A UX RESEARCHER

- As you'll see from some of the examples in this book, we have worked with more than one development team who believe they are designing a useful product but in practice there is no user need for it. Thinking of the product you are working on at the moment, what evidence do you have that it is solving a user need? If you were to play Devil's advocate, how would you critique that evidence?
- It's not uncommon for a development team to be given a solution by senior management or marketing and then told to build it. This skips validation of the problem hypothesis. Does this happen in your own organization? How could you push back against it?
- The world is awash with waste materials and waste products. Do you have an ethical responsibility to insist your organization first validates the problem hypothesis before developing a product that may ultimately fail and cause yet more waste?
- If your organization follows an Agile development process, like Scrum, does it include sufficient time in early sprints to validate the problem hypothesis? How would you adapt the process to ensure there was sufficient time allocated to "discovery"?
- How easy or difficult would it be to adapt a usability test to also include questions around the participant's need for the product? In the first essay in this book ("The seven deadly sins of UX research") we pointed out that simply asking people if they need a product is flawed. So how would you find out if the user genuinely needed your solution in the context of a usability test?

Anatomy of a Research Question

Surprisingly, many UX research studies do not begin with a considered research question. Instead they are motivated by uninteresting and superficial objectives such as the need to "do some research," "get some insights," "hear the voice of the customer," or "find some user needs." The first step of any research endeavor should be the development of a research question that will provide the central core around which an investigation, its methodology and its data analysis, can be developed.

What do we mean by a "research question"? We're not talking about lists of questions you might generate and expect respondents to explicitly answer, either in an interview or in a questionnaire. We're referring, instead, to the underlying question that describes the purpose of the research, and that guides the design and focus of a study.

For example, your question list may well ask a respondent, "Do you like coffee?" or "How many cups of coffee do you drink in a day?" or "What's your favorite brand of coffee?" but your underlying research question is, "Does drinking coffee affect employee productivity?" This is not a question you can directly ask of anyone and get a useful answer but it is the focal point and driving force behind your investigation.

Without a specific research question, studies lack the ability to penetrate a problem. They skim the surface and risk becoming purely method driven. Instead of exploring new territory, they simply retread the same worn pathways, collect the same old user responses, and culminate in the same tedious research presentations that are guaranteed to put your development team to sleep.

In contrast, an effective research question will:

- Be interesting.
- Ask something that is important.
- Be focused and specific.
- Lead to a testable hypothesis.
- Allow you to make predictions based on measurable data.
- Advance your company's knowledge by going beyond the obvious.

"Going beyond the obvious" means pushing limits, asking new questions and venturing into new territory, or venturing deeper into territory you may have only tentatively visited before. In the last essay we talked about thinking like a detective, but at this stage of research planning we must think like an explorer—and as an explorer, you need to break new ground, otherwise you're doing it wrong.

We're often so eager for answers and solutions that we overlook the importance of a strong research question. But it is the question—not the answer—that is the most important part of research. As Jonas Salk put it: "What people think of as the moment of discovery is really the discovery of the question."

We can avoid recycling the same old questions simply by shifting the starting point for our thinking. Let's describe one way to do that.

On Safari

In the previous essay, we used an analogy to differentiate field visits from traditional interviews. We pointed out that a user interview is like a visit to the zoo whereas field research is like going on safari.

This analogy leads us to an interesting way of shifting our research thinking. Imagine trying to learn something new and interesting about a particular animal by observing it in a zoo. Stripped of its need to fight for survival or hunt for food, it will probably be either pacing its cage or sitting motionless for hours, or sleeping in a corner. Worse still the animal may have developed abnormal behavior, sometimes called "zoochosis": repetitive, invariant behavior patterns that have no obvious goal or function. Any opportunity for observing natural behavior is lost because the animal's natural environment is missing. That's why you never see Sir David Attenborough on his hands and knees observing animals in a zoo.

The same is true of interviews. Just like in a zoo, you typically remove the respondents from their real world environment and put them in a room where their unrepresentative "made up" behaviors can be observed from a distance.

In contrast, on safari there are no constraints placed on the animals and they are running wild. They are in their natural environment with all of its pressures and dangers, and their natural behaviors and reactions to all kinds of situations are on display. The same is true when we conduct UX research and observe people going about their real world activities.

So, the zoo v. safari analogy raises interesting questions. But what if we push this analogy a step further? What if we acknowledge the self-evident, though seldom voiced, fact that all UX research is actually the study of animal behavior?

We sense a few raised eyebrows. But let's agree that this at least puts a different spin on things. Now let's see where it might lead...

Tinbergen's Four Questions

In 1963, Nobel Prize winning zoologist Niko Tinbergen published *On the aims and methods of ethology*[13] in which he outlined four questions (sometimes referred to as Tinbergen's four problems).

He argued that, far from simply recording any specific behavior and taking it at face value, the behaviors of animals (including humans) can be characterized by answering each of the four questions. Professors Paul Martin and Patrick Bateson summarize Tinbergen's four questions in their own book, *Measuring Behavior*[14] (a "must read" for any UX researcher, by the way). As we can't improve on their summary, we're going to paraphrase them here:

What Is the Behavior for?

This question concerns the behavior's function. What is the behavior currently used for and what is its survival value? How does the behavior help the individual to survive and reproduce in its current environment?

How Does the Behavior Work?

This question concerns proximate causation or control. How do causal factors control the behavior? What kinds of stimuli elicit a behavioral response? What are the neurological, psychological and physiological mechanisms that mediate the behavior?

How Did the Behavior Develop?

This question concerns ontogeny—the development of the behavior for that individual. How did the behavior arise during the individual's lifetime? What internal or external factors influenced the behavior's development? How do the developmental processes work? What is the nature of the interaction between the individual and its environment during development?

How Did the Behavior Evolve?

This question concerns phylogeny—the evolutionary development of the behavior in that particular species. What factors could have shaped the behavior over the course of evolutionary history?

These seem like very good questions, and it is clear that they will help us avoid easy, quick and superficial explanations, and guide us towards a more thorough, insightful and detailed understanding of a specific behavior.

But, before we consider how we might use these questions in our UX research, let's take a look at an example that Profs. Martin and Bateson use to show how the four questions result in four different kinds of answers: Why do we stop at red traffic lights?

Why Do We Stop at Red Traffic Lights?

Because it's the law. The answer is obvious and not very interesting. But what would the answer be if we explained this behavior in terms of Tinbergen's four questions?

Function

We want to avoid causing an accident, being injured or injuring someone else. We also want to avoid being pulled over by a cop and getting a ticket.

Proximate Causation

We perceive a visual stimulus that excites our color receptors and we process this information in our central nervous system, which triggers a specific response. The response results in us taking our foot off the accelerator pedal and pushing it down on the brake pedal.

Ontogeny

We learned this rule by studying the rules of the road, from our driving instructors, and by noticing that other cars, including cars on TV and in movies, also stop at red lights.

Phylogeny

Historically, a red light has come to be an almost universal signal for controlling traffic at road junctions. They were first used in 1868 in London and involved gas lighting and semaphore arms. The first electric traffic light appears to have been employed in Salt Lake City in 1912.

All of these answers are correct, all of them are valid, but all of them are different. The resulting explanations complement each other and reveal facets of the specific behavior that we may otherwise have missed. The four questions are logically distinct, and one way to think about them is as a set of four new tools (tools for probing, lenses for looking through) that you can use to approach a topic from new and different directions.

Behavior is complicated. Simplistic, trite, unimaginative, and uninteresting questions leading to obvious answers are inadequate. Tinbergen's four questions can give us a way of revealing insights that we might otherwise miss.

Going Beyond the Obvious

These four questions fit nicely into our field research toolbox. Now, instead of focusing primarily on just observing and recording behaviors, we can get more focused and start to "unpack" a given behavior or user interaction, and collect data that our previous "blunt" questions could not detect.

Let's take a look at each of the four questions again, but this time in the context of a field visit in which the behaviors of interest now include specific product or system interactions.

The "Function" Question (What Is the Behavior for?)

This is the closest to the kind of implicit question we typically ask.

- What is this solution or interaction about?
- What is the product or system or feature used for?
- What is the user trying to accomplish by using it?
- What user goals are being met?
- How does this behavior or interaction help the user (and the company, if we are observing a work environment) to be successful?
- Compared to not carrying out this behavior (or not using this product or system) what advantage does the user now have over competitors or other users?

The "Proximate Causation" Question (How Does the Behavior Work?)

This question invites us to ask:

- What triggers the behavior or interaction?
- How is the interaction being controlled?
- What are the steps or events and actions leading up to it?
- What is the behavior or interaction a response to?
- What other activities or functions are involved in mediating this behavior?
- What's going on in the system right now?

- What's going on in the mind of the user?
- What mechanisms are working to support the behavior and what things are getting in the way?
- Is the user in control?

The "Ontogenesis" Question (How Did the Behavior Develop?)

This question requires us to understand how the behavior came about.

- How did this particular user learn this particular action or step?
- What training was required?
- How easy or difficult was it to learn this behavior?
- What level of skill is required?
- Is the user's skill level increasing over time?
- What were those early learning steps like for this user?
- Was he/she anxious or confident during first use?
- At the company level, what support is given?
- Are training courses available?
- What do training materials look like?

The "Phylogeny" Question (How Did the Behavior Evolve?)

We can often move our understanding forwards by first going backwards, and this question invites us to do just that. Thankfully, we don't have to worry about geological time scales, but we can certainly go back decades, if necessary, and discover the history of a product or system and the origin of a behavior.

- What was the origin of the behavior/interaction/interface/product?
- What was it originally trying to solve?
- What previous versions have existed?
- When did the problem first appear?
- What behavior existed before this solution?
- How was the task carried out back then?
- What has prompted design or technology changes over the years?
- Would we have solved the original problem differently?
- If so, where might evolutionary iterations of our original (hypothetical) solution have brought us to by today?

Try asking these four questions next time you carry out your field research. Ask them of each example of user behavior you identify. Use them as a framework around which to design a study that avoids asking mundane "top of mind" questions that generate banal answers, and not very insightful insights—not to mention mind-numbingly dull presentations.

THINK LIKE A UX RESEARCHER

- Practice this technique by taking a UX research study you already completed, especially one that felt perfunctory or returned findings that you felt were too obvious, and apply Tinbergen's four questions retroactively. How would this fresh perspective change your study design?
- Jonas Salk's observation that the moment of discovery is really the discovery of the question, reminds us that uncovering new questions is the *raison d'être* of research. Think about UX research studies you have done where, along the way, you found yourself asking new and intriguing questions. How can you prepare your stakeholders for the possibility of ending up with more questions than you started with?
- Our zoo v. safari analogy depends heavily on exploring natural behaviors in natural environments. This works well for field studies, but usability tests are often carried out in controlled lab sessions. Can we still use these four questions to motivate a lab study? What limitations might you encounter and how might you overcome them?
- Consider a few of the example questions that we've listed under each of Tinbergen's four questions. How would you design a UX research study to answer them? What techniques would you use to get your answers?
- Even the most penetrating questions can be nullified if the resultant answers are poorly delivered. How would starting out with Tinbergen's questions change the way you report your findings?

Applying Psychology to UX Research

When planning UX research studies, there are four fundamental principles from psychology that UX researchers must know. These are: Your users do not think like you think; your users don't have good insight into the reasons for their behavior; the best predictor of your users' future behavior is their past behavior; and your users' behavior depends on context.

Check the requirements for most UX research jobs and you'll see that they often ask for a background in psychology or behavioral science. People usually assume this is because psychologists know secret mind hacks, things like reciprocation, social proof and framing that can be used to manipulate people.

In truth, there are a small number of fundamental principles that (a) psychologists know, (b) most people don't and (c) are relevant to UX researchers.

Four of the most important are:

- Your users do not think like you think.
- Your users don't have good insight into the reasons for their behavior.
- The best predictor of your users' future behavior is their past behavior.
- Your users' behavior depends on context.

Your Users Do Not Think Like You Think

Of all the principles in psychology relevant to UX researchers, this is the easiest understand intellectually—but the hardest to appreciate intuitively. In fact, not only do most people on development teams fail to appreciate this principle, most adults don't appreciate this principle. It's the principle that we need to consciously remind ourselves of on every new project—because all of us forget it from time to time.

This principle tells us that our users don't think like we think.

- *They don't value what we value*: optimizing our product's splash screen may be important to us but nowhere near as important to our users as having a larger font size.
- *We do not see things like our users*: they think that the gray placeholder text inside the form field needs to be deleted before they can enter a value.

- *We do not know what our users know*: they use workflow shortcuts, acronyms, and jargon that are entirely missing from our application.

One area where this is most obvious is in users' technical skills. Development teams almost always overestimate the technical competence of their users.

Since your users will never stop surprising you, there is only one solution to this: You need to put the development team (and yourself) in front of users at every opportunity. This will help you gain empathy for your users and help you see the world through their eyes.

Your Users Don't Have Good Insight Into the Reasons for Their Behavior

We like to think that our decisions are rational and made after conscious deliberation. That's why it's tempting to believe participants when they tell us why they did what they did. But people are poor at introspecting into the reasons for their behavior. In reality, people want to tell a good story—a "narrative"—of their life and will change what they say to fit the view of who they are and to whom they are talking.

One of many studies proving this is the case comes from the field of choice blindness. In this study, a researcher showed participants two pictures of different men or different women and asked the participant to point to the most attractive. If you were a participant in this study, you would have seen the experimenter hand you your chosen picture, discard the other photo, and then ask you to justify your choice.

Unknown to participants, the experimenter was a part-time magician, and using a sleight of hand technique he was really showing the participant the picture of the man or woman thought *less* attractive. He now asked participants why they had chosen that picture.

Remarkably, even when the photos weren't that similar, the majority of participants didn't spot that they were now looking at the person they thought was less attractive. Even more curiously, participants now provided "explanations" for their choice. So, for example they might say, "Well, I chose this picture because I like blondes," even though the participant had really chosen a brunette (whose picture was now face down on the table). People made up reasons to justify their choice.[15]

In practice, this principle means that asking people to introspect on the reasons for their behavior is seldom useful. You are much better off designing experiments where you can observe people's behavior. Which takes us to our next principle.

The Best Predictor of Your Users' Future Behavior Is Their Past Behavior

Opinion polling and exit polling provide a nice demonstration of this principle.

An opinion poll asks people to predict what they would do in the future (their intention). An exit poll asks people what they did in the past (their action).

Intention research is the field of market researchers and the tools of choice are usually surveys and focus groups. These are devised to ask questions like, "How likely are you to recommend our company?," "Would you use this feature in the next release of the system?" and "How much would you pay for this product?" Unsurprisingly, the results are variable and often have little predictive value, despite the fact that sample sizes are often huge.

For example, opinion pollsters failed to predict the Leave vote in the UK's EU referendum in 2016 as well as the results of recent political elections in the UK and the United States. In contrast, the results of exit polls where voters are asked to recast their vote on leaving the polling station were spot on.

Action research is the field of UX researchers. With action research, we interview users about how they behaved in the past and we spend time observing how users are behaving now. How are people solving this problem at the moment? What is the workflow across multiple channels? What systems, tools or processes do people use? How do people collaborate?

Because we are observing real behavior, action research has strong predictive value, even though the sample sizes are often small. This is because the best predictor of future behavior is past behavior.

Your Users' Behavior Depends on Context

Back in the 1930s, psychologist Kurt Lewin proposed a formula,[16] $B = f(P, E)$. The formula states that behavior (B) is a "function" of the person (P) and his or her environment (E). Lewin's equation teaches us that the same person (such as our user) will behave differently in different environments. This means the best way to predict the way our user will behave with our system is to observe them in their natural environment. Context is like a skeleton key for unlocking user needs—which in turn leads to new feature and product ideas.

With in-context field research you observe real behavior; you see what people really do in a particular situation, not just listen to what they say they do or see them act it out. In short, you go where the action happens. This doesn't mean that out-of-context research offers no value, we just need to find some way of incorporating the user's context. One way you can achieve this with out-of-context interviews is with cognitive interviewing. With this technique you put the user back in the situation by having them restate the context. Research shows this aids memory retrieval.

With usability testing, you can recreate the context with realistic task scenarios. There's a big difference between "pretending" to buy car insurance and "really" buying car insurance. No matter how well intentioned they are, participants know that, if they get it wrong, there are no consequences. You can mitigate this risk by giving participants real money to spend on the task—in Chapter 3 (see the essay, "Writing effective usability test tasks"), we call these "skin in the game" tasks. If, in contrast, you find yourself asking the user to "just pretend" in a usability test, don't expect to observe authentic behavior.

Applying These Principles in the Field

These principles are easy to understand intellectually but they are a little counter-intuitive. Knowing something in your head is different from believing something in your gut. This means it may take a while before they change your own behavior. But these principles repay reflection, because behind every good UX research plan is an intuitive understanding of these four principles.

THINK LIKE A UX RESEARCHER

- One of the most difficult things for us (UX researchers, designers, people in general) to do is to see things from the point of view of other people. But some people are really good at it: teachers, doctors, carers, counsellors, detectives, magicians and con artists, for example. Actors too have to be able to see situations as if they were someone else. Method acting helps an actor to "get into character." What can we learn from these other professions to help development teams "get into the character" of our users?
- The market research world still relies heavily on asking people what they are thinking or what they want or what their opinion is about something, often prioritizing literal "voice of the customer" data over behavioral data. Where does your company sit on this issue? Find out how much your company relies on opinion-based

(Continued)

THINK LIKE A UX RESEARCHER (Continued)

methods and think of two or three arguments that can persuade your colleagues to tilt the balance towards objective behavioral data.

- Interviewing people about how they have done things in the past is one method used by UX researchers, but people's memories are often unreliable. What other techniques can you think of that might reliably tap into people's past experiences?

- How well do you know the context of use for the application or product you're currently working on? Write down as much as you can describing a typical use environment. Then identify how much of your understanding is based on verifiable evidence and how much is based on assumptions. Draft an action plan to challenge any assumptions and to reinforce with evidence where needed.

- As the science of human behavior, psychology covers a wide range of disciplines that include cognition, sensation and perception, emotion and motivation, learning, human development, language and thought, social behaviors, personality and many others. Many of these disciplines can inform the design of user interactions and user experiences. Dip into any introductory psychology book or website, pick a topic that interests you and think about how you can use it to get a better understanding of your users.

Why Iterative Design Isn't Enough
to Create Innovative Products

Iterative design is a proven approach for optimizing the usability of a product or service. Teams create prototypes, test them with users, find problems and fix them. But iterative design does not guarantee innovation. To develop innovative designs, we need to question the way we have framed the problem and instead focus on our users' underlying needs.

The twenty-first century organization, we're told, needs to be innovative, creative and customer centered. Senior executives implore their staff to get out of the building. HR departments clear desks from a meeting room and replace them with beanbags, a foosball table and a games console. Teams install whiteboards and plaster them with sticky notes and flow diagrams.

Then the work starts. Users are recruited for research. Customer conversations are analyzed, interpreted and then presented as fundamental truths. Iterative design and usability testing becomes a new mantra. Teams adopt an iterative development methodology like Scrum. And the benefits are immediate. Week by week, products get better. It seems to work.

But then a startup appears, disrupts the industry and changes the rules of the game.

Iterative design can be deceptive. It does a great job of delivering incremental improvements. Those improvements build upon each other after each iteration.

But iterative design is not enough.

We end up with incrementally better versions of the same product. But what if we need an entirely different product? How do you truly innovate?

Two Kinds of Research

In 2005, the UK's Design Council introduced a design process known as the Double Diamond.[17] Divided into four distinct phases (Discover, Define, Develop, and Deliver) the model maps the divergent and convergent stages of the design process, showing the different modes of thinking that designers use.

Figure 1.1: The Design Council's Double Diamond model (with additional annotations). Many teams skip the "Discover" and "Define" stages because they have preconceived ideas about user needs

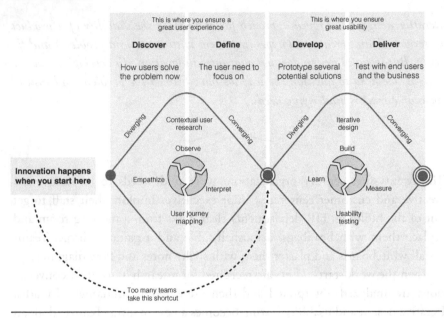

We have re-drawn the following diagram and annotated it with some additional thoughts (Figure 1.1).

On first glance, this may feel like a familiar process. But our experience with development teams shows that they don't spend much time, if at all, in the "Discover" phase of this model (where they are understanding how users solve the problem now) or in the "Define" phase (where they decide on the user need they will serve). Yet it's in these two areas where teams have the best chance of innovating and creating a great user experience.

Instead, teams rush to optimize the usability of a solution based on pre-conceived ideas before they have properly explored their users' goals, needs and motivations. This is a common problem in organizations that use Scrum, because managers want to see developers developing.

Yet an exploration phase is critical to innovation because *you will never iterate toward a transformative solution.* If you start with a website and iterate, you'll end with a website. It may be the best possible kind of website, but it's still a website. To be truly innovative, you need to spend serious time in the

Discover and Define phases to give you the ideas you need to create innovative solutions in the Develop and Deliver phases.

Teams aren't always aware that they are making this mistake because they do indeed explore a range of alternatives in the later, "Develop" phase. In this phase, teams run usability tests of prototypes and modify the designs based on the results. It's easy to mis-characterize this kind of iterative design work as "Discovery" and "Definition."

Don't misunderstand. We think usability testing is a terrific tool. However, a usability test is inward-looking. It focuses on the detail of the thing you've designed. But the aim of a usability test is to discover how people do specific tasks with a product and what problems they experience when using it. Since you will only ask people to do tasks in a usability test that your product will support, you're unlikely to spot significant gaps in your thinking.

A field study, on the other hand, is outward-looking. It focuses on the big picture: how people currently solve their problem. The aims of field research are to discover the workflow across multiple channels, user behaviors, needs, goals and pain points. With field research, you don't know what you don't know. It's here where true innovation happens.

How can you tell if you're doing it wrong? Seth Godin has famously said,[18] "You don't find customers for your products. You find products for your customers." So to check if you're in the "Discover/Define" phases and not in the "Develop/Deliver" phases, ask: "Are we showing users a prototype?" If the answer is Yes, you're actually in the "Develop" phase because you're already thinking in terms of solutions. This isn't the way to become innovative. Innovation happens only when teams fundamentally question what they are designing—and the best way to raise these questions is by understanding users' needs, goals and motivations.

From Field Research to Innovation

So to be truly innovative, we need to discover the boundaries of the research domain and the rough shape of the experience for which we are designing. We make progress by creating hypotheses about the context of use and we then test these hypotheses to help us understand what's going on.

One of the interesting challenges with field research is that you are not making predictions about an *audience*. With innovative, discovery research, you are making predictions about an *experience*. This can cause difficulties for development teams who believe they already know who their users are. The team may expect you to speak with representative users, but if you do this, you'll be digging in the wrong place. With research in the discovery phase, when we are trying to innovate and come up with new product ideas, we don't know our audience.

As an example, let's say we want to understand how people use headphones because we want to innovate in the headphone product space. We need to start somewhere, so let's begin with a commuter who wears headphones on the train. Then we ask: "Who is most different from that user? Who would be the 'opposite'?" That should lead us to someone who has an entirely different context: perhaps an audiophile who uses headphones only at home. But we still haven't explored this space fully. Let's look at some of the edges: professional musicians; sound recordists; teenagers.

These types of users will probably fall squarely within the preconceptions that the development team has about its users. But now let's look further afield. To adopt the terminology of jobs-to-be-done, we might question what "job" the headphones are doing. If people are using headphones to shield out noise at work from co-workers, then maybe we want to understand the experience of people who wear ear defenders. If people are using headphones to learn a new language on their commute then maybe we want to look at the way people learn a foreign language. By expanding into these less obvious areas we start to establish the limits of the research domain.

How to Stop a Startup

If you work in a large organization, there will be established ways of working that may pose a problem for this approach:

- Perhaps you're already struggling to get senior managers to move from a waterfall-based development methodology to a more iterative, Agile approach. In this case, you may find you are neither innovative nor iterative.
- And if you are already using an Agile approach, like Scrum, you may have another kind of problem: the team may be so fixated on iteration that development starts on Day 1, before suitable time has been spent in Discovery.

But there's a startup snapping at your heels who is trying to eat your lunch. No amount of iterative design will stop them. Iteration is not enough; you need ideation, too. So don't just create the best possible thing with iterative design. Create the best thing possible by uncovering what users actually need.

THINK LIKE A UX RESEARCHER

- Your development team has skipped the discovery stage and has conceived a new product by brainstorming in team meetings. Now your usability test participants are telling you that they would never use the new concept for the kinds of tasks you have given them. Clearly the team's vision was off target. Your boss wants you to go out and do field research retroactively and find confirmatory evidence to support the team's design. What will you do? What can you do to get things back on track?

- In an earlier essay ("Think like a detective") we likened UX researchers to detectives. Now we're likening UX research to explorers. Think of three explorers—they can be historical or contemporary—read up on them to get a sense of what motivated them and what their objectives, challenges, and discoveries were. What can you learn from them that can be applied to user experience discovery research?

- If you don't know what you don't know, how can you be sure your field research doesn't just wander about aimlessly? What can you do to keep it focused? Or does having focus in advance defeat the purpose of exploring?

- When it comes to innovating, explain why talking only to your typical users is a case of "digging in the wrong place." What are the implications of this for participant recruiting?

- Who is the opposite of your target user? Who are the less obvious users of your product and how are they using it? Make a list of ways that your product (or competitor products in the same domain) are being used in ways the development team never intended. What user needs does this reveal?

Does your Company Deliver
a Superior Customer Experience?

Many companies think of themselves as user focused, but this judgment is often based on anecdotal or biased data. To truly deliver a superior customer experience, companies need to progress through four stages of maturity, finally arriving at a point where feedback is not simply welcomed or solicited—but demanded.

A while back, Bain & Company surveyed over 350 companies and asked them if they thought they delivered a good customer experience.[19]

What was interesting about their survey was that some companies claimed to deliver not just a good experience: they claimed to deliver a "superior experience." These companies are fascinating. They are the small proportion of companies that place user experience on a pedestal. These companies are user experience heroes, the companies to work for, the leaders in the user experience field.

Who were these companies? A rarefied group? Perhaps 5% to 10% of the firms in the survey?

Here's a question for you: what percentage of firms do you think this was? What percentage of firms in Bain & Company's survey do you think claimed to deliver a "superior experience" to their customers?

The answer? A whopping 80%.

This wasn't because the researchers had chosen a biased sample of overachievers. We know this because the researchers took the unusual step of asking the firms' customers the same question.

When researchers asked customers for their views, they heard a different story. Customers said that only 8% of companies were really delivering a superior experience.

This is reminiscent of the illusory superiority bias,[20] where most people tend to rate themselves as above average. For example, 93% of U.S. drivers describe themselves as better drivers than average and 88% say they are safer drivers than average.[21]

Nowadays nearly every company pays lip service to user experience, but it's a fact that many of them are simply out of touch. A small amount of reflection on your own interactions with various brands will probably bear out Bain & Company's research; just a small percentage of companies actually deliver on the promise of a superior user experience.

What causes this disconnect in customer feedback, and how can we resolve it?

In our experience working with a range of companies, we find that customer feedback programs tend to move through four phases. Think of this as the customer feedback maturity model.

The First Phase: Criticism Is Rejected

This is a region where you'll find both startups and established companies. These firms don't involve their customers because, they assert, customers don't know what they want. Senior execs live in a reality distortion field where they believe they know better than their customers. Indeed, these people often invoke this quotation from Steve Jobs: "It's really hard to design products by focus groups. A lot of times, people don't know what they want until you show it to them."

These people tend to ignore at least one important fact: they are not Steve Jobs. Steve Jobs was a visionary who prioritized design and surrounded himself with the best designers in the business. And we don't just mean Sir Jonathan Ive; some members of Apple's earliest design team (like Bruce Tognazzini, Jef Raskin, Don Norman and Bill Verplank) went on to define the field of user experience.

The Second Phase: Criticism Is Welcomed

In this phase, a company has no formal plans in place to collect and analyze feedback from customers. Nevertheless, informal feedback still arrives—in the form of a letter, an email, a newspaper report, a tweet or a forum post. These aren't ignored because the company prides itself on welcoming feedback. Indeed, they may be collated into a digest and forwarded to the chief executive with a cheesy title like, "Brickbats and bouquets."

The problem with this kind of feedback is that it tends to come only from customers who are either delighted with your product or from customers who absolutely hate it.

These represent a small fraction of your overall customer base and tailoring your design to customers who shout the loudest is rarely sound business practice. This may be partly the cause of the firms in Bain & Company's research being so out of touch with their customers.

Things are improving, but we've a way to go.

The Third Phase: Criticism Is Solicited

In this phase, the organization prides itself as a company that not just welcomes but solicits feedback. Surveys are constructed to answer specific business questions and these surveys appear on its website. A new product may come with a postage-paid mail-in card that asks about the purchaser's experience. To answer specific issues, the organization may ask an outside firm to run focus groups. Someone in the organization will have the responsibility of collating the feedback and providing rolling summaries to senior management.

The most obvious problem with this approach is, again, the biased sample of respondents. Most people tend to complete surveys when they already have some goodwill towards the brand: "OK, as it's you, I'll spend five minutes on your survey." Again, this misses the bulk of customers, and the criticisms that you do hear can often be muted.

But there's a second, more subtle problem. With these techniques (and this includes focus groups), people are asked to recall their behavior. Our memories are imperfect and sometimes we don't tell the truth, or the whole truth. We also know that people tend to say one thing but do another. The truth is that we aren't very good at explaining the "why" behind our behavior.

The Fourth Phase: Criticism Is Demanded

The most mature companies—and these are probably the 8% in Bain and Company's survey—take a different approach.

These companies demand criticism.

They achieve this not by asking for anecdotes, but by observing the experience.

Researchers carry out field visits to the places where the product is used. They sit and observe people using the system. They discover the deeper problems that people experience with a system that people may not be able to describe or articulate. They run usability tests, where representative users carry out real world tasks without help, and the researchers observe where people fail. This provides real data that can be used to drive design decisions, rather than *ad hoc* opinions.

These techniques enable researchers to peer into the gap between what people say and what people do—and this is where some of the best design ideas are hiding.

Solving the addiction to bad data is like solving any addiction: The first stage is to admit you have a problem. This means identifying your own position on this maturity model and relentlessly moving forwards.

THINK LIKE A UX RESEARCHER

- Identify your company's position on this maturity model. Does your company think of itself as customer focused? If you asked your customers, what do you think they would say? Do they love, hate or simply tolerate your product?
- Find out how your company uses the customer feedback it gets. Does it ever reach the user experience and design teams? What would you have to do to tap into this important source of information?
- Spend an hour each week listening in to customer support calls. Encourage your development team to do the same. Discuss the feedback you hear.
- Find out what your company's most common customer or user complaint is. Does it come as a surprise? Does it affect design? Can you make it the focus of your next user experience field research project?
- Phase 4, demanding criticism, requires the user experience function to step up to the plate and to actively collect customer and user feedback by observing real users working with your product. Let your marketing colleagues know that you plan to do this and join forces, taking them with you into the field.

2

Planning User Experience Research

Defining Your UX Research Problem

Without a clear understanding of a research problem one cannot expect UX research to deliver useful findings. Here are four techniques to help better define a research problem and sharpen your research question.

"If I had 20 days to solve a problem," observed Albert Einstein, illuminating an approach to research that may come as a shock to some in the corporate world, "I would take 19 days to define it."

In a culture somewhat preoccupied with solutions, the idea of deliberating over a research problem may seem heretical to some. Of course, logic and common sense tell us that you can't arrive at a solution if you don't understand the problem. And that's a rather worrying thought because companies spend a lot of money on customer and UX research and it would be nice to think it was solving something.

According to the Council of American Survey Research Organizations[1] (CASRO) an estimated $6.7 billion is spent each year in the USA, $2 billion in the UK, and $18.9 billion spent globally on just one method—survey research (research concerned with measuring the opinions, attitudes, perceptions, and behaviors of population samples).

Alas, most of the research is inadequate because it doesn't move knowledge forward. In fact, Rohit Deshpande,[2] Harvard Business School professor and former executive director of the Marketing Science Institute, estimates that 80% of all customer research serves only to reinforce what companies already know, rather than testing or developing new possibilities.

Can we identify such inadequate research? Yes we can. Brace yourself, this might ring some bells. In his book *Research Strategies*, William Badke[3] explains that inadequate research:

- Merely gathers data and regurgitates it.
- Deals in generalities and superficial surveys, avoiding depth and analysis.
- Asks no analytical questions.
- Does not advance knowledge, but is happy to summarize what's already known.
- Is boring.

We sense you are nodding. Most of us have experienced research presentations or reports that bear some of these hallmarks. We've sat behind the one-way mirror fighting ennui as the moderator goes through the motions of rolling out the same old method, asking the same old questions, revealing the same old "insights," and generally inspiring what writer Douglas Adams would have called an acute attack of no curiosity.

But then, from time to time, we get to experience research that blows us away, that's sharp and incisive and positively exciting, and we want to tell everyone about it.

So why are some research studies so lame while others are so inspiring?

It's obvious from the list above that inadequate research lacks a clearly defined and interesting research problem. There are two main reasons why this happens with UX research:

- The superficial motivation to hear what people think about X, or whether they prefer X, Y or Z is often enough to meet an internal requirement to "do some research" even though it's not addressing anything interesting. A "problem" may be assumed to exist, but it turns out to be next to impossible to find anyone who can actually write the research question on a whiteboard and put a question mark at the end of it.
- In lieu of an actual research question, UX research often ends up being "method led" or sometimes "technology led." That is to say, we do a survey or a card sort because doing surveys or card sorts is what we do. We do eye tracking because we have eye tracking equipment. Hammer therefore nail.

But Einstein knew a thing or two about doing research. Not for nothing is his name synonymous with genius. He knew that the research problem dictates the research method and the study design, and that every aspect of an investigation follows from that point. So let's take his approach a bit further.

What If You Had 19 Days to Define a Research Problem? How Might You Go about It?

Here are four techniques you can use to help you better understand a research problem, determine clear objectives, and sharpen the research question:

- Find out what other stakeholders need to know.
- Deconstruct the construct.

- Measure something.
- Shake out the issues.

Find Out What Other Stakeholders Need to Know

It's very tempting—especially if timelines are short—to simply take your brief from the initial kick-off meeting, or from a Request for Proposal (RFP) and assume you've learned all there is to know about a project. In reality, an initial brief can be quite weak, especially for internal researchers who may not get a formal RFP. Perhaps your sponsor has not really had an opportunity to prepare anything or think things through other than to know that it's time for some research. But, rather than guessing or making assumptions, there's an opportunity for the UX researcher to add real value right at the outset, by helping to define the research problem.

Keep in mind that the person who commissions your work and gives you the initial brief is representing a larger development team, and the team has a lot of knowledge and experience that you can, and must, tap into. Different disciplines within the team are likely to need your research data in order to make business, design or engineering decisions, so you need to find out what they want to know and how they think about the research problem.

Begin by creating a list of possible stakeholders, and then arrange to meet with them. Your list is likely to include marketers, market researchers, engineers, designers, customer support agents, other user experience specialists, technical writers, business analysts, and even legal experts. Find out what they know about the research problem, how it is being experienced, what's been tried already, what will happen if nothing is done, why this problem, why now, what success will look like, and what each person's needs, wishes and concerns are. Find out what the pressure points are, identify any constraints, discover the timeline and the budget, get the background and the history. Peel back the layers to get at what's motivating the call for help. Seeing the research requirements through the eyes of these key players will help you understand the kind of research that's needed.

It's not uncommon for UX research activities to happen without a development team even knowing about it, because no one thought to share the plan or invite contributions from the different stakeholders. In our experience, members of a development team are always pleased to be consulted, and value the opportunity to contribute. After all, when the dust has settled, these are the people who are going to put your design recommendations into action, so you need them involved from the beginning. This is not only a way of seeing a problem in a new light, but it is also a great way to connect with the team and get early buy-in.

Remember that the goal here is to better understand the initial research problem. However, you will invariably collect a shopping list of other research wants and needs. Feed these back to your project manager or client and work together to determine the priorities. But at all costs, resist the temptation to address every need in the same study—that's a recipe for disaster.

Deconstruct the Construct

Another way of defining a research problem is to deconstruct the phenomenon that is being investigated.

Most of the phenomena that UX researchers are likely to study are constructs. That is to say they do not exist in any physical sense and cannot be directly observed. Usability is an example of a construct. You can't weigh it or put it in a box like you can with, say, pencils or jars of marmalade. Quality is also a construct. So are emotions, desires, intelligence, attitudes, preferences and the propensity to buy. This doesn't mean we can't research them or measure them, but in order to do so we have to deconstruct them to reveal their constituent elements and then find ways to operationalize those elements. Not only is this an essential step in designing research, it's really the essence of what's meant by "drilling down" into a problem.

The construct "quality" gives us a good example. You know what quality is and how to judge it, but have you ever tried defining or explaining it to someone? Of course, you could simply ask users what they think of the quality of a product, but you can have no idea what they are really responding to or whether their concept of quality is the same thing that you're talking about. Even experts can't agree on a definition of quality, though there have been some very useful attempts (Joseph Juran's "fitness for use" is our favorite[4]). In fact, if you were thinking that quality is straightforward take a look at Robert Pirsig's exploration of the metaphysics of quality in his classic work *Zen and the Art of Motorcycle Maintenance*.[5] Thankfully, in the world of product development and system design, we don't need to delve as deeply as Pirsig (who drove himself to a nervous breakdown in his pursuit of understanding), but we do need to unpack the construct if we are to design a study around it.

When we do this we get to see that quality is not some homogeneous blob of stuff: It is (at least in the context of a product) a construct made up of sub-components such as performance, features, reliability, conformance to standards, durability, serviceability, and aesthetics. Suddenly the research problem starts to look clearer, and immediately we can see ways of measuring the components. The same holds true for usability—the research problem leads us directly to the test design when we deconstruct the concept into elements such as system effectiveness, efficiency and user satisfaction (following ISO 9241-11[6]).

Begin by reading about the construct under investigation. Don't simply make up, or guess at, component elements. Most concepts and constructs that we encounter in UX research are the result of decades of work by psychologists and standards organizations. The constituent elements, and how to measure them, are often well documented.

Measure Something

Whatever kind of UX research you are doing, you are measuring some aspect of human behavior. Understanding a problem and understanding what can be measured are inextricably linked such that focusing on the measurements you will make is a way of clarifying the nature of the problem. So ask questions like:

- What specifically do we need to measure?
- What kinds of metrics will differentiate specific concepts or different levels of a variable?
- What will my dependent variable be and what will I need to manipulate in order to detect differences?
- What variables will I need to control?
- Will these kinds of data convince the development team?
- Can I just use subjective rating scales or are there some objective behavioral measures I can use?
- How will I analyze the data?
- How can I connect my metrics back to the business?

Avoid just regurgitating the raw data or reporting obvious descriptive statistics. Analyze the data properly. There are hidden gems. Interrogate the data and make it work for you.

Shake Out the Issues

UX research can require a sizable investment in time and costs. Because the outcome will dictate the direction of a project and influence its success, there's too much at stake to risk mishaps or misunderstandings happening during the research. Although it seems increasingly common in the corporate world to skip this step, you should always conduct a pilot study prior to commencing the full research project.

The term "pilot" derives from the Greek word for rudder, and refers to steering and adjusting the course of something. TV shows are always piloted to get early audience reaction; engineers test jet engines on the ground before they use them to fly aircraft; and military leaders send out an advanced scouting party to check the lie of the land before any major action, all so that they can make adjustments to the plan. Doing research is no different. In fact, we would be remiss in our obligations to our client or development team if we jumped straight in to a "stage production" study without first giving everything a good shake down.

Typically, a research pilot test is conducted quite late in the preparation stage and resembles the kind of full dress rehearsal that theatrical actors would perform. It is typically used to check that the test design will return valid data, give the test administrators and data loggers an opportunity to practice, make sure the timing and logistics are in order, and check for any potential glitches in testing or recording equipment.

But we can also run a much earlier and much less formal pilot to help us better understand the research problem. This "pre-pilot" is more akin to actors doing an early read-through of a script. It requires no costumes or stage props. It requires virtually no budget and no recording equipment or testing lab. It's not about collecting real data, it's just about airing the research problem and getting it in front of some users to help flush out any issues before advancing further.

The Chinese have a phrase: "Hitting the grass to startle the snake." This is the same thing. It's a way of "hitting" the problem to see what jumps out, and it can be a useful way of testing any assumptions you might have made, and discovering any previously unknown facets to the problem, prior to moving on to the test design step.

It's also a good way to identify any stakeholders you might have missed. For example, a while back Philip did a UX research study for an organization that required store visits to generate personas. During the planning phase he made sure that senior managers were aware of the research. At the time, the organization was in the middle of a merger. As he started preparing for the pre-pilot, word came back down the chain to delay the store visits because store managers were concerned that their staff would see Philip's team as management consultants in search of cost savings. If staff thought this was a time and motion study as part of a downsizing exercise this would create confusion and anxiety, and we would be unlikely to get any good data. By planning an early pre-pilot, we created an opportunity for this potentially damaging issue to reveal itself.

If you're planning a pilot test or a pre-pilot, remember to include members of the development team and invite them to join you so they can give you feedback and help shape the final test design.

THINK LIKE A UX RESEARCHER

- If we take the Albert Einstein quotation literally, he would spend 95% of his time planning a project and 5% of his time executing the plan. Although we wouldn't recommend such a dramatic split, it does raise the question of what proportion of your time you should spend planning a project. Thinking of a project you are working on at the moment, what percentage of time has been, or will be, spent in the planning phase? Do you think this is sufficient? In an ideal project, what split would you aim to achieve? Might some projects require a different split between planning and execution—and if so, which ones?
- We list five indicators of inadequate research, as defined by William Badke. Assume you have been asked to audit a project to assess the quality of its UX research. Choose one of those indicators and identify two assessment criteria that would indicate good or poor quality research.
- We point out that the development team are important stakeholders, as are your users. Sketch a diagram illustrating the range of stakeholders on your project. Use a circle to indicate each stakeholder and vary the size of the circle to indicate that stakeholder's relative importance. Does this visualization help you consider who you should involve in defining the research problem?
- We discuss the notion of breaking down a construct (like "quality") into a set of sub-components (like performance, features and reliability) that can be separately evaluated. Try applying this idea to a research question on your current project (for example, "Is our mobile app easy to use?") Identify five sub-components that you could assess and that would answer your research question.
- Remembering that a pre-pilot is about "hitting the grass to startle the snake," what would a pre-pilot look like on your current project?

How to Approach Desk Research

Desk research is another name for secondary research. Broadly speaking, there are two types of research activity: primary research (where you go out and discover stuff yourself); and secondary research (where you review what other people have done). Desk research is not about collecting data. Instead, your role as a UX researcher carrying out desk research is to review previous research findings to gain a broad understanding of the research question.

Before carrying out a field visit, developing a prototype, running a usability test, or embarking on any project that you want to be user centered, it makes sense to see what people have done in the past that relates to the product domain. Although it's unlikely that anyone has carried out the exact research activity you're planning, someone has almost certainly tried to answer related questions. Reviewing this research is the quickest and cheapest way to understand the domain.

Carrying out desk research is a critical first step, for at least three reasons:

- If you don't know what has gone before, you won't know when you've discovered something new.
- You'll sound credible when you get face-to-face with users and stakeholders. If you've not done this "due diligence" you'll ask silly or irrelevant questions and may find your participants cut your sessions short.
- Failing to do preparatory research is disrespectful of your participants' time. You may get less than an hour with a user of your system. Do you really want to waste half that time understanding the domain issues that you could have covered elsewhere?

How Do You Approach Desk Research?

At this point, we've had many UX researchers tell us that they're working on a bleeding edge design project so there isn't any desk research to do. There's a common misconception that no research exists.

In our experience, there is almost always something you can build upon. Here's an approach we take to go about finding it. It helps us stay focused but also makes sure that we remember to check all the possible nooks and crannies where relevant research findings may be hiding.

Figure 2.1: A Venn diagram showing users, goals and environments. Where these three overlap is the sweet spot for UX research

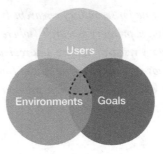

The Venn diagram (Figure 2.1) describes the context of use: your users, their goals and the environments where the action occurs. The best kind of research is where all three of these dimensions overlap: field visits that focus on your users trying to achieve their goals in context. This kind of research is so specific and relevant to your project that it may be hard to find, so don't get discouraged if you can't turn anything up in this area.

But there is potentially useful research in the other areas of overlap on our Venn diagram (Figure 2.2). This falls into three broad areas:

- Research about your users and their goals, but that was not carried out in context. This kind of research will take the form of surveys, user interviews and focus groups.
- Research that addresses the goals your system will support and the environment it will be used in, but doesn't tell us much about users. Examples include call center or web analytics.
- Research that uncovers information about your users in their environment, but that may not address the goals that your system will support. This will take the form of field research by teams who are designing a product for the same kinds of user but to meet different needs.

The most likely place you'll find customer and user research is within your own organization. But you need to be prepared to dig. This is because research findings, especially on Agile projects, are often treated as throwaway by-products that apply to a specific project. The findings aren't shared outside the development team but typically make a fleeting appearance on a research wall or end up buried in someone's email inbox. Even when

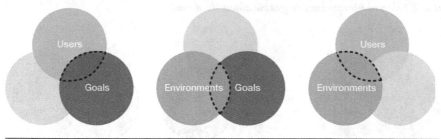

Figure 2.2: This set of Venn diagrams shows that research into the overlap between users and goals, environments and goals and users and environments can also yield useful insights

research findings are written down, and even when the report is archived somewhere, people typically don't know how to go about finding it. Organizations are generally poor at creating a shared repository of knowledge and rarely teach staff how to use the intranet or where past reports might be located. The result of these obstacles is that companies waste time and money either doing research that already exists or asking the wrong research questions.

So within your organization, you should:

- Talk to your stakeholders. Get to know the product owner and understand their goals, vision and concerns.
- Examine call center analytics or web analytics (if there is an existing service).
- Talk to front line, customer-facing people who currently interact with users.

Once you've covered the areas of overlap, your next step is to look for more generic information about your users, the environment in which they'll use the system, and the kinds of goals your system will support (Figure 2.3).

- What research has been done with your users, even if it's not directly relevant to their goals when using your system?
- What research has been done on the kind of goals your system will support, even if the research has been done with a different user group?
- What research exists on the kinds of environment where you expect your system to be used (environment means hardware, software and the physical and social environments in which your system will be used).

Figure 2.3: In almost every project, you'll find some research that exists into users, goals and environments. This may not be directly relevant to your specific research questions but it will help you become knowledgeable about the domain

In this step, you'll find it useful to:

- Review existing research done by government organizations. For example, in the United States there are numerous government websites with census and statistics data (www.usa.gov/statistics is a good starting point that links to many other United States and international sources); in the UK, the Office for National Statistics (www.ons.gov.uk) has a wealth of information about citizens that may be useful to understand your users, such as demographics about internet users, consumer trends and facts about online retail sales.

- Review research carried out by relevant charities. For example, if you're developing a new kind of tool to help diabetics measure their sugar levels, you should bookmark the research done by a diabetes charity. Websites like America's Charities (US) and Charity Choice (UK) allow you to browse through and locate hundreds of different charitable organizations so you're bound to find at least one that's relevant.

- Search Google Scholar to find relevant research carried out by universities. Although you may struggle to appreciate the nuances of certain academic arguments, you could always use this route to find the researcher's contact details and give them a call.

- If your system will be used in a work context, study interviews at careers websites. For example, *The Guardian*'s "How do I become..." section[7] has interviews with people working as tattoo artists, forensic scientists, and even as a royal footman so the chances are that you'll be able to get some context for whatever job title your system is aimed at. You should also check *The Guardian*'s "What I'm Really Thinking" series.[8]

Judging the Quality of the Research You Find

Beware of dismissing research just because it was done a few years ago. People new to research often make the mistake of viewing research reports like so many yogurts in a fridge where the sell-by dates have expired. Just because it was done a couple of years ago, don't think it's no longer relevant. The best research tends to focus on human behavior, and that tends to change very slowly.

THINK LIKE A UX RESEARCHER

- Other than Google Search, list five kinds of desk research you could do to find out more about the users of the system you are researching at the moment. (Review the diagrams in this essay for ideas.)
- How important is it to validate research carried out in the past or by third parties, such as academics? Is there any kind of desk research that you would accept or reject unconditionally?
- Assume your desk research uncovered a well executed, large scale survey of your users. If the project manager said, "Great! There's no need for us to do the UX research now," how would you argue the case for contextual research over desk research?
- We point out that research findings are often treated as throwaway by-products. How might you store or summarize the findings from your desk research and your UX research so that future researchers don't duplicate your effort?
- In the previous essay ("Defining your UX research problem") we discussed William Badke's indicators of inadequate research. One indicator is that it deals in generalities and superficial surveys, avoiding depth and analysis. How would you define "depth" and "analysis" to evaluate the outputs of your desk research? How might you use Badke's other criteria to evaluate the outputs?

Conducting an Effective Stakeholder Interview

There are few things more likely to make your design project difficult than a poorly conducted kick-off meeting with stakeholders. Structuring your stakeholder interview around a few simple techniques will ensure you get off to a good start and set you up for success.

Though it may consume two of hours of your life, involve people saying lots of words, and require much watching of PowerPoint, when distilled to its barest essentials, the typical stakeholder meeting often goes something like this:

> Client: "We need you to design a new wibble."
> Development team: "OK"

In this scenario, development teams, whether internal or external to a company, often end up simply designing what they are asked to design, or rolling out the usual "one-size fits all" usability test. Project requirements arrive by decree from on high and go unchallenged. The trail of data and decision making linking the thing being designed to the potential user is tenuous or non-existent.

Designers and UX researchers find this approach frustrating and disheartening because it sells them short. We know we can design the best wibble imaginable, or carry out the best usability test. We just don't know for sure whether a new wibble or a usability test is really what's needed.

There's a better way.

Let's Get Real or Let's Not Play

The structured technique we will describe in this essay is guaranteed to flush out the information you need to properly diagnose your stakeholder's needs and to help them be successful. It's an approach based on our favorite, and most thumbed, business book, *Let's Get Real or Let's Not Play* by business development consultant Mahan Khalsa.[9] In it, he describes some simple steps designed to give a new project opportunity a bit of a shakedown.

We'll use Khalsa's framework and prompt questions as our guide, and we'll look at each step in turn and see what we can learn from his masterful understanding of how to help stakeholders and clients succeed. But first Khalsa warns us of an important rule upon which these steps are predicated: *No guessing!*

We too often think we have understood a stakeholder's needs properly—especially if we work for the same company—when, in fact, we haven't quite grasped something. We often make assumptions without even realizing that they are just assumptions. We may assume that the design or research requirements have been derived from reliable information and careful decision making. We may hesitate to ask the right questions if we think it makes us look like we don't know what we're doing.

But it's important not to guess, or to think that the answer to your question doesn't matter. It will matter at some point during the project. Not knowing may result in you making the wrong design or research decisions, and by then it may be too late. If you don't understand something in the stakeholder meeting, the chances are other people don't understand it either. So avoid guessing. "Supposing is good," advised Mark Twain, "but finding out is better."

Move Off the Solution

Here's what Khalsa advises you do instead: Move off the solution.

Your stakeholders often want to talk about solutions. "We need a new design for X" and "Can you test Y?" are requests for solutions. Most stakeholders are looking for a quick fix, or a magic bullet, because they have already self-diagnosed their needs. The formal "Request for Proposal" (RFP) works this way. A typical RFP offers little real insight into the client's needs and usually assumes no one will ask any questions. Face to face discussion is actively discouraged. The client has already decided what needs to be done, has written down the solution, and now just wants someone to deliver: "A pound of UX research please and two bags of design. Thank you very much."

It's possible, of course, that your stakeholder has indeed arrived at a correct diagnosis, but the real difficulty lies in the fact that they may not know how your design or user experience process works, so they don't know what you need to know before you can start thinking about designing a solution. We can get ourselves in a fix if we allow ourselves to get swept along by the promise of solutions. After all, we love talking about what we can do. It's easy. Besides, it's what the stakeholder expects the meeting to be about.

So why avoid talking about solutions?

Because we don't know what the problem is yet. Solutions have no inherent value. They can't exist in isolation from a problem. The fact that stakeholders think they can is because the word "solutions" has entered the lexicon of meaningless business jargon. But if we're going to create a real solution, there must be something to solve. In Khalsa's words, the solution must "alleviate some pain" that the stakeholder or company is experiencing, or it must "result in some gain" that the stakeholder or company desires.

The one thing you can bank on is that the stakeholder will bring the solution (design a new X) to the meeting table. Respond by shifting the focus. Change the direction of the conversation away from solutions and, ever so subtly, take control of the dialogue. Khalsa suggests asking questions like these:

- "It's likely that we can design a new X, but what issues are you hoping a new X will address?"
- "By not having an X, what kind of problems are your users (or your company) experiencing?"
- "If we designed the best X imaginable, what problems will it solve for you?"
- "Let's say we designed the world's best X. What results would you achieve that you can't get today?"

The stakeholder may respond by giving you a list of problems, or may go all vague on you and wander off into a pointless ramble. Bring them back to your question.

- "Thanks for describing the general situation. Let's get a bit more specific. What particular problem have you identified that you think a new X will solve for your users?"

Don't get trapped into talking about solutions.

Get Out All the Issues

Next, have the stakeholders generate a quick list of issues. The items you write on the whiteboard should describe a specific problem or a desired result or outcome. Don't dwell on any one issue at this point—you don't know which issues are important yet—and don't allow the conversation to spiral away from you as stakeholders debate among themselves. Just focus on creating the list. If you are working with a group of stakeholders you can ask individuals to write down what they believe the main issues are on sticky notes, then have them place them on a whiteboard. That can prevent the meeting from becoming a free-for-all.

As the list unfolds, keep pushing for it to be a complete list:

"What else are you hoping X will achieve?"

Don't start discussing any issues just yet. When the stakeholders have exhausted their input, if your own expertise is telling you something is missing, you can prompt with:

"I notice no one mentioned anything about (for example, improving ease of learning). Is that an issue for you?"

Next, you need to know which issues matter the most. Sometimes the stakeholders will easily identify the main issues. Other times they may say, "All the issues are important." Respond to this by acknowledging that you want to understand all of the issues, and then ask:

"Which one would you like to talk about first?"

Finally, double-check:

"If you could make progress against the issues on this list, and nothing else, would you have a solution that exactly meets your needs?"

If the answer is no, there's still something you're not being told. Find out what it is and add it to the list.

Develop Evidence and Impact

Now you're ready to ask a question that may take your stakeholders by surprise, so be prepared for hesitation, uncertainty, or even a very long pause, as you look at the list and ask:

"How do you know these are problems?"

Cue hesitation, uncertainty and a very long pause.

- "What evidence do you have that these problems actually exist?"
- "How is your organization (or your users) experiencing the problems?"

- "What do you currently have too little of (sales, profits, customers, etc.), or too much of (complaints, product returns, service calls etc.)?"
- "Do you have any data to show that a solution will provide the results you want?"

Our questions about evidence are likely to result in one of four possible outcomes that Khalsa identifies:

- *There is no evidence*: There is nothing to indicate that the problems really exist or that our work will have the desired results.
- *There is soft evidence*: This may be in the form of anecdotes, or word of mouth feedback collected from customers in focus groups or in small-sample surveys.
- *There is presumed evidence*: This may be in the form of articles in publications or other media. It may be data that are generally true but that may or may not apply in the current case.
- *There is hard evidence*: The company has done reliable research and actual data exist that describe the problems, or provide verifiable measurements about the current and desired state.

It goes without saying that we would like to see hard evidence. But if it doesn't exist, or if the evidence is weak or unreliable, all is not lost. In this event, we can offer help to get the evidence. We know how to do design research, so we can put feet on the ground and collect real evidence based on real user behavior. Or we can help search for existing evidence within the company. What we can't do is brush the matter aside and just "wing it." No guesswork, remember.

We not only want evidence that the problems are *real*—we also want to know how *important* the problems are and how big an impact solving them can have:

- "How are you measuring the problem?"
- "What is the current measurement?"
- "What would you like it to be?"
- "What is the value of the difference?"
- "What is the value of the difference over time?"

Once we get into this kind of discussion, if the problems are important and the impact is big, we can present rough calculations like this:

"So, overall, returns cost you $12 million a year. But only 25% of these products are actually faulty: the rest are returned because they are just too difficult to use. Our user experience work will eliminate the usability problems that are causing the returns. This will save you $9 million a year, and $45 million over the next five years. Let's get started."

Remove the Solution

What if the problem is not very important or the impact will be small? Khalsa has a clever technique: Remove the solution.

What if you did nothing? Here's where you can pull back a little and let the stakeholders convince themselves that the project is important. Remember that people like to buy, but they don't like to be sold to. You can help move the discussion along like this:

- "It sounds like living with the problem may be cheaper than fixing it."
- "It seems like you have other problems that could take priority over this one."
- "It sounds like you can do this work yourself. How do you think we can add value?"

This may seem like you're playing hard to get and it may feel counterintuitive, but if the opportunity is really not that important to the stakeholder then even your best solution will fall flat, and it might be in the best interests of both parties to step back and revisit the opportunity at a later time.

Explore Context and Constraints

Once we have a clear understanding of the problem, some evidence that it is real, and a measure of its importance, we can start to expose the background and history and some of the constraints and obstacles we may encounter once we get started. Ask questions like:

- "What you've described is clearly an important problem. How long has it been going on?"
- "Have you tried anything to solve this problem before?"
- "Did something stop you from succeeding in the past?"

At this point you may get responses such as:

- "We didn't have the right skills to fix it ourselves."
- "The timing wasn't right."
- "It was a low priority back then but now it's really hurting us."

Khalsa calls these "good constraints." They are good because they used to exist but don't anymore. Or you may get responses such as:

- "We had no budget."
- "We couldn't get buy-in from upper management."
- "We tried but another group had a vested interest in killing the project."
- "Politics always gets in the way."
- "It wasn't considered important enough."

If you hear these kinds of responses, you must ask:

- "So, what's different now? What's changed?"
- "If we try again now, will we still hit these same obstacles?"

And it's OK to ask, "From what you've been saying, it sounds like some of these obstacles still exist. What do you think we should do?"

Remember, your objective is to help your stakeholder find a way through to a solution and to help them to be successful. This may involve helping them troubleshoot whatever obstacles are in the way.

Caveat: Don't Blindside Your Stakeholders

This approach to an initial stakeholder interview will help put you in control of the meeting and get you the information you need. But a word of caution: *Don't catch your stakeholders off-guard.* Your objective is to get information, not to expose the fact that they haven't done their homework.

We always give clients advanced notice of the kind of meeting we are going to conduct, and the kinds of questions we are going to ask, so they can do some preparation if necessary. This serves two purposes: first, the meeting will be pointless if the stakeholder can't answer our questions. And second, this ensures we are going to be meeting with the right people. These will be decision makers who are accountable for the project's success, and who have authority to make decisions and manage the budget.

We've tried these techniques in our own stakeholder meetings and not only do they deliver the goods, and make for a very productive meeting, but they also create a strong first impression of our ability to help solve the problem. This leaves the stakeholders feeling confident that we know what we're doing and that they are in safe hands.

THINK LIKE A UX RESEARCHER

- This approach to stakeholder interviews draws heavily on Mahan Khalsa's book, *Let's Get Real or Let's Not Play*. Is it possible to work as an internal consultant and refuse to "play" by your company's rules if you feel they are outdated?
- This essay includes some phrases to help shift stakeholders from thinking about the solution to thinking about the problem. Choose one of these to memorize—or re-write the phrase using your own words that would work with your stakeholders.
- Clients and development teams often approach the UX researcher with a "method led" request (such as "Please run a focus group"). Imagine you have been asked to deliver a UX research method that you feel is inappropriate but you are told, "That's all we can do with the time and budget available." Which is the more ethical approach: to carry out the research method that's asked of you or to decline to run the research at all? Why?
- Usability testing is a valuable method but when it is the only UX research method carried out it is often an indicator of a development team with low user experience maturity. What would you say are the main user experience issues with your existing product? Do you think usability testing is the most appropriate UX research method to fix these problems? What alternatives could you offer your development team?
- Think of a product or software app that you use frequently and that you feel suffers from user experience issues. What evidence exists to support your point of view? Is this evidence "soft," "presumed" or "hard"? What methods could you use to collect "hard" evidence? How could you use that evidence to express the impact of these user experience issues on the business?

Identifying the User Groups for Your UX Research

*One challenge faced by teams new to UX research is simply getting started.
Enthusiasm quickly gives way to frustration as teams don't know where to
begin—especially when their product is aimed at "everyone." A practical solution
is to identify a group of users who are easiest to get to and who provide the best
opportunity for validated learning.*

David once asked a product manager to describe the users of his product.
"That's easy," he replied. "It's aimed at everyone." This reminds us of an
ironic internet meme that read, "The target audience is males and females
aged zero and up."

Thinking of your audience as "everyone" is the best way we've come across
to make a product fail. One reason for this is that designing for everyone
removes all constraints. Focus becomes impossible. When a product is aimed
at everyone, you can make a valid argument for every feature, every platform
and every context.

If that's how your team is thinking of your audience, we have an idea that
may help. We don't want to discourage you from world domination; we simply want to convince you that the best way to get there is by taking informed
baby steps—rather than a giant leap into the unknown.

How to Design for Everyone

As an example, let's look at a case study of a successful website used by pretty
much everyone: Facebook. If you examine the history of Facebook, Mark
Zuckerberg and his team didn't set out to design for everyone. The site was
initially aimed at Harvard students. It then expanded to students at other Ivy
League universities. Although Facebook next expanded outside the United
States, the target audience was still university students for the first two years.
Keeping the target market reasonably focused enabled Facebook to test out
what worked and what didn't. Facebook then opened up membership to
employees of companies like Apple and Microsoft before finally opening the
doors to anyone over the age of 13 with a valid email address.

As another example, Amazon began life as a web-based bookseller,
with a product aimed mainly at web-savvy users. Amazon then diversified

in two ways: first, it offered the same functionality to a different segment (it sold books to anyone who could use a web browser). Then it offered slightly different functionality to the same segment: for example, Amazon began to stock software and CDs. The rest, as they say, is history.

In both of these examples, the end goal may well have been "everyone, everywhere" but this wasn't where the product started.

So where *do* you start?

An Exercise in Focusing

Get your development team together for a 30-minute exercise. Give each person a stack of sticky notes and, working alone, ask each person to write down at least five different user groups for your product (one group per sticky).

For example, a passport service might have "business travelers," "someone with no fixed address" and "a retired person." A photography app might have groups like "day trippers," "food enthusiasts" and "Instagrammers." A sports website might have "Football fans," "Rugby fans" and "People who watch the Olympics but little else."

If your team struggles to come up with more than one or two stickies, here are some specific prompts you can use to generate more user groups:

- Who do you see as the "typical" users of your product?
- Which users contrast with typical users (the "opposite")?
- Who are the early adopters—people who will want to use your product before anyone else?
- Who are the power users—people who will use the product frequently?
- Who might struggle to use the product?
- Who would use the product only if "forced" to do so?
- What different sorts of people use the product? How might their needs and behaviors vary?
- What ranges of behavior and types of environments need to be explored?
- What are the business goals of the product? Do these goals suggest which users to focus on?
- Which users do you know least about?
- Which users are easy to get to?
- Which interviews are easy to set up?
- Which users are keen to talk to you and provide input?

Using the Grid

Once the stickies have been generated, remove any obvious duplicates and then organize the remaining stickies in the following grid (Figure 2.4).

The vertical axis on this grid is labeled, "Amount we expect to learn from this group of users." This is because the purpose of UX research is validated learning: the process of identifying and testing your riskiest assumptions. Some groups of users will provide a better test of your riskiest assumptions than other groups. Simply divide your sticky notes into two groups: one group from which you expect to learn more and another group from which you expect to learn less.

The horizontal axis is labeled, "Ease of access." This means how easy it is to get to your different groups of users. For example, some of your user groups may be in another country, or may work night shifts, or may be too busy to see you. Those groups are harder to get to than user groups who live in your local town or that have free time on their hands. Your job is to subdivide your groups of users into these categories and place the stickies on the appropriate part of the grid.

At this point, step back and look at your work. This grid provides a pragmatic way for you to get started on your research quickly.

Figure 2.4: A 2 × 2 grid to help you pick the user groups you should research first

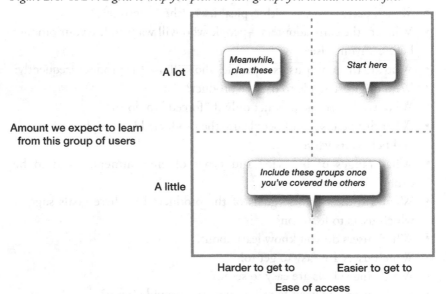

You'll start with a group of users from the top right of this grid. Think of these as the "gold" user groups since these are users who will teach you a lot about their needs from your product and who are also easy to set up. You should be able to arrange sessions with these groups of users in the next few days. Once you start talking to these users you'll discover some assumptions you made that are wrong. You'll also start to learn new stuff that's relevant to the use of your product. You'll begin to generate new assumptions. This is validated learning in action.

But let's not forget the other important quadrant: users who you expect to learn a lot from but who are hard to get to. Think of these as your "silver" user groups. You should add these groups to your UX research backlog. While your existing research is in progress, take time to plan visits to this group of users. This will give you the chance to test more of your assumptions.

We could characterize the user groups in the lower right quadrant as our "bronze" user groups. Consider the "bronze" user groups only once you've exhausted your "gold" and "silver" user groups.

And what about that final quadrant: users who are hard to get to and who probably won't teach you much? Given that there's never enough time or budget to do research with everyone, don't feel bad about skipping this group of users entirely.

A Final Word

A common reason that teams don't do UX research is not that they don't think users matter but because they simply don't know where to start. There's a paralysis of analysis that prevents action. This approach, although simple, will help you cut through the clutter and help you get started on your UX research immediately.

THINK LIKE A UX RESEARCHER

- The notion of "validated learning" was popularized by Eric Ries in his book,[10] *The Lean Startup*. The idea is to get user feedback based on actual observed behavior then continually iterate your product and market strategy based on that feedback until you hone in on exactly what your customers want. This leads us to an interesting conclusion. It means that the best development teams aren't the ones who *ship* quickest. The best development teams are the ones who *learn* quickest. If you joined a development team that claimed to use "validated learning" in its approach to product development, what kind of behaviors would you expect the team to demonstrate?

- Thinking of your current development team, what labels do they use to describe users? Do they use job titles (such as "financial analyst"), user segments (such as "gamers"), persona names (such as "Caroline") or other terms that make it clear they are not designing for everyone? Or do they use generic terms, like "users" or "customers"? If they use generic terms, how might you change their thinking to focus on specific groups of users?

- One of the best ways to explore the usefulness of the 2 × 2 diagram introduced in this essay is to try it out yourself. Either do the exercise alone or—even better—get your team together to identify the key user groups and classify them as "gold," "silver" and "bronze" user groups.

- Imagine a scenario where you had several groups of "gold" users (user groups who are easy to get to and who you expect to learn a lot from). It's entirely possible that you could use your entire UX research budget focusing on users in this single quadrant. What would be the risks of ignoring the "silver" users entirely? What can "hard to get to" user groups tell us that we can't learn from "easy to get to" user groups?

- One advantage of 2 × 2 diagrams is that they stop us thinking in one dimension. For example, development teams often think in terms of "expert" and "novice" users, ignoring the fact that the vast majority of users are probably somewhere in between these two extremes. How might you change one or both of the axis labels on the 2 × 2 diagram to help your team think in a more nuanced way about users?

Writing the Perfect Participant Screener

"Know thy user" is the first principle of usability, so it's important that you involve the right kind of people in your usability study. These eight practitioner guidelines for screening participants will show you how to recruit articulate, representative participants for your research, quickly filter out the people you don't want and help you avoid the dreaded "no shows."

A few years ago, the BBC interviewed Guy Goma about an Apple Computer court case. Mr Goma was presented as an IT expert but in fact was really at the BBC for a job interview. The researcher had collected him from reception by mistake, leaving behind the real "Guy," IT expert Guy Kewney. Mr Goma's facial reaction (which you can see on YouTube[11]) when he suddenly realizes he is live on air and about to face a series of questions about music downloading is a sight to behold.

In this instance, having the name "Guy" was a necessary but not a sufficient condition to take part in the interview. "Participant screening" is where you sift through all the possible candidates to identify people who are truly suitable—the participants. It's where you filter out the Guy Gomas and filter in the Guy Kewneys.

Here are eight practitioner guidelines for writing great participant screeners:

- Screen for behaviors, not demographics.
- Ask precise questions.
- Identify unsuitable candidates early.
- Get value-for-money participants.
- Manage each participant's expectations.
- Pilot test the screener.
- Avoid no shows.
- Brief the recruiting company.

Screen for Behaviors, Not Demographics

When faced with a new product or website, a user's past behavior will predict their performance much more accurately than their demographic profile.

Demographic factors like gender may be important segmentation variables for marketers but they have very little impact on the way someone actually uses a product. It's important to work with marketing managers to be sure you understand the target users but at the same time encourage them to describe users in terms of their behaviors rather than (say) their income level.

If the marketing folks seem vague, or can only describe the user in high-level terms ("We have two customer groups, people who use laptops and people who use desktops") then this should raise a red flag and suggests some field research is warranted.

But which behavioral variables should you use? On web projects, two behavioral variables used by every UX researcher are digital skills (the user's experience of web idioms like navigation, form filling and search) and task knowledge (the user's knowledge of the domain, for example photography, share dealing or genealogy). Design your screener so you can classify each candidate's ability as "high" or "low" on both these factors, and recruit people accordingly.

It may be hard for you to get your screener past the product or marketing team without including any demographic questions whatsoever. In that case, place the demographic questions towards the end of the survey and just aim to get an appropriate mix.

Ask Precise Questions

If you want to distinguish "high" and "low" digital skills, don't just ask people how long they spend online. One person's "frequently" is another person's "sometimes." Instead, ask what they do online and whether they do it on their own or with assistance. People with high digital skills probably buy things online using a credit card, download and install software, belong to social networking sites, manage their photos online, actively manage their privacy, and comment on blogs. People with low digital skills will do fewer of these activities or seek help from a friend or family member.

Identify Unsuitable Candidates Early

Broadly speaking, screeners contain two kinds of question: exclusion questions (where one answer will exclude the candidate, such as answering "Yes" to the question, "Do you work for a competitor company?") and balance questions (where you want to get an equal number of people in different categories, for example a balance of "high" and "low" digital skills). Because of this, it's helpful to think of your screener as a funnel: ask the exclusion questions early to filter out unsuitable candidates as quickly as possible.

Incidentally, a quick aside on that question, "Do you work for a competitor company?" We've often seen screeners that start with a question of the form: "Do you, or does anyone in your household, work for any of the following organizations..." Any candidate faced with this question knows the "correct" answer and may lie to get selected (a process known as "faking good"). Avoid this by simply asking an open question: "Where do you work?" or "Tell me about your job."

Sometimes candidates can pass all your screening questions but still not be what you want. For example, one of our colleagues was testing a website that sold eyeglasses. Everything went fine during the usability test until it got to the product selection part of the test. It turned out that, in real life, the participant said he took his partner along to the opticians to choose his eyeglasses. So if you're testing a B2C website, make sure that your participants make the purchase decisions too (or alternatively, make sure they bring their influential partner along to the test).

Get Value-for-Money Participants

If you are recruiting for a thinking aloud study, you need to screen out candidates who are shy or inarticulate. You can usually judge this by including an open question in your screener: for example, "Tell me about the way you shop for products online." But if you find that you're screening out lots of potential candidates with this requirement—an audience of teenage boys for example—you may need to rethink your methodology.

Also, if you are recruiting for an eye tracking study, you'll need to exclude people who wear bifocals, rimless eyeglasses—or lots of mascara. (We've yet to find a subtle way of asking if the participant wears lots of mascara. It's probably easiest to ask your participants not to wear mascara on the day of the test.)

Manage Each Participant's Expectations

At the beginning of the screening session, make sure your participant realizes that answering the screening questions is a pre-requisite for taking part in the research, not the research itself. Clarify that the screener isn't the actual deal. Explain that the incentive will be paid in cash once they attend the session.

Once you have recruited participants, manage their expectations for the session. Most people's preconception of consumer research is the focus group, so if you're running a typical usability session make it clear that the participant will be interviewed alone. This is also a good time to let participants know that the session will be recorded to video and that they will be asked to sign a consent form and a non-disclosure agreement. If any of these are deal-breakers, now would be a good time to find out.

At the same time, don't reveal too much in case participants decide to do their own research prior to the test. For example, if you tell participants that you'll be asking them to evaluate BigCo's website this gives them the opportunity to go to the site and work on it in advance of the test, so as to "practice" for the test. Provide enough information to reassure the participant of the nature of the study, but not the specifics.

Pilot Test the Screener

Test the screener on a handful of people you know you don't want, and on a handful you know you do want and make sure they fall into the right "bins." And critically, be sure that internal stakeholders sign off on the screener so that later they cannot dismiss the value of the study by saying you recruited the wrong participants. When a frustrated colleague observes your usability study and asks you, "Where did you get such clueless users?" you want to be sure you have a watertight response.

Avoid No Shows

Participants who fail to turn up are the bane of the researcher's life. Not only is this frustrating and a waste of time, it's expensive and embarrassing— especially if you have a couple of senior managers in the observation room twiddling their thumbs. You need to avoid participant no-shows at all cost. Try these suggestions:

- Once you've recruited the participant, emphasize how important he or she is to the research. Phrases like this help: "This product has been designed especially for people like you," and "You are exactly the kind of person we need for this research."
- Send the participant a map and directions to the facility. Send a proper letter, in the post, since this makes the event appear more real and tangible. Also send an email with a link to a web page that contains the same information, just in case the participant loses the letter.

- Give participants your phone number to call if they can't find the venue or if they are running late.
- Make sure all letters and emails are sent from a named individual rather than from a faceless group, such as "The Usability/UX/Web/IT Team."
- Get the participant's mobile phone number so you can call him or her. On the day before the session, ring the participant to confirm everything is still OK and re-send instructions by email. On the day of the test, send a text message reminding the participant of the start time.

Following these suggestions will help, but there are no guarantees. So it's also worth getting back-up cover. Recruit "floaters," who are people who agree to turn up at the facility at the same time as the first participant and stay until that day's last participant has arrived. The floater's life is boring but it's well paid. We tend to pay floaters two to four times as much as regular participants. (Just make sure you have lots of magazines and newspapers for them to read.)

For critical projects, you should also consider double-recruiting, where you recruit two participants for each slot. If both participants turn up, ask your observers to review each participant's screener and choose the person they want to take part. The other participant should remain at the facility for 15 minutes or so, just to make sure the chosen participant is up to scratch. Then your other participant can be sent on their way with the full incentive.

Brief the Recruiting Company

If you use an external agency to do the recruiting, walk through the screener carefully with the recruiter and make sure there are no ambiguities. Make sure you speak with the actual recruiter: most recruitment agencies have a legion of subcontractors who actually do the leg work, and it's that person you need to speak with, not his or her manager. Explain to the recruiter why getting the wrong people is a serious problem for your study. You should also identify the questions where you can allow some flexibility and those questions where you can't—this will make your recruiter's life a lot easier.

UX research with unrepresentative participants is a waste of time and money. It makes no sense to cut corners. Use these guidelines to set up and manage your own participant recruitment program and you won't go far wrong.

THINK LIKE A UX RESEARCHER

- We argue that you should recruit for behaviors, rather than demographics. People often argue that age (a demographic characteristic) is an important recruitment criteria because they believe that older users are less competent with technology, lack the physical capabilities to use it or are generally less able. If you took our advice and ignored age, what behaviors could you use instead to get an appropriate mix of participants? (By the way, common assumptions around age and digital abilities are often incorrect.[12])

- Assume you need to recruit people who may be applying for a driving license. What question could you ask on a screener? If you said, "Are you thinking about applying for a driving license in the next 12 months?" that's a good question that focuses on behavior—but it makes it obvious what you're looking for. How could you ask this question and simultaneously obscure the purpose of your study so potential participants can't "fake good"?

- Recruitment companies tend to recruit from their own panel of participants. They keep this panel fresh over time by recruiting new people and weeding out people who no longer want to take part. Recruitment companies almost always build these panels by asking people to complete an online registration form, directing people to the form using channels like social media advertising. What biases might this introduce? What difficulties could this cause if you wanted to expressly recruit people with low digital skills? How could you engage participants in your research that avoid social media entirely or use technology to block online advertising?

- We provide five suggestions for avoiding "no shows." Rank order these suggestions in terms of their likely effectiveness with your own users.

- Consider a situation where, for whatever reason, the participant has been incorrectly recruited. She is so different from the recruitment requirements that there's no point using her in the usability test. If the project sponsor told you to send the participant away and keep the incentive for another participant who is a better fit, what would you do? How could you have prevented this situation from occurring in the first place?

Arguments Against a Representative Sample

Engaging a representative sample of participants in UX research sounds like a good idea but it is flawed. It requires lots of participants, does not work in an Agile development environment, stifles innovation and reduces your chances of finding problems in small sample usability tests. When combined with iterative design, theoretical sampling (where theory and data collection move hand in hand) provides a more practical alternative.

Sooner or later when you present your design research findings, someone will question your sample's demographic representativeness. "How can you possibly understand our audience of thousands by speaking with just 5, or even 25, people?" you'll be asked. "How can you ensure that such a small sample is representative of the larger population?"

This question is based on the assumption that demographic representativeness is an important characteristic of design research. But this assumption is wrong for four reasons. The first two reasons are practical:

- Representative samples require lots of participants.
- Representative samples are difficult to achieve in an Agile development environment.

And the second two reasons are methodological:

- Representative samples stifle innovation.
- Representative samples reduce your chances of finding usability problems that affect a small number of users.

Let's look at each of these in turn.

Representative Samples Require Lots of Participants

An obvious argument to make against demographic representativeness is that it results in sample sizes that are too large for almost all design research. For example, to make a sample representative of a demographic, you would aim for an equal balance of gender (male and female), domain knowledge (experts and novices), technical knowledge (digital savvy and digital novices), device types used (desktop and mobile), geographical location (urban and rural), age (Gen X and Millennial) as well as additional, specific characteristics important for your particular product. To get even rudimentary coverage of these characteristics you will need a large sample size.

For example, with the characteristics we have listed earlier, you'll need a sample size of 64 to end up with just one person representing a target demographic:

- To achieve a representative demographic sample, our 64 participants will comprise 32 men and 32 women.
- Our 32 men will comprise 16 domain experts and 16 domain novices.
- Our 16 male, domain experts will comprise 8 participants who are digitally savvy and 8 that are digital novices.
- Our eight male, domain expert, digitally savvy participants will comprise four desktop participants and four mobile participants.
- Our four male, domain expert, digitally savvy, desktop participants will comprise two participants in an urban location and two participants in a rural location.
- Our two male, domain expert, digitally savvy, desktop, urban participants will comprise one Gen X and one Millennial participant.

And what if that one participant is unusual in some other, non-representative way? Can one participant ever be representative of a segment? It seems that all we've done is move the issue of "representativeness" further down the chain. Boosting the sample size in each segment from one to (say) five participants (to make it more representative) means we now need a sample size of 320 participants. Very quickly, our sample size escalates dramatically as we build in more "representativeness."

This isn't practical for design research.

Representative Samples Don't Play Nicely with Agile

A second reason a representative sample is impractical is because it doesn't work with Agile development. Recall our sample size of 64 participants from the previous section. This belongs to a world where we can define our research problem up front and plan exactly how to arrive at a solution. Yet no modern software development team works like this because requirements can't be nailed down in advance. Instead, development teams rely on iteration—and this is the same approach we should adopt as UX researchers.

For help, we can turn to a different approach to participant sampling used by qualitative researchers. This approach is very different to the criteria researchers use for statistical sampling. In particular, the qualitative researcher does not sample participants randomly. Instead, theory and data collection move hand in hand. The qualitative researcher simultaneously collects and analyses data while also deciding what data to collect next and what participants to include. In other words, the process of data collection is controlled by the researcher's emerging understanding of the overall story. This sampling technique is known as "theoretical sampling."

This means the UX researcher should select individuals, groups, and so on according to the expected level of new insights. You want to find participants who will give you the greatest insights, viewed in the context of the data you've already collected.

It's easy to see how you can adapt this approach to working in sprints with an Agile team. Rather than do all of the research up front, we do just enough research to help the team move forward. Our sample size and its representativeness both increase as the project develops.

These two practical issues of representativeness—that it requires a large sample size and it doesn't fit with Agile ways of working—are important. But they do not fully address the point made by our critic. Practical research methods are fine but we can't use impracticality as a defense against shoddy research.

But these are not the only issues.

There are methodological issues too. Aiming for a "representative" sample in UX research stifles innovation and it reduces your chances of finding problems in small sample usability tests. Let's turn to those issues now.

Representative Samples Stifle Innovation

A third problem with representative samples is that they stifle innovation. With research in the discovery phase, when we are trying to innovate and come up with new product ideas, we don't know our audience.

Stop for a second and let that sink in: we don't know our audience—or at least, we know it only roughly. There is no list of people we can select from because we don't have any customers—we may not even have a product. Indeed, part of the UX researcher's role in the discovery phase is to challenge what their team thinks of as "the product." The role of the UX researcher is to help development teams see beyond their product to the user's context, to understand users' unmet needs, goals and motivations.

Since we don't know who our final audience will be, it's impossible to sample the audience in any way that's representative. It would be like trying to sample people who will be driving an electric car in 15 years' time. Even if we already have a list of customers who use an existing product, we can't use *only* those people in our discovery research, because then we are speaking to the converted. This reduces opportunities for innovation because we are speaking only to those people whose needs we have already met.

Instead, to be truly innovative, we need to discover the boundaries and the rough shape of the experience for which we are designing. Rather than make predictions about an *audience*, innovative discovery research tries to make predictions about an *experience*. You're creating tests and hypotheses to help you understand what's going on.

One of our favorite examples comes from IDEO. They were designing a new kind of sandal. They expressly included outliers in their sample, like podiatrists and foot fetishists, to see what they could learn. This is what we mean by understanding the boundaries of the research domain.

Representative Samples Reduce Your Chances of Finding Usability Problems that Affect a Small Number of Users

We can't use this same defense when it comes to usability testing. Now we know the rough shape of our audience: it would be foolish to involve (say) teenage music fans in a usability test of headphones aimed at working musicians. We need to match our participants to the tasks that they carry out.

But recall that a usability test typically involves a small number of participants (five has become the industry standard[13]). This is because five participants give us an 85% chance of finding a problem that affects one in three users. However, some important usability problems affect a small number of users. On some systems, testing five participants may find only 10% of the total problems, because the other 90% of problems affect fewer than one in three users. (We elaborate on this in the next essay.)

To get the most value out of our usability test, it therefore makes sense to bias our sample to include participants who are more likely to experience problems with our product. This type of person might be less digitally savvy or may have less domain expertise than the norm.

This means you want to avoid having too many participants in your usability test sample who are technically proficient (even if they are otherwise representative of your audience). This is because these types of participant will be able to solve almost any technical riddle you throw at them. Instead, you should *actively bias* your sample toward people with lower digital skills and lower domain knowledge. Including people like this in your sample will make it much more likely you'll find problems that affect a low proportion of users. This helps you make the most of your five participants.

Just to be clear, we're not saying you should test your product with total novices. Participants in a usability test should be (potential) users of the product you're testing. If your product is aimed at air traffic controllers, that's where you draw your participant sample from. But to make most use of your small sample, recruit air traffic controllers who have less domain knowledge or lower digital skills than the norm for that group. In other words, bias your sample towards the left of the bell curve.

Your Defense Against Non-representativeness Is Iterative Design

There's always the (unlikely but statistically possible) chance that every one of your participants in a round of research is unrepresentative in an important way. This will send the development team off at a tangent and risks derailing the project. For example, recruiting usability test participants who are less digitally savvy than the norm may result in false positives: mistakenly reporting a usability problem when one doesn't exist. Why isn't this more of an issue?

The reason this isn't a serious issue is because of the power of iterative design. We involve a small sample of participants in our research and make some design decisions based on the outcomes. Some of these decisions will be right and some will be wrong (false positives). But with iterative design, we don't stop there. These decisions lead to a new set of hypotheses that we test, perhaps with field visits to users or by creating a prototype. In this second round of research we involve another small sample of participants—but crucially a different sample than before. This helps us identify the poor design decisions we made in earlier research sessions and reinforces the good decisions. We iterate and research again. In this way, iterative design is the methodology that prevents us from making serious mistakes with our research findings. This is because it leverages the power of the experimental method to weed out our UX research errors.

Our goal as UX researchers is not to deliver a representative *sample* but to deliver representative *research*. UX researchers can achieve this by combining iterative design with theoretical sampling.

THINK LIKE A UX RESEARCHER

- Assume that you followed our advice and all of the participants in a research round had an obvious demographic bias (for example, all participants were the same gender or all were over 40 years of age). Which, if any, of the arguments in this essay would be most effective to persuade your development team that this bias was unimportant?

- If you accept the point that demographic representativeness is unimportant for UX research findings, is there still an argument for attempting to have a degree of balance if this makes the development team more likely to listen to your results? What problems might this concession lead to in later rounds of research?

- A key defense of this approach is that iterative design and testing will weed out your research mistakes. A single round of research with five participants is clearly not iterative, but how many rounds *are* enough? How could you change your way of working to double, or quadruple, the number of research rounds you carry out at the moment?

- If you wanted to bias your sample to the left of the bell curve—for example, to include participants in a usability test who had lower domain knowledge than the norm—how might you go about finding participants? What questions could you ask on a screener to identify this type of candidate?

- We provide an example showing how aiming for a balanced demographic can quickly increase the sample size beyond what is practical for design research. Sketching this on a whiteboard is a persuasive way to convince the development team to reconsider their demands for a balanced sample. If you were to recreate our example for your product, what specific demographic factors would your development team expect you to balance in your participant sample?

How to Find More Usability Problems with Fewer Participants

A common myth in usability testing goes like this: "Five participants are all you need to get 85% of the usability problems." Understanding why this is a myth helps us generate ideas to help us increase the number of problems we find in a usability test.

David spends a lot of time working with early- and mid-career UX researchers. Among other skills, he coaches them on how to do usability tests. There's a question he asks early on to check their level of knowledge: "How many participants do you need in a usability test?"

Inevitably, they have heard that five is a magic number. Some of the more experienced go further: "Five participants are all you need to get 85% of the usability problems." Not all of them mention 85%. Some say 80%. Some say "most."

Although this belief is widely held, it's a myth. Testing five participants will not find 85% of the usability problems in a system. It's entirely likely that testing five participants will find a fraction of the total number of usability problems.

The Myth of the Magic Number Five

The myth isn't due to problems with the original research but in the way the research has been interpreted. The statement needs an important qualification. The correct formulation is: *"Five participants are enough to get 85% of the usability problems that affect one in three users."*

On first reading, this may sound like we're being pedantic. But in fact it's critical to understanding how you can find more usability problems in your test, with or without increasing the number of participants.

To explain why this is the case, assume your interface has a single usability problem. Let's say you have a novel kind of slider that people use to enter a number in a form. That's not a great way to enter numbers in a form and some people will struggle to use it. How many participants will you need to test to detect this problem?

The answer is: it depends. It depends on how many participants it affects. For some people, the usability problem may not be an issue. They may be tech savvy and find it a breeze to use the control. For others, it may prevent them from completing the task. They may not even know where to start with the slider.

Because a usability problem rarely affects every single user, we need to refine the question and ask, "How many participants will we need to test to find a problem that affects *a fixed percentage* of users?" Researchers typically set this percentage at 31%[14]—let's call that one in three users to make the sums easy.

Now let's run a test.

Our first user comes in. By definition, we have a one in three chance of spotting the problem. Our second user comes in and we have a one in three chance of spotting the problem. Our third user comes in and we have a one in three chance of spotting the problem. You'd think, given that we've now tested three participants, we should have found the problem, but probability doesn't work like that. It's like tossing a coin: sometimes you might have to toss a coin more than twice to get a heads even though the likelihood of getting a heads is 50%. Because of the way probability works, you actually need to test with more than three participants to find a problem that affects one in three users.

How many? Again, we can't be exact: we have to be probabilistic. What we can say is that, if you test with five participants, you have an 85% chance of finding a problem that affects one in three users. (If you'd like more details on this, Jeff Sauro has a fine article that includes calculators you can play with to understand probability.[15])

Some Critical Usability Problems Affect Few Users

The reason this matters is that some important usability problems affect a small number of users. For example: hint text inside form fields. Some people mistake hint text for a form field entry: they think the field is already completed. Other people get confused trying to delete the place-holder text. For most people (say 90%) it's not a problem. But for the 10% of users who do experience this problem, it means they really struggle to complete the form.

If you're designing a system to be used by a wide range of users (like a government system) this really matters. Because what if a problem affects not one in three users but one in ten users? How many participants will we need to test to find that problem? It turns out you need to test 18 participants to have an 85% chance of finding that problem.

So to say that five participants will get 85% of all the problems in a system totally misrepresents the research. On some systems, testing five participants may find only 5% of the total problems, because the other 95% of problems affect fewer than one in three users.

Increasing Your Chances of Finding Usability Problems

If this is leaving you frustrated and thinking that you need to run usability tests with larger samples, fear not. There is a way to find more problems without increasing the number of participants in your study. Here are three ideas:

- Include in your participant sample people with low digital skills. In other words, don't just recruit the ones who are tech savvy. Including people with low digital skills will make it much more likely you'll find problems that affect a low proportion of users. This is the idea we introduced in the last essay of recruiting people on the left of the bell curve.
- Ask participants to do more tasks. How many tasks participants try turns out to be a critical factor for finding problems in a usability test.[16]
- Arrange to have several people from the development team observe the test and independently note down the problems they find. Research shows that the chances of you missing a critical usability problem that other observers find is about 50–50.[17]

If you still want to test more participants, bravo! But rather than run one big test with lots of participants, we would encourage you to run multiple usability tests with smaller samples (perhaps every sprint). So long as your testing is part of an iterative design process (where you find problems, fix them and then test again), with a sample size of five you will eventually start finding some of those gnarly problems that affect fewer than one in three users.

THINK LIKE A UX RESEARCHER

- Can you explain what's wrong with the statement, "Five partici-pants are all you need to get 85% of the usability problems"?
- We point out that some important usability problems affect a small number of users. Imagine you were running a usability test of a product where real-world user errors could be catastrophic, such as a medical device. Would it still be acceptable to use five participants, assuming this was combined with multiple rounds of research? Why, or why not?
- This is another example of where we recommend including in your UX research participants who are less digitally savvy, or have less domain knowledge, than the norm. If this type of participant was the development team's first exposure to users, what might the risks be with our recommendation? How might you mitigate those risks?
- Given that we can never know how many usability problems exist in a product, how can we decide when we have done "enough" usability testing?
- Typically, when development teams first start usability testing, they tend to run one round of research late in development. More experienced teams plan for a small handful of usability tests, but only the most sophisticated teams run sessions every sprint, as we recommend here. Where is your development team on this spectrum? How could you persuade your team to run usability tests more frequently?

Deciding on Your First Research
Activity with Users

A usability test is the wrong research method when you want to discover if there's a real user need for your product; when you want to understand the environment where your system is used; and when you want to find out how people use your product in their daily lives. So why do we almost always recommend a usability test as a team's first UX research activity?

UX research is, in part, a scientific activity: you generate hypotheses and test them by collecting data. Then you revise your hypotheses in light of your findings. But unlike science, UX research is also a *political* activity. For example, some organizations treat UX research, and indeed the whole field of user experience, as merely a passing trend or fashion. Some managers need to be convinced that UX research is needed. And some development teams just don't understand what UX researchers do all day.

The politics of UX research may also explain why development teams often prefer to start their user experience journey by commissioning an expert review. An expert review doesn't involve users: instead, a handful of usability experts evaluate the design against good practice. We think expert reviews are attractive to development teams not simply because they are quick and cheap but because they don't require the team to engage with users: the team can claim they have "done usability" when in fact there were never any real users involved. It is also easy for the team to dismiss any critical findings from an expert review as being "just the view of the consultant." Ignoring the behavior of users is much more difficult.

Given that "user experience research" implies we need to involve users in our research, the most (scientifically) logical UX research activity is a field visit, especially in the early stages of design. This gives you the opportunity to test out your hypotheses around user needs. But if you find yourself in the kind of environment we've described above, your decision should not be based on logic but on emotion. You need to answer the question: *what UX research activity will have most impact in making this organization user centered?*

And in our experience, the answer is often a usability test, for five reasons:

- You'll identify the business objectives.
- You'll discover the key user groups.
- You'll reveal the key tasks.
- You'll flush out the stakeholders.
- You'll establish if there's an appetite for UX research in your organization.

You'll Identify the Business Objectives

To run a usability test, you need to know the business objectives of your product because otherwise you don't know where to focus your test. What is the business trying to achieve with this thing? It's not unusual for different business units within an organization to hold competing, contradictory or inconsistent business objectives. So getting a direct answer to this question is crucial for any future UX research and design activities you engage in.

To make sure you have this clear in your own head, use our earlier advice (see "Conducting an effective stakeholder interview" in this chapter) and *remove the solution*. Ask, "If we didn't run the test, what would be the main business risks?"

You'll Discover the Key User Groups

Development teams are often dysfunctional. It's common for them to suffer from a kind of groupthink where no one really knows who will use the thing they are designing but at the same time no one wants to admit that this is a problem. There's a general belief that someone will use this thing, otherwise "management" would shut the project down. To run a usability test you need a clear description of the main user groups, otherwise you won't know who to recruit for the test. And in the same way that a psychotherapist needs to make a dysfunctional family confront the elephant in the room, you'll do the same when you plan your test. (See "Identifying the user groups for your UX research" earlier in this chapter for some suggestions on identifying the key user groups).

You'll Reveal the Key Tasks

Development teams maintain a backlog of technical work that they want to complete and when this gets overly long you'll find someone adds "simple to use" to the list. But "simple" isn't a feature. You can't build "simple" into a product. You have to weed complexity out.

To achieve this, you must identify the key tasks and maintain a laser focus on these during development. Few development teams have this focus because their development process is geared towards coding discrete functions and features, not towards the tasks that users carry out. You can't run a usability test by asking people to *play* with a feature: instead, you need to ask them to *carry out tasks* that require the use of several features and functions. By asking the team to identify the key tasks, you'll go someway to turning the development process on its head and making it more user centered.

You'll Flush Out the Stakeholders

Once people hear that you're running a usability test, you'll initially think you're the most popular person in the organization. Messages will arrive from people you've never heard of, often with "VP" in their job title. They'll want to know why you are doing this work, who authorized it, why you are speaking to our customers, what the output will be and why you can't just speak to the Head of Sales instead (after all, his team members speak with customers every day). These people may also provide a whole host of reasons why you shouldn't go ahead with your test. You'll find this uncomfortable but it's an obstacle you need to overcome if you're ever to do any kind of UX research in the future.

You'll Establish If There's an Appetite for UX Research in Your Organization

If you can't get permission to run a usability test, you won't get permission to do more in-depth UX research, like field visits. But once you get the green light, it will make it much easier for you to carry out other, more "logical" UX research activities. A usability test will also give you insight into your development team's appetite for UX research: it's easier to get your team to observe a usability test (even if it's just watching a highlights video) than it is to get them to come out on a field visit. If they're not even willing to watch a usability test video, you've got a lot of convincing to do. It might even be time to start looking for a UX research job elsewhere.

In reading over this essay, we're aware that we sound a bit like men with hammers, seeing a world full of nails (when a screwdriver might be a better tool). So in case we've not made ourselves clear, we don't think that usability tests should be your *only* UX research activity. However, if you're in an organization that's taking its first steps in user experience, then a usability test is almost always the best UX research activity to try first.

THINK LIKE A UX RESEARCHER

- Is it ethical to do a "wrong" (or at least, sub-optimal) UX research activity if it helps change the culture in an organization and paves the way to doing the "right" UX research later on?
- What are the potential consequences of doing usability testing in the absence of field research to uncover user needs? Could this result in a highly usable product that nobody wants? Is doing field research the only way of mitigating this problem or could we still gain some insights from usability testing?
- Because usability testing has so much face validity, it's been likened to a UX research gateway drug. One risk with this is that the development team may begin to see usability testing as the only UX research method. What arguments would you use to encourage a development team to use other UX research methods alongside usability testing?
- How would you deal with a situation where a member of the development team declined to observe a usability test (either live or recorded), saying, "You're the UX researcher, just tell me what to fix"?
- Early in his career, David received a terse phone call from a VP asking him to justify his research program (which had received media interest). The VP had no understanding (and even less interest) in the technicalities but wanted to know, in simple terms, why the business was doing this research. If you received a similar call from a high-ranking manager in your organization and had 60 seconds to justify your research, what would you say?

3

Conducting User
Experience Research

Gaining Informed Consent
from Your Research Participants

Gaining informed consent is a cornerstone of the social sciences. But it is some-times poorly practiced by UX researchers. They fail to explain consent properly. They mix up the consent form with a non-disclosure agreement. And they mix up the consent form with the incentive. Improving the way you get consent will also improve the data you collect because participants can be more open and because it makes UX researchers more empathic.

As a UX researcher, you have an ethical duty to ensure that your UX research does not harm the people who take part. Informed consent is the process of helping research participants make an educated decision about whether they want to take part in your research.

Why You Need to Get Informed Consent

Your first reaction might be, "How can a usability test harm anyone?"

It's true that a usability test is unlikely to cause someone physical harm (although once David had a participant who tried to lift an 80 kg large format printer on his own, despite warnings on the outside packaging). But a usability test can cause psychological distress to your participant. For example, how might your participant feel if:

- A researcher shows a video of her at a conference where she curses about a product?
- She hears people in the observation room laughing as she tries to find the correct option on a web page?
- She gets frustrated and ends up in tears because the interface is so hard to use?

And by the way, these aren't made up scenarios: We've seen all three of these situations in real life.

You face similar ethical problems when you carry out field research. The participant has a right to know how you will use the notes, photographs, and videos that you take. Who will see this information? Will participants' comments be anonymous? How will you ensure anonymity if your video shows the participant's face?

As well as an ethical requirement, you also have legal obligations. Article 8 of The Human Rights Act protects the right to a private and family life. This includes respect for private and confidential information, respect for privacy and the right to control information about one's private life. Additionally, Europe's General Data Protection Regulation (GDPR)[1] has specific requirements around the use of personal data. Other regulations may apply if you're doing research with children and vulnerable adults.

Common Problems with the Way UX Researchers Get Consent

We commonly see three problems with the way UX researchers get informed consent:

- Failing to explain consent properly.
- Mixing up the consent form with a non-disclosure agreement.
- Mixing up the consent form with the incentive.

Failing to Explain Consent Properly

We've seen some studies where the researcher asks the participant to read the consent form and then sign it. This is a poor way to get consent. This is because participants want to show willing, and they may sign the form on trust (in the same way that many of us agree to software terms and conditions without actually reading them). Instead, before the participant signs the form, highlight the key concepts. For example, you could say, "Before you sign the form, I just want to point out some things on it…" Then highlight issues such as confidentiality and freedom to withdraw.

We once saw an excellent consent form where participants had to tick each clause to confirm they had read it. For example, "I confirm that I understand the purpose of the study"; "I understand my participation is voluntary"; "I agree to my screen being recorded"; "I agree to my session being video-recorded." When overdone, this can become death by checkbox but used appropriately we believe it ensures participants actually read the form (see Figure 3.1). It has the added benefit that it puts the participant in control of the consent.

Figure 3.1: An example consent form. Note that we are not lawyers, so we can't guarantee this consent form will meet legal requirements around privacy in every jurisdiction

What this study is about

The purpose of this study is to understand how people use [INSERT PRODUCT NAME]. Your participation in this study will help us make the product easier to use.

Your participation in this study is voluntary

You can take a break at any time. Just tell the researcher if you need a break. You can leave at any time without giving a reason.

Information we want to collect

We will ask you to show us how you use the product. We will watch how you do various tasks and we will ask you some questions. We will record the session and we will take notes to record your comments and actions.

How we ensure your privacy

People on the design team may view the sessions from another room. Other people involved in the design of the product may watch the recording of your session in the future. These recordings will be treated as confidential and will not be shared outside our company.

We may publish research reports that include your comments and actions but your data will be anonymous. This means your name and identity will not be linked in our research reports to anything you say or do.

Before you leave today, the researcher will give you a copy of this form. If you want to withdraw your consent, contact the person named below who will destroy any personal data we hold about you (such as the recordings). Otherwise, we will delete your personal data after 12 months.

[INSERT DATA CONTROLLER'S NAME AND CONTACT DETAILS]

Your consent

Please sign this form showing that you consent to us collecting these data.

I give my consent (please tick all that apply):

☐ For people to observe me during the research.

☐ For the session to be recorded.

☐ For people on the design team to watch the recording in the future.

Your name: ....

Signature: ....

Date: ....

Mixing Up the Consent Form with a Non-disclosure Agreement

Sometimes researchers ask participants to use products that are not released. Clients want to protect their intellectual property so they get participants to sign a non-disclosure agreement (NDA). But you don't want to mix up an NDA with the process of getting consent. Treat the NDA as a separate form for the participant to sign.

Mixing Up the Consent Form with the Incentive

Participants are eligible for the incentive once they have arrived at the test facility. So give them the money, gift voucher or other incentive on arrival. If they then decide to withdraw from the study, that's life. (We've never had a participant withdraw after receiving their incentive in this way. Folks are generally honest.) So don't include anything about the incentive on your consent form. They are (or should be) unrelated.

To Sign or Not to Sign?

It's understandable that researchers want a signed consent form. They believe this will protect them from a study participant claiming he did not give consent. In practice, consent forms are rarely drafted by lawyers. So unless a court has tested your consent form, this protection may be illusory.

But we want to discourage you from thinking about informed consent as a legal transaction. Informed consent is not about protecting you; it's about protecting the participant. If you see informed consent as protecting you from, say, being sued, your attitude is wrong. The correct attitude is to ensure your participant understands what consent means.

This doesn't mean that you shouldn't ask participants to sign anything. It's just that this may not always be the right approach in all situations. For example, asking people to read and sign a form may be a problem if your participant has dyslexia or if he or she has low literacy skills (a real issue for organizations, like governments, who are designing for everyone).

At the very least, asking the participant to sign on the dotted line may affect the mood music. One minute you're the good guy, building rapport. Next minute, you're the bad guy with the legal-looking form.

Depending on the situation, it may be more appropriate to get verbal consent. You can still make a record of this once you turn on the voice or video recorder. For example, start the recording, then say: "For the purposes of the recording, I just want to check that you understood the conversation we had about the purposes of the research and that you give your consent for me to record our conversation." After the participant agrees, you could follow up with, "And just to re-iterate, you can refuse to participate at any time; you can take a break at any time; you can ask questions at any time; and anything you tell me will be kept confidential."

Isn't this Just Bureaucracy Gone Mad?

Why bother with informed consent? After all, it's not going to improve the quality of the UX research, is it?

In fact, we would argue that it will improve the quality of your UX research, for at least two reasons.

First, if your participants see that you are taking their concerns seriously, they are more likely to relax. Rather than worry that the video will appear on the internet, they know that only the development team will see it. A relaxed participant means you are more likely to observe realistic behavior. Observing realistic behavior is the goal of all UX researchers.

Second, gaining informed consent encourages UX researchers to be more empathic. UX researchers that empathize with their participants' concerns about privacy are more likely to be sensitive to participants' concerns about the product. Imagine two alternative research studies: one where the researcher gained informed consent and one where she didn't. We would expect the one where the researcher gained informed consent to offer more insights. This is because the UX researcher is probably more experienced and empathic.

It's true that you could just shove a consent form under your participant's nose and tell them to sign it. But try treating the process of gaining consent as an important step. You'll find you end up with more reliable data in the long run.

THINK LIKE A UX RESEARCHER

- We point out that asking someone to sign a form may affect the "mood music." How might you prepare your participant in advance so the consent form doesn't come as a surprise?
- Imagine a participant arrived at your study, looked at your consent form, and said: "There's lots of words here! I'm going to struggle with this as I have dyslexia." How would you proceed?
- If a researcher withholds the incentive until the participant completes the study, is the participant's consent freely given? Or might the participant feel coerced into completing the study to get the incentive?
- Many clients we work with insist that participants sign a non-disclosure agreement (NDA). If you wanted a participant to sign an NDA to take part in your study, would you ask them to do this before or after asking for consent? What's behind your decision?
- Put yourself in the situation where a participant contacts you three months after a study and asks to withdraw consent. This means you would need to destroy any recordings you have made of this participant and any notes you have taken. What implications does this have for how you should organize and store your research data?

What Is Design Ethnography?

A common mistake made by novice researchers is to ask users what they want from a new product or service. Although this seems like the correct way to do UX research, in most cases users don't know, don't care, or can't articulate what they need. It is the development team's job to establish the underlying problem, identify the best solution and then validate that their solution works. Design ethnography is the first step on that journey.

Predicting what will work best for users requires a deep understanding of their needs. Research methods like focus groups and surveys have obvious face validity but they continually fail to provide the insights that development teams need in product discovery. The reason is that these techniques require users to predict their future behavior, something that people are poor at doing.

An alternative method is to examine what people do, rather than what they say they do. This approach is based on a simple premise: The best predictor of future behavior is past behavior. What people do is a better indicator of the underlying user need than what people say.

To avoid simply asking users what they want, UX researchers have appropriated methods from ethnography and applied them to UX research. This technique is broadly known as "design ethnography" but it differs in important ways from traditional ethnography.

What Is Ethnography?

Ethnography is the study of culture. Branislaw Malinowski,[2] who studied gift giving among natives in Papua, wrote, "The final goal is to grasp the native's point of view, his relation to life, to realize his vision of his world."

Replace the word "native" with the word "user," or extend the metaphor and think of your users as a "tribe," and you can see why this approach could offer value in product and service design.

Some of the defining characteristics of ethnography are that:

- Research takes place in the participants' context.
- Participant sample sizes are small.
- Researchers aim to understand the big picture: participants' needs, language, concepts, and beliefs.

- Artifacts are analyzed to understand how people live their lives and what they value.
- Data are "thick," comprising written notes, photographs, audio, and video recordings.

To some degree or another, design ethnographers adopt each of these characteristics in the work that they do.

In addition to the work of Branislaw Malinowski, other examples of ethnography include:

- Margaret Mead,[3] who studied "coming of age" rituals in Samoa.
- Sudhir Venkatesh,[4] who embedded himself with Chicago drug gangs to understand drug culture.
- Matthew Hughey,[5] who spent over a year attending the meetings of a white nationalist group and a white antiracist group.

So how does design ethnography differ from traditional ethnography?

It's a struggle to use a traditional ethnographic approach in modern product development, mainly because of the timescales. That's not to say it's impossible: Jan Chipchase (who specializes in international field research) says he spends half the year traveling around exotic destinations.[6] But most people who practice design ethnography in business would agree with these distinctions:

- The purpose of traditional ethnography is to understand culture. The purpose of design ethnography is to gain design insights.
- The timescale of traditional ethnography is months and years. The timescale of design ethnography is days and weeks.
- Traditional ethnographers live with participants and try to become part of the culture. Design ethnographers are visitors who observe and interview.
- With traditional ethnography, data are analyzed in great detail over many months. With design ethnography, there is "just enough" analysis to test the risky assumptions.
- The findings of traditional ethnography are shared in books and academic journals. The findings from design ethnography are restricted to a team or an organization.

How Should You Approach Design Ethnography?

Instead of asking people what they want, with a design ethnography approach the UX researcher tries to discover *why* people want those things. Through observation and interview, they answer questions like these:

- What goals are users trying to achieve?
- How do they currently do it?
- What parts do they love or hate?
- What difficulties do they experience along the way?
- What workarounds do they use?

You answer these questions by observing users and interviewing them.

As someone who spent several years on a single research project in the Trobriand Islands, we don't know what Malinowski would think of the compromises made by today's design ethnographers. Our view is that, if we liken traditional ethnography to a prize heavyweight boxer, then design ethnography is more akin to a street fighter. It doesn't follow all of the rules, but it gets the job done. That's usually acceptable for most design projects but be aware that too much compromise can jeopardize the quality of your results.

Let's look at some of the ways we've seen that happen.

Avoiding Some Common Mistakes

When we work with companies and we suggest a design ethnography exercise, we often hear, "But we already do that."

It's true that many companies carry out some up-front customer-focused field research activities (that are different to their traditional market research). They often dub it "insights research" done by their Insights Team or by their Innovation Team.

But these activities frequently amount to nothing more than going to a customer site to carry out the same interviews or surveys the team would normally do out of context, with little to no observation of behavior taking place. We've even seen it done with versions of "concept testing" where researchers simply write a descriptive paragraph of their idea and ask respondents to read it and say what they think of it—which has to be just about the worst kind of UX research imaginable.

The consequence of this is that development teams often set out creating the wrong product or service. The team continues blindly on until the user experience team gets involved and usability tests it. Now the development team gets to see real users at work, at which point they get an inkling they have built the wrong concept. But now the team is too far along in development and too wedded to their idea to pivot.

The mistakes we see most often are:

- Doing research in the field—but doing the wrong kind of research.
- Not knowing what is and what is not data (because there is no focus) so user opinions and comments are prioritized over user behavior.
- Not sending experienced field researchers—instead sending people familiar with interviewing only.
- Doing it after the company has already decided what the design solution is going to be—therefore looking only for confirmatory evidence and missing other opportunities.

If you've not tried it in the past, we encourage you to add design ethnography to your current practice. Turn to the next essay for a step-by-step approach to running an ethnographic interview.

THINK LIKE A UX RESEARCHER

- Design ethnography requires you to keep an open mind when you visit participants: You should expressly avoid presenting solutions to them until you understand the problem. Product-focused members of the development team might dismiss this as aimless, "blue sky" research. Do they have a point? How would you respond?
- Although it's unlikely your research will expose you to drug gangs or white nationalist groups, as a UX researcher you are still vulnerable when you leave your office and spend time in a participant's environment. What can you do to maintain your own personal safety when you do this kind of research?
- Is there still a place for in-depth, contextual UX research like design ethnography in Lean product development? Or does Lean's build-measure-learn cycle move too quickly for this kind of research?
- The majority of stakeholders who we work with do not talk to users. Does ethnographic research make it more or less likely that stakeholders would attend UX research sessions?
- One of the mistakes we highlight in this essay is "Not sending experienced field researchers—instead sending people familiar with interviewing only." How would you explain the difference between interviewing and field research to a member of a development team?

Structuring the Ethnographic Interview

Running an ethnographic interview is a fundamental step you'll take in trying to understand your users' needs, goals and behaviors. You can learn a lot from any customer conversation, such as a "pop up" interview in a café or library, but you'll learn even more by running the interview in context: in your user's home or workplace.

As with most things in life, there is more than one way to run an interview. Most of us are familiar with out-of-context interviews, such as those we might encounter in a doctor's office, or in a government building, or the kind of interview we may see on a television chat show. Out of context interviews can certainly provide the beginnings of an understanding for UX research, but to gain significant insights you need to get into your user's context.

What's So Special about Context?

A good customer interview during the discovery phase is not aiming to find out *what* people want—it's aiming to find out *why* people want it. You are trying to get answers to three basic questions:

- *Motivations*: What is the user trying to get done?
- *Activities*: How does the user do it at the moment?
- *Problems*: What are the pain points / happy moments with the current process?

The issue with out-of-context interviews is that you can never be sure that you're getting at the truth. People often do not understand why they do things a certain way and therefore can't tell you. Even when they do understand why they are doing things, they may not want to tell you. And when they do tell you, they may think they are being helpful by describing a "simplified" view of the way they work which misrepresents how they actually work. And, of course, people can lie.

The most effective way to deal with this is to get people to show you how they achieve their goals at the moment and then observe them. Asking people to show you how they achieve their goals is a good way to get closer to authentic behavior because it's hard to fake.

As a trivial example, imagine a researcher asked you to describe how you make instant coffee. You might describe the various steps in making instant coffee, such as boiling the kettle, grabbing a teaspoon, adding coffee and hot water to the cup, then adding milk and sugar to taste. But if instead the researcher observed you in context, he or she might notice that you do other things while the kettle is boiling and sometimes you need to boil the water again. Other times you may not have a teaspoon to hand so instead you tip out a teaspoon-sized amount of coffee directly from the jar into the cup. These behaviors aren't unusual, but users won't describe them because they want to tell the researcher a good story. And these behaviors lead to design insights such as a kettle that whistles when it boils; or a new instant coffee jar that includes a kind of Pez-dispenser in the lid to deliver a teaspoon of coffee.

Getting Prepared

Let's review what you need for a contextual interview. To begin with the obvious, you need some participants to visit. But how many is "some"?

Ask two UX researchers, "How many participants?" and you'll probably get four different answers. There are a few reasons for this. First, any interviews are better than none, so even one participant will teach you something. Second, if the people you want to interview divide into clear types, start with four to six of each type. Third, if you don't know what different types there are, start with eight people (the types will emerge from the patterns in their different experiences). Typically, we tend to involve around 20 users in our first round of research and then visit smaller samples to address specific questions later.

As well as your participants, you should have an outline discussion guide to act as a framework for eliciting stories. This discussion guide will contain the key assumptions you need to validate. Make sure your discussion guide is brief: Don't see it as a Q&A but as a kind of scaffolding to elicit and structure stories.

There's one more thing you need, and that's a member of the development team who will join you on the field visit. You need some help taking notes, and this is the role you will give to your colleague. But the main reason you want a member of the development team with you is because UX research is a team sport: You want to ensure everyone gets to spend time observing users.

But even though you want the team to observe, there's a limit to how many people should come along on any one visit. A two-person research team is ideal: With three or more, the dynamics change. It's hard to stop observers interrupting the flow or changing the direction of the session. It can be a bit like people trampling over a crime scene and spoiling the evidence.

To manage this, and to ensure that everyone gets to observe users, swap the note-taker for someone else on the development team after the first couple of participants. The note-taker could be a developer, designer, project owner, Scrum master, or domain expert (the latter is especially helpful when there is domain-specific jargon with which you're not familiar).

On the field visit, your role will be to develop rapport with the user; conduct the interview; and apprentice with the user. Your colleague will be the note-taker. His or her role is to take photographs of the user, the environment and any artifacts; audio record the interview; make written observations; and ask clarifying and follow-up questions.

A good field visit tends to have five stages:

- Build rapport with the user.
- Transition from a traditional interview to a master-apprentice model.
- Observe.
- Interpret.
- Summarize.

Let's review these in turn.

Build Rapport with the User

In this phase, which should take only five minutes or so, you will introduce yourself and describe your separate roles (UX researcher/note-taker). Then you should explain the purpose of the study so the participant knows what you care about. A good way to start is to get an overview of the participant's background, so use questions like, "Maybe you could give me a tour of your place," "Tell me about the first time you started doing this activity," or "What got you interested in this kind of thing in the beginning?" These are all good, safe, natural questions that should give you clues as to what to look for once the participant starts to demonstrate their work. Then move on to the opening question on your discussion guide.

As part of building rapport, you should also review your "shot list" and get the participant's consent to take photographs. Photographs provide an incredible amount of additional insight and you don't want to be the researcher who's too shy to take photographs. But taking photographs can often appear intrusive and rude. The way to deal with this is to put control of the situation in the hands of your participant. For example, show them a list of things you want to photograph, such as:

- You.
- Your desk.
- Your computer.
- Your computer screen.
- The technology you use.
- Papers you use for your job.
- Manuals.
- The wider environment.

Then say to the participant, "We need to take photographs while we're here today to help the development team understand your context. Here's a list of the things we'd like to photograph. If there are any things on here you want to keep private, just put a line through them and we won't photograph them."

This puts control of what you photograph in the hands of the user but at the same time it means you won't need to continually ask for permission before every photograph. Another good question to ask is, "What things do you think we should photograph to understand the way you do this?"

Now is also the time to ask for permission to record the session to a digital voice recorder. The participant's verbal protocol is central to your analysis, so you want to make a recording of the session. You should also consider transcribing your recordings (typically, transcription firms charge around $1 to $1.50 per minute of audio).

If this is moving you outside your comfort zone, you could always prime the participant about photographs and recordings before the visit. When you initially recruit people for your research, along with the background to the study you could send them your shot list and mention the audio recording. Then it shouldn't be an obstacle when you first meet the participant.

Transition

In this phase, which should take just a minute or so, the session moves from a traditional interview to a master-apprentice model. You should tell the user that you want to learn by watching and asking questions, as if you were an apprentice learning how to do their job.

As you become more experienced, you'll realize that good interviewing isn't a set of questioning techniques: It's more a way of being. Hugh Beyer and Karen Holtzblatt, who invented a particular approach to customer interviews known as contextual inquiry,[7] explain why this is important: "Running a good interview is less about following specific rules than it is about being a certain kind of person for the duration of the interview. The apprentice model is a good starting point for how to behave."

The master-apprentice model is a useful method for engaging participants in your discovery process because everyone has experienced "teaching" somebody something. It also gives you, the researcher, license to ask naïve questions to check your understanding.

Observe

The observation phase is where you should spend the bulk of your time during the session.

Sometimes the best thing you can do is to sit back and watch the way your user is behaving. Don't think that you need to continually ask questions. Especially if you have asked for a demonstration of something, it's fine to just watch and simply ask the odd question to clarify your understanding. In fact, to someone looking from the outside, this may not look like an interview at all. That's because few people have experience of running these kinds of interview. A good contextual interview should help you validate your riskiest assumptions, give you insight into the problems your users have and help you understand what matters in your users' lives.

Keep observing. Anytime something tweaks your antenna, drill down with follow up questions. Point to things in the participant's environment and ask what they are for. Get copies or pictures of artifacts, samples, forms, and documents. Use the discussion guide to remind you what you want to cover but don't worry about covering every topic in every interview.

You'll discover that it's much easier to run a contextual interview than a pop-up interview because you don't need to keep firing questions at your participant. Most of the time, just remembering two question stems will keep the session moving along nicely:

"Tell me a story about the last time you…"
"Can you show me how you…"

Interpret

In this phase, you verify your assumptions and conclusions with the participant. Skim back over your notes and review what you learned. Make suggestions for why the participant performed an action; the participant will correct you if your assumption is wrong.

Summarize

Immediately at the end of each session, grab an unlined six-inch by four-inch index card. You will use one index card for each of the participants in your study. The purpose of these index cards is to summarize your immediate thoughts: They won't be a replacement for the transcripts or your more considered analysis, but this step is useful to help stop your different participants blending one into the other. Arrange your index cards in portrait orientation and at the top of the card write your participant's first name. Print out a passport-sized picture of your participant (or draw a sketch if you were too shy to take photographs) and stick that to the card. Then write down some concise, bullet-point descriptions about this participant. Aim for about five or so descriptions: These should be the things that really stood out to you. The best kinds of descriptions capture participant's behaviors, needs and goals.

THINK LIKE A UX RESEARCHER

- How does the approach to field research that we describe in this essay compare with the approach you have used in the past? In what ways is it better and in what ways is it worse?
- How would you feel about asking permission to take photographs in a participant's home? If you were unable to take photographs, how else could you share the participant's context with the development team?
- The person you bring with you as note-taker will often have questions for the participant too. How would you structure the session so that the note-taker can ask questions—yet at the same time ensure you lead the session?
- If you record the sessions it's useful to have them transcribed. What ethical issues might arise if you use an external agency to do the transcription for you? How can you get the session transcribed and maintain the participant's privacy?
- The master-apprentice model helps you avoid positioning yourself as the "expert" in the participant's domain. This stops you telling the participant how something should be done. But what if you notice the participant stepping through a process in entirely the wrong way? Would you tell the participant that they are doing it wrong?

Writing Effective Usability Test Tasks

The magic of usability tests is that you get to see what people actually do with a product (rather than what they say they do). This gives you profound insights into how people behave and how to improve your design. But if your tasks lack realism you'll find that people just go through the motions and don't engage with the test—reducing the credibility of your results. Here are six practitioner takeaways for creating great test tasks.

Usability test tasks are the beating heart of a usability test. These tasks determine the parts of a product that test participants will see and interact with. Usability test tasks are so critical that some people argue they are even more important than the number of participants you use: It seems that how many tasks participants try, not the number of test participants, is the critical factor for finding problems in a usability test.[8]

But for test tasks to uncover usability problems, usability test participants need to be motivated: They need to believe that the tasks are realistic and they must want to carry them out. So how do we create test tasks that go beyond the mundane and engage participants?

To help our discussion, we're going to classify usability test tasks into six different categories. You don't need to create tasks in each of these categories— you simply need to review the categories and decide which kind of task will best motivate your participants.

The six categories are:

- Scavenger hunt.
- The reverse scavenger hunt.
- Self-generated tasks.
- Part self-generated.
- "Skin in the game" tasks.
- Troubleshooting tasks.

Let's look at each of these in more depth.

Scavenger Hunt

This type of task is a useful way for you to find out if users can complete tasks with your product. With a scavenger hunt task, you ask users to do something that has one clear, ideal answer. An example of this kind of task (for a website that sells luggage) might be: "You're traveling abroad next month and you're looking for a good-sized bag that you can take on an airplane as hand luggage. You want the bag to be as big as possible while still meeting the airline's maximum luggage dimensions (56 cm × 45 cm × 25 cm). You have a budget of $120. What's the most suitable bag you can get?" With a good scavenger hunt task there will be one perfect answer, so quiz the development team to find out the best solution to this task and then see if participants can find it.

The Reverse Scavenger Hunt

With this type of task, you show people the answer (for example a picture of what they need to look for) and then ask them to go about finding or purchasing it. For example, if you're testing out a stock photography application, you could show people an image that you want them to locate and then ask them to find it (for example, by searching with their own keywords). This kind of task works well if you think that a textual description of the task might give away too many clues.

Self-Generated Tasks

Scavenger hunt and reverse scavenger hunt tasks work well when you know what people want to do with your website. But what if you're less sure? In these situations, try a self-generated task instead. With this type of task, you ask participants what they expect to do with the product (before you show it to them), and then you test out that scenario.

For example, you might be evaluating a theatre-ticketing kiosk with regular theatre-goers. You begin the session by interviewing participants and asking what they expect to be able to do with the kiosk. For example, you might hear, "book tickets for a show," "find out what's on," and "find out where to park."

You then take each of the tasks in turn, and ask the participant to be more specific. For example, for the task, "book tickets for a show," you'll want to find out what kind of shows they prefer, such as a play, a musical or a stand-up routine. How many tickets would they want to book? On what day? For an evening or a matinee performance?

Your job is to help participants really think through their requirements before letting them loose with the product, to make sure that the task is realistic.

Part Self-generated

These tasks work well when you have a good idea of the main things people want to do with the product, but you're less sure of the detail. With a part self-generated task, you define an overall goal (for example, "Analyze your electricity usage") and then ask the participant to fill in the gaps. You can do this by asking participants to bring data with them to the session (such as electronic versions of past electricity bills) and allowing them to query their own data in ways that are of interest (for example, "What are your hours of peak usage?").

"Skin in the Game" Tasks

A problem with usability test tasks is that you want participants to carry out the tasks as realistically as possible. But there's a big difference between *pretending* to do a task and *really* doing a task. No matter how well intentioned they are, participants know that, if they get it wrong, there are no consequences. You can mitigate this risk by giving participants real money to spend on the task.

The easiest way to do this with a commercial website is simply to give participants a redeemable voucher to spend during the test, or reimburse their credit card after they have made a purchase.

A related approach for other systems is to incentivize the participant with the product itself. For example, if you're testing a large format printer that creates photographic posters, you could ask people to bring in their digital photographs and then get them to use the printer to create the poster they want. The poster itself then becomes the participant's incentive for taking part.

As well as getting as close as possible to realistic behavior (mild concerns become pressing issues), this approach also gives you the confidence that your participants are the right demographic, because their incentive is based on the very product you're testing.

Troubleshooting Tasks

Troubleshooting tasks are a special category of test task because people may not be able to articulate their task in a meaningful way. It would be misleading to give a participant a written task that you've prepared earlier since by its very nature this will describe the problem that needs to be solved. For example, a smartphone may display an arcane error message if the SIM card is improperly inserted. Or a satnav system may not be able to plan a route because it fails to locate a GPS satellite. As far as the participant is concerned, the product is simply not working and they don't know why.

For these situations, it makes sense to try to recreate the issue with the product and then ask the participant to solve it either by starting them at a search engine or at your company's troubleshooting page. You'll then get useful insights into the terminology that people use to describe the specific issue, as well as seeing how well your documentation stands up to real-world use.

Once you've created a good set of tasks, your next job is to moderate the usability test. That's what we'll turn to next.

THINK LIKE A UX RESEARCHER

- Pick some tasks that you used in your most recent usability test and try to classify them according to our taxonomy of test tasks. Do they fit? Are there other categories of test task that we missed?
- With scavenger hunt tasks, you need to be quite specific in your task scenario (in our example we include the dimensions of a piece of luggage). How would you balance this with the need to create test scenarios that don't lead the participant or provide the answer?
- Consider a situation where you are running a usability test of an innovative product that is the only one of its kind ("It's Uber for parcel deliveries!"). Would it make sense to use a self-generated task?
- How could you adapt a "skin in the game" task for a website that sells an expensive product (such as jewelry, package holidays or a new car) where you couldn't give the participant the product as an incentive?
- One way to engage the development team in a usability test is to ask them to create test tasks. Would sharing our taxonomy of test tasks with your team help them create useful tasks? How else could you get the team to create effective test tasks?

The Five Mistakes You'll Make
as a Usability Test Moderator

What are the most common mistakes that test moderators make? We've observed usability tests moderated by consultants, in-house researchers, junior UX researchers and experienced practitioners and there are some common mistakes we come across time and again. These mistakes are like a rite of passage on the route to becoming a UX researcher, but even experienced practitioners aren't immune from making them.

Moderating a usability test is full of bear traps. The moderator may fail to set expectations (by reviewing the purpose of the test and describing the moderator's role), forget to reassure the participant ("We're not testing you"), or fail to check for understanding (by asking the participant to repeat the task in his or her own words). Other common mistakes include asking leading or biased questions, and quizzing participants on how they would design the interface.

But there are five mistakes that we see usability test moderators make frequently and that eclipse all of these. They are:

- Talking too much.
- Explaining the design.
- Answering questions.
- Interviewing rather than testing.
- Soliciting opinions and preferences.

Talking Too Much

When moderating a usability test, you need to fight against the tendency to talk too much. This can happen in two places: at the beginning of the test; and during the session itself.

It's true that you need to provide an introduction to the session to put the participant at ease; and you also need to explain the kind of feedback that you want from the thinking aloud technique. But you shouldn't go overboard in your introduction: Five minutes or so is usually enough.

Usability testing is about observing participants while they carry out realistic tasks. This means the golden rule is to shut up. Although moderators tell us they know this, we still see many of them (even some experienced ones) failing to practice it. In the white heat of the test session, they can't stop themselves from filling the silence.

This happens partly because people are not comfortable with silence and partly because there's a misconception that if the participant isn't speaking, then you're not learning anything. But because you're interested in participant behavior, it's fine to have periods of silence. Of course you want participants to think aloud—but at the same time, you need to allow participants space to read, make judgments and generally think about what they are doing.

You can avoid this trap by learning to embrace the silence. Ask participants to do the task. Then shut up, observe, and listen to what they say. If you feel the urge to speak, use a phrase like, "Tell me more about that." If you force yourself to use the same stock phrase, and none other, it will help you stay silent (you'll sound stupid if you use it incessantly to fill the silence)—and you won't do too much damage because you'll encourage the participant to talk.

Explaining the Design

If you ever find yourself saying to a test participant, "What the developers are trying to do here is...," or "The reason they designed it this way is because...," or "What you don't understand is...," then you should slap yourself. When you explain the design of your product to a test participant, it causes two problems.

First, you're no longer able to find out how someone will really behave when they first encounter the design. This is because you've given the participant some background information that real users probably won't have.

And second, even if you were never involved in the design of the product, you affiliate yourself with it. Because what the participant hears isn't an *explanation* of the product but a *defence* of the product. This prevents you being seen as a neutral observer and makes it more likely that participants will self-censor their comments.

The point where this problem occurs most frequently is during the test tasks themselves. The participant may use the product the "wrong" way and the moderator feels the need to explain how to use it "properly." Or the participant may be critical of something in the interface, and the moderator feels the urge to defend the design with a phrase like, "The development team thought about doing it that way, but…" Or the participant may completely misunderstand something in the interface, at which point the moderator will want to correct the participant's misunderstanding. In particularly bad situations, this moderating style risks turning the usability test into a coaching session, or even an argument.

Believe us when we say that no usability test moderator ever won an argument with a participant.

If you ever feel the urge to explain the interface or use a phrase like, "Yes, but…," then instead say, "Tell me what you're doing right now." You'll then get behind the behavior without influencing it too much. If you really, really want to explain how to use the product or correct any misconceptions, then wait until the end of the session, once participants have tried it without your help.

Answering Questions

Here's another trap we see moderators walk into. It's like watching a slow-motion replay of a dog chasing a stick over a cliff. The participant sets the trap and the moderator runs towards it.

Like most traps, it seems fairly innocuous. The participant simply asks a question.

Now, participant questions are like gold dust. You want participants to ask questions because this indicates they are experiencing a problem with the product: They're not sure how to proceed, so they ask you.

Gold dust, but not gold.

You find the gold by observing how the participant answers their question: What do they do to solve the problem? Do they find it easy to fix or do they consistently take the wrong path? It's their behavior that helps you distinguish a low priority problem from a critical one. This means the route to the gold is to refuse to answer the question.

But to any normal human being, refusing to answer a question is alien. From childhood, we're conditioned to think that ignoring a question makes us appear either rude or stupid. That's why so many test moderators walk blindly into the trap of answering participants' questions.

Here's the way to fix this in your own practice. First, in your preamble, tell participants you want them to ask questions but you won't answer, because you want the session to be realistic. Use a phrase like, "Just do what you would do if I wasn't here." This then gives you permission not to answer any questions you're asked.

Then, when the inevitable question comes at you during the session, use the "boomerang" technique: Answer the question with a question. So, if the participant asks, "How do I get back to the beginning?," you respond: "How do you think you get back to the beginning?" If the participant asks, "Whereabouts is the registration form?," you reply: "Where would you look for it?"

Interviewing Rather than Testing

If you've invested time in getting participants to attend your session, it makes sense to get as much out of them as possible. So you should certainly run a pre-test interview with participants before they start the test tasks to find out more about them and their relevant goals. But while the participant carries out the test tasks—which should represent the bulk of their time in a usability test—you're an observer.

Here's a common situation that causes a usability test to degrade into an interview: When the development team don't know much about users. The team may not have done any field research in the past and want to milk this session for all its worth. This shows itself when the participant is interrupted mid-task and asked questions about the way they do this task at home. Or when the marketing lead asks you to shoe-horn in a shopping list of questions during a task. As a consequence, the research falls between two stools: It's neither an interview nor a usability test.

Another situation where this can happen is when you have a particularly loquacious participant who wants to engage the moderator in conversation, rather than do the tasks. The participant will continue to look over to the moderator for reassurance and try to make eye contact.

The best approach is to prevent this problem from happening in the first place. Adjust your body language to be more of an observer than an interviewer. Position yourself so you are behind and to one side of the participant. If you sense the participant looking toward you, pretend to take notes and decline the offer of eye contact.

Also make it clear to the development team that you'll run a post-test interview to get an overall assessment and encourage comments regarding topics not raised during the session, and that's where you'll cover their shopping list of questions.

Soliciting Opinions and Preferences

This final mistake is one we see often in people who are new to moderating a usability test. This is because they have confused usability testing with market research. They think their role is to solicit opinions rather than to observe behavior.

The way this manifests itself in a test is the moderator will ask the participant to compare different designs to see which one they prefer, or they will continually ask the participant if they like or dislike some design feature.

Usability testing isn't about finding out what users like, but rather what works best for them.

How to Continuously Improve as a Test Moderator

These mistakes almost always occur in novice test moderators as they earn their spurs. But even experienced test moderators make these kinds of mistake during a usability test. The best way to avoid mistakes is to continuously reflect on your own moderating skills. After each usability test, look back over the recordings, especially sessions that you feel went particularly well or badly. Make it part of your personal development to identify three things you can build on or that you could have done better.

THINK LIKE A UX RESEARCHER

- It's difficult to assess one's own competence as a usability test moderator. We mention listening back to a participant recording, but it can be hard to be objective. One way around this is to use the five mistakes as a checklist as you reflect on your performance. Another approach, but more challenging to listen to, is to ask for critical feedback from usability test observers after each participant session.

- Some members of development teams misunderstand the purpose of a usability test and expect you to solicit opinions and preferences. They may want you to ask if the participant likes the design or prefers one version over another. How would you manage that expectation?

(Continued)

THINK LIKE A UX RESEARCHER   (Continued)

- We've run tests in the past where it's clearly the test participant's style to continually ask questions. It's how they think aloud. "Where's the link for the basket? Oh, there it is. But how do I find out the shipping costs? Maybe I need to click the basket icon. Where's the basket icon?" You get the idea. These can be one of the more challenging participants to moderate because the "boomerang" technique can become wearing after a while (both for you and the participant). When is it acceptable to ignore a participant's question and treat the question like a statement? How could you practice dealing with a participant like this?

- We discourage you from explaining the design to the participant but of course you'll need to step in if the participant gets totally lost or confused. At what point should you step in to bring a participant back on track? How "lost" do participants need to get for you to know this is really a problem and not one that they can solve themselves?

- Imagine you have a test participant who seems more interested in turning the session into an interview than in doing the test tasks. He turns away from the screen, faces you and tells you anecdotes tenuously related to what he's meant to be doing. How would you bring the participant back on track?

Avoiding Personal Opinions
in Usability Expert Reviews

When properly carried out, usability expert reviews are a very efficient way of finding the usability bloopers in an interface. But there are four common mistakes made by novice reviewers: failing to take the user's perspective; using only a single reviewer, rather than collating the results from a team; using a generic set of usability principles rather than technology-specific guidelines; and lacking the experience to judge which problems are important.

Some people approach a usability expert review like a dogmatic movie critic, prepared to give their opinion on an interface's strengths and weaknesses.

This is the wrong mind set.

A design review is not about opinions, it's about predicting how users will interact with an interface.

Here are four problems that you'll need to address to ensure your review avoids personal opinion and will lead to a better interface.

Problem #1: The Reviewer Fails to Take the User's Perspective

The hardest part of being a good user experience practitioner seems, at first sight, to be the easiest: taking the user's perspective. It's an easy slogan to spout, but like most slogans it's also easy to forget what it means. We often hear reviewers preface a "problem" they have identified with a sentence like, "I really hate it when I see..." or "Personally, when I use this kind of system..."

Here's the difficult truth: It doesn't matter what you like.

The interface may offend your aesthetic sensibilities, look clichéd or old-fashioned. It doesn't matter—because you are not the user. As Kim Vicente[9] has said: "Ironically, the strength of the Wizards—the often-brilliant designers of high-tech products and systems today—is also partially responsible for their downfall: since they have so much scientific and engineering expertise, they tend to think that everyone knows as much about technology as they do."

This means that if you're a member of a development team, you're unlikely to be representative of your users. And if you review the interface from your own perspective, you'll do a very poor job of predicting the problems that real users will have.

So before even starting the review you need a firm idea of your users and their goals. (If you can't do this, consider testing with real users rather than carrying out a usability expert review.) This step isn't just a formality—it really helps you steer the review because it enables you to predict the future. "Predict the future" sounds like a bold statement, but consider this:

- If you know the users' goals, then you should be able to predict why the user is using the product.
- If you know why the user is using the product, then you should be able to predict the specific tasks that the user will be carrying out.
- If you know the tasks, then you should be able to predict the most important features or functions that the user will be looking for to complete those tasks.
- Putting all this together: you should now be able to predict where users are most likely to look, what other elements might distract them, and even where they are likely to click, tap, or swipe first.

A good usability expert review will begin with a data-driven description of the users of the product and a detailed description of the users' tasks. If your review omits these, you're almost certainly evaluating the product from your own perspective and as a consequence your findings will lack the predictive validity that your development team needs.

Problem #2: The Review Is Based on the Opinion of One Reviewer

David carries out an exercise on one of his training courses where the class has a shoot-out between a single reviewer and a team of three. With regularity, the single reviewer (no matter how experienced) finds only around 60% of the usability issues found by the team. This isn't a new finding: Researchers have known for some time that you need three to five reviewers to get adequate coverage of usability issues in an expert review.[10]

Adding multiple reviewers helps find more problems for a number of reasons:

- Some reviewers have more domain knowledge than you (for example, they know a lot about finance if it's a banking application), which means they can find problems you'll miss.
- Some reviewers tend to be sensitive to a sub-set of usability issues—for example, they may be more sensitive to visual design issues or issues to do with information architecture—and they tend to over-report those

issues at the expense of other, equally important ones (like task orientation or help and support).

- Some reviewers have had more exposure to users (either via usability tests or field visits), and this means they are better at identifying the usability issues that trip up people in the real world.

In short, different people just see the world differently.

But ego is a terrible thing. It's almost as if people think that by asking other people to collaborate in the review, they are diminishing their status as "the expert." In fact, the opposite is true: Involving extra reviewers demonstrates a wider knowledge of the literature. Despite this, the majority of expert reviews that we come across are still carried out by a single reviewer.

A good usability expert review will combine results from at least three reviewers. If your review is based on the work of a single reviewer, it's likely that you've spotted only around 60% of the usability issues that you would have found if you had worked as a team.

Problem #3: The Review Uses a Generic Set of Usability Principles

All reviewers have their favorite set of usability principles, such as Nielsen's heuristics[11] or ISO's dialogue principles.[12] These principles are based on decades of research into human psychology and behavior, which is a good thing as you can be sure that—unlike technology—they won't change over time.

But this strength is also a weakness.

By their very nature, these principles are fairly generic and may even seem a little vague when applied to a new technology, like fitness trackers or virtual reality headsets. This is why an experienced reviewer will develop a usability checklist to interpret the principle for the technology and domain under review.

For example, take a principle like "User control and freedom." This is one of Nielsen's principles and is expressed as follows: "Users often choose system functions by mistake and will need a clearly marked 'emergency exit' to leave the unwanted state without having to go through an extended dialogue." This principle was developed for the graphical user interfaces that were in existence at the time. As a reviewer, this would remind you to check (among other things) that dialogue boxes had a cancel button and that the interface supported undo. Fast forward to the web and these checks aren't relevant to most web pages. To re-interpret this principle for web pages, we'll probably want to check (among other things) that the website doesn't disable the back button and that there's a clearly marked route back to "Home" from all pages in the site.

So the guideline is still relevant but the way we check for compliance is different.

It takes some effort to generate a checklist for a specific technology. But it's time well spent because having a checklist to hand when you carry out a review will ensure that you get full coverage of the principles and ensure none get forgotten.

To summarize, a good usability expert review will use a checklist to interpret the principles for the specific technology under test. If you use the high-level principles only, you risk missing important usability issues.

Problem #4: The Reviewer Lacks Experience

Many user interfaces are so bad that finding usability problems with your checklist is simple. But a checklist does not an expert make. You now have to decide if the "problem" is a genuine issue that will affect real users, or if it's a false alarm that most users won't notice.

Sadly, there's no simple way to distinguish between these two choices. Here's a relevant quotation from Nobel prizewinner, Eric Kandel[13]: "Maturation as a scientist involves many components, but a key one for me was the development of taste, much as it is in the enjoyment of art, music, food or wine. One needs to learn what problems are important."

This analogy with "connoisseurship" applies equally to the issue of identifying usability problems. You need to learn what problems are important.

Philip's friend, a ceramics artist, told him the following story: She was asked to judge the ceramics section of an art show (about 20 artists) but included in her section were about five "mixed-media" artists (including media like wood, metalwork, and glass). For the ceramicists she was able to evaluate their work thoroughly—the aesthetics, the skill involved, the originality of the work, the craftsmanship—and she was able to give a rigorous critique of their pieces. But for the mixed-media art she could only use her personal opinion of what she liked or didn't like. When it came to judging the craftsmanship she had no knowledge of what is involved in, say, blowing glass, or welding metal. And because she was uncertain, she found herself giving the mixed-media artists the benefit of the doubt and rating them *higher*.

Generalizing from this story: If you don't understand the domain or the technology, you may tend to be more lenient—perhaps because if you are very critical you may have to justify and explain your judgment, and that could expose your lack of experience with the domain.

The risk is that you'll fail to report some important usability problems.

One way you can develop "taste" in the field of user experience is to break down the wall that so often separates you from users. For example:

- Run as many usability test sessions as you can and observe the seemingly trivial user interface elements that stump test participants.
- Do field work with your users in their home or place of work so you truly empathize with their goals, aspirations and irritations.
- Listen in on customer calls to discover the kinds of problem your users face.
- Be a usability test participant yourself.

A good usability expert review needs to be led by someone with experience. Without this practical knowledge you won't be able to reliably distinguish the critical show stoppers from the false alarms.

Usability expert reviews are an efficient way to weed out usability bloopers from an interface—but only if they avoid personal opinion. Pay attention to these four common mistakes and you'll find your reviews are more objective, more persuasive, and more useful.

THINK LIKE A UX RESEARCHER

- As the UX researcher on a team, you'll often be asked by a developer to cast your eye over a design and give your opinion on its strengths and weaknesses. How could you approach an informal review like this and still avoid the four problems highlighted in this essay?
- How can you ensure you take the user's perspective at the start of each design evaluation and avoid falling into the trap of evaluating a design from your own perspective?
- Select one guideline from your favorite set of usability guidelines (such as Nielsen's heuristics). Then apply the generic guideline to the specific domain in which you work. Create around 10 checklist items that you could use to evaluate an interface objectively.
- If you work in a "UX team of one," how could you involve more than three reviewers in a usability expert evaluation? Do reviewers need to be experts in user experience?
- We provide some examples of how you can develop "taste" in the field of user experience. If you wanted to help an entire development team improve its sense of taste, how would you go about it?

Toward a Lean UX

In The Lean Startup, *Eric Ries describes a design process to help manage risk when developing new products and services under conditions of extreme uncertainty. This essay describes three established user experience techniques we can use to support this design process: narrative storyboarding; paper prototyping; and the Wizard of Oz.*

In 2011, Eric Ries[14] published an influential book titled *The Lean Startup*. What we like about the book is that it puts user experience at the very heart of new product design—and does so in language that makes managers sit up and take notice.

Here's our version of the digested read.

1. Designing new products or services is risky because there are so many uncertainties.
2. The development team has a set of hypotheses—for example, about users, their goals, and what they will pay for—and to reduce uncertainty, these hypotheses need to be tested.
3. We identify these hypotheses and then design experiments to test them out. We run these tests on minimal versions of the product with limited functionality because these minimal systems are quick and easy to create.
4. Design takes place within an iterative cycle of build-measure-learn where we test ideas with users as early as possible.
5. Based on the test results, we continue to develop the idea, or we "pivot" (change direction) and develop a product that has more value for customers.

Sound familiar? There's obviously a lot more to *The Lean Startup* than these five points but we're sure that you can see how congruent this approach is with user centered design.

UX researchers have a lot to contribute to this way of working, but we wanted particularly to focus on item number four in the list above: iterative design and testing. Through necessity, people in user experience have developed many speedy techniques for gleaning feedback from users and we wanted to review some of those. Ries mentions a few in his book (such as a video demonstration and what he calls a "concierge minimum viable product" where you create a highly personalized version of the system to uncover customer needs), but we wanted to mention three other techniques.

These techniques have three things in common.

First, they cost virtually nothing and can be completed in a few days, so they support Ries' notion of moving through the build-measure-learn loop as quickly as possible.

Second, they focus on user behavior rather than people's opinions so they address another issue that Ries highlights: the fact that customers often don't know what they want.

Third, Ries points out that development teams are often reluctant to involve users until they have something fairly complete to show to them. These techniques allow us to test our business idea while it's still an idea—before developers have written a single line of code.

The three methods we will discuss are:

- Hypothesis testing with storyboards.
- Hypothesis testing with a paper prototype.
- Hypothesis testing with the Wizard of Oz.

Hypothesis Testing with Storyboards

With this approach, you create a narrative storyboard—a short cartoon—and then ask your potential users to review it. The storyboard needs to consist only of a handful of panels, but it should convey:

- The user problem you're trying to solve.
- How the user encounters your solution.
- How your solution will work (from the user's perspective).
- How the user will benefit.

As storyboards are inherently visual, let's look at a storyboard for a new product development idea.

Imagine we're thinking of developing a new way for people to pay for train tickets at rail stations using an electronic payment service on their smartphone (a "mobile wallet"). Our initial idea is that people will start the task by using a kiosk at the station where they can choose their ticket. At the

Figure 3.2: A storyboard showing how people might interact with the system. We created the images by tracing over suitably-posed photographs and then we combined the sketches with photographs taken at a train station

USER ARRIVES AT STATION, SEES KIOSK AND LONG QUEUES FOR THE TICKET OFFICE

USER SELECTS DESTINATION

ON PAYMENT SCREEN, HE SELECTS 'MOBILE WALLET'

HE SCANS THE CODE

HE FOLLOWS INSTRUCTIONS TO PAY AND HAS TICKETS DELIVERED

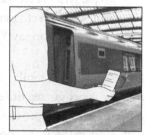

GETS ON TRAIN WITH TICKETS DELIVERED TO HIS PHONE.

payment stage, they will scan a code that's generated on the kiosk screen. Scanning the code takes the user to a payment site where they can pay and get the tickets delivered to their phone.

Let's represent that as a storyboard (see Figure 3.2).

It's clear that there are a few risks that we need to explore with customers. We already know that people use kiosks at rail stations, so we can be confident that people will get over the first couple of steps. But here are some more serious leap-of-faith questions that occur to us about this idea:

- Will people be willing to use their smartphone to pay, or might they prefer to just put their credit card in the kiosk and pay that way?
- Do most people have the software on their phone to scan codes? Do people even know what "scanning a code" means?
- How will people feel about electronic ticket delivery? Do people have any anxieties about not having a physical ticket?

Now we have something that we can show to rail travelers: It will take them less than a minute to digest what's in the storyboard. We can then test two hypotheses:

- Is the problem (not being able to pay via smartphone) serious enough to warrant the solution? If we spend an hour at a railway terminus and speak with 50 people and only three of them report this as a problem, then we need to pivot and find out what the problem really is.
- If the problem is serious enough, then we test the second hypothesis: Is our solution appropriate? We test this by first giving them some context to the activity and then asking them to talk us through the sequence of steps. After each frame we ask a simple question: "Is this a step that you can see yourself, personally, doing?" Again, we can count the numbers of people who say Yes or No at each step.

For example, as a result of testing this solution with customers, we might find that most people see little benefit in paying by phone because it simply adds more steps to the process. So instead, we might "pivot" and come up with a new idea: Perhaps we should display a poster near the kiosk with codes next to the most popular journeys from the station. People can then scan their journey and complete the whole process on the phone without needing to use the kiosk at all. We then storyboard this new idea, and test again.

Hypothesis Testing with a Paper Prototype

A second lean way to evaluate your business idea is to create a paper prototype that shows in detail the steps that you expect the user to take to achieve their goals. Paper prototypes combine hand drawn buttons, labels, and user interface elements with sticky notes to help you craft an interactive experience.

The idea is that you sit users down in front of the prototype, give them a scenario ("Buy a ticket from New York to Boston"), and tell them to use their finger as the mouse. As each new selection is made, you update the screen with sticky notes to reflect the choices that have been made.

Paper prototypes are quick to create—if you spend more than a couple of hours, you're taking too long—and will give you definitive feedback on the usability or otherwise of the workflow you've created. At the end of the test, you'll know the percentage of users who could complete the task: the acid measure of usability.

When we talk about paper prototyping with UX researchers, people are quick to comment that paper prototyping is old fashioned and that electronic prototyping tools are much more efficient. We don't see this as an either-or: There's room in the design process for both types of prototyping. However, the time for electronic prototyping isn't at the initial stage of an idea. As Ries points out, you want to minimize your time through the build-measure-learn iteration loop so you can learn most quickly. Paper prototyping is perfect for that initial phase because it's much quicker than electronic prototyping and easily amenable to modification as you test it out with users.

Hypothesis Testing with the Wizard of Oz

With a Wizard of Oz test, the user interacts with a system that appears to be fully programmed but in fact all of the system's responses are being controlled by a human operator, just like in the eponymous movie. One of our favorite examples of this—the Mechanical Turk—actually predates the movie by nearly 200 years and serves as a wonderful example of the technique.

The Mechanical Turk was a large, chess-playing machine built around 1770. If you played a game of chess against the machine, you would sit down at a proper-sized chess table opposite a mannikin wearing Turkish dress (hence the name). The mannikin would grasp and move chess pieces around the table in response to your moves. It would also probably beat you—the Turk was able to beat most human chess players that it played against, including (apparently) Napoleon and Benjamin Franklin.

The machine, however, was a fake. Hidden inside was a human chess player who moved the pieces around using magnets. Although some people suspected it was a hoax, the illusion was so well created that it was many years before the machine's inner workings were revealed.

For our purposes, what's critical about the Mechanical Turk is that people thought they were really playing against a machine. They had no idea that a human operator was hidden inside the box and animating the mannikin.

To show how we can create a similar illusion with our business idea, let us give you a more up-to-date example.

A while back David was working on the design of an interactive voice response system for a cinema booking system. The idea was that people could ask the system questions over the telephone (a bit like Amazon's Alexa or

Apple's Siri, although this was a long time before good speech recognition was in place). David pre-recorded a small number of responses that he knew he would have to use (such as, "Can you say that again?") but because he didn't know the specific questions that people would ask, he couldn't pre-record all the answers.

Instead, he used text to speech technology to create the illusion that the system was working, with David playing the Mechanical Turk. The user would ask a question, such as, "What films are showing this afternoon that are suitable for families?" and then David would quickly type in, "We have four films suitable for families." The system would read this to the user over the phone in a text-to-speech, computerized voice. While this was being spoken, David would then type in the names of the films.

It was hectic and required fast typing skills, but David's users believed they were interacting with a live system that could do excellent speech recognition. David was able to use this to test out the business idea and identify the most common questions before the client invested in the extensive (and expensive) technology to support it.[15]

What this means for Your Design Process

There are some fundamental principles in user centered design captured in the Lean approach to product development:

- Early and continual focus on users and their tasks.
- Iterative design.
- Empirical measurement of user behavior.

We're delighted that Ries (a former entrepreneur-in-residence at the Harvard Business School) has brought these principles to the attention of senior managers and development teams. It makes our job much easier as we push to make sure the idea of testing business ideas by developing prototypes—dozens of prototypes, not just a couple of iterations—becomes commonplace.

THINK LIKE A UX RESEARCHER

- The key principles of Lean have been around since the early days of human-computer interaction (HCI). Yet Eric Ries' book captured the attention of senior managers and business people in a way that HCI struggled to do. What do you think was different? What does this tell us about engaging that audience in UX research?

- This approach requires the development team to quickly create a prototype to test out a design concept. Do you have someone on your development team who can prototype this quickly? Do you have the necessary skills to prototype? If not, how could you build these skills?

- The Lean approach emphasizes minimizing your time through the build-measure-learn iteration loop so you can learn most quickly. This means it's fine to create and test rudimentary prototypes (like a paper prototype) mentioned in this essay. How do you think stakeholders or the development team would react if you wanted to show a paper prototype to customers? If a stakeholder asked you to delay the test for a few weeks to give the team time to create a more polished prototype, how would you respond?

- We describe how David used the Wizard of Oz technique to test out an interactive voice response system for a cinema booking system. How might you use this technique to create a chatbot (a computer program designed to simulate conversation with human users)?

- One advantage of creating a storyboard is that it shows the user experience "big picture" without too much focus on the specific knobs and dials in a user interface. But testing a concept is very different from testing a prototype where you can ask people to carry out tasks. How could you test a storyboard with users without asking them to predict their future behavior (which people are bad at) or asking them if they like the idea (which provides weak data)?

Controlling Researcher Effects

We take a look at some subtle yet pervasive researcher effects, at ways they can bias the outcome of UX research, and at what we can do to control their influence.

Nothing is more guaranteed to shatter the illusion of reality that's building up nicely in that best seller you're reading, than the author suddenly appearing out of the blue and talking to you directly. Grandly known as "authorial intrusion," it's the moment the author yanks the reader's attention out of the story, reminds us of the real world, and breaks the golden rule of fiction writing and journalism: Keep yourself out of the story. It's right up there with the film crew recording its own reflection in a passing shop window.

Research has its own version of these unfortunate moments. They happen when the researcher blunders into view and ruins things by influencing the outcome of a study. We call these blunders *experimenter effects*.

Experimenter effects contaminate the research process, but we know their origin. They are almost always the result of the experimenter having prior expectations about the hypothesis of a study.

Some classic examples remind us how insidious experimenter effects can be. Recall the case of Clever Hans the counting horse. When given numbers to add, subtract, multiply, or divide, Hans would tap out the correct answer with his hoof. Psychologist Oskar Pfungst showed that, rather than doing arithmetic, Hans was simply picking up involuntary ideomotor cues from his trainer when the correct number of hoof taps was reached. When asked a math problem his trainer did not know the answer to, Hans' performance collapsed.

And it's not just horses. In 1963, psychologists Lucian Cordaro and James Ison[16] asked two groups of college students to observe and count head turns and body contractions made by *planaria* (flatworms). One group of students was led to believe the target behaviors would occur infrequently, while the other group was led to expect a high rate of head turns and contractions. The flatworms in each group were identical and (as is often the case with flatworms) had no expectations about anything. Sure enough, the group expecting a high rate of body movements reported a much higher count than the group expecting a lower rate—an outcome carried entirely by experimenter expectation.

Robert Rosenthal's extensive work on experimenter effects[17] (an investigation spanning 30 years and including both animal and human behavioral research) reveals that 70% of experimenter effects influence outcomes in favor of the researcher's hypothesis.

Experimenter effects are also common in UX and market research, though we'll switch to calling them "researcher effects" as most user experience methods are not really experiments in the conventional sense. Field studies, focus groups, interviews and usability tests are all susceptible to researcher effects because researchers have expectations, and because UX and marketing research create social situations, and because being truly objective is difficult.

The Double-Blind

Science has a powerful antidote to researcher effects: the Double-Blind.

In a double-blind study, neither the participant nor, critically, the experimenter (nor anyone involved in moderating, observing, recording or analyzing the data) knows the research hypothesis, or knows which condition participants are assigned to, or which design is the "before" and which is the "after," which product is "ours" and which is "theirs," etc. A double-blind eliminates the most problematic researcher effects and is effectively used in clinical trials and in debunking pseudoscientific claims.

Can we apply this to UX research? Unfortunately, conducting a double-blind in UX research, while not impossible, is very challenging in practice and is not something we are likely to see. A UX researcher typically works with the development team on a daily basis and has been instrumental in guiding design. In any evaluative situation, there's no way the UX researcher can suddenly have no knowledge or prior expectation of study conditions. Bringing in an external UX researcher doesn't solve the problem either, because this person also must know the design or product at least well enough to conduct an effective study. And remember, the double-blind must extend to data recording, analyzing, interpreting, and reporting the results. In most cases, running a double-blind would turn a quick user experience study into a major covert operation.

The double-blind may be the gold standard but, if we can't use it, how else might we prevent researcher effects? The first step is to raise awareness among project teams that researcher effects exist, and that they can have serious consequences. The second step, since we can't totally eliminate these effects, is to find ways to control them.

Here are some ways that researchers influence the outcomes of their own research, and some thoughts on how we might control biases in these situations.

Biases When Interacting with Participants

These are the "Clever Hans" biases that stem from unintended communications with the participant before and during a study. They result from verbal and non-verbal cues and gestures that influence the participant's thinking or behavior during the UX research, and they become damaging when they systematically favor one particular outcome. For example, Philip observed a study during which the moderator did a good job of remaining neutral when introducing competitor designs, but she leaned forward and nodded whenever she spoke about the sponsor's design.

In reality there are an almost infinite number of biasing behaviors that can creep into a study, from the blatantly obvious, "We hope you'll only have good things to say about our product," (we're not making that one up, we actually heard a researcher say this), to the almost imperceptible smile when the participant clicks the correct button in an interface. Other influencing behaviors can include the researcher's mood and demeanor, tone of voice, frowning, sighing, tensing up, relaxing, shuffling on their chair, raising their eyebrows, and pulling faces. Even note-taking can introduce a bias ("Oh dear, he just wrote something in his notebook, I must have done it wrong"). And this is before we even start to think about the biasing effects of leading and loaded questions, reassurances such as, "You're not the only one to have done that wrong today," or paraphrasing the participant's remarks with a little extra topspin, or allowing one's own opinions to creep into the dialogue.

We can't eliminate all of these biasing factors: They are far too pervasive, and we would end up behaving like automatons if we tried to monitor ourselves down to this micro-behavioral level. So what is the solution? Since a double-blind test is not possible, here are some techniques that can help:

- *Standardize everything*: the research protocol, the moderator script, the questions, and so on. Follow the same protocol in the same way for every participant in every condition. Present task scenarios on cards for the participant to read aloud. Stick to the script.
- *Have a second researcher monitor the first researcher*: Monitor for "protocol drift."

- *Stay out of the participant's line of sight*: In summative usability testing, leave the room if you can during a task.
- *Practice*: Run mock studies that focus on controlling biasing behaviors.

Video-record yourself administering a study or moderating an interview. Critically analyze your performance, and have a colleague help you note any systematic biasing behaviors and inadvertent signals you may be giving.

Biases When Recording, Interpreting and Reporting Findings

Researcher effects can contaminate a study in a number of ways, such as:

- Systematic data recording errors.
- Participant actions or responses that are given undue weight.
- Jotting down what you thought the participant meant rather than what she actually said.
- Trying to interpret data on the fly and too early into a test.
- Making careless recording errors.
- Failing to pay attention.
- Struggling to keep up with the participant.
- Making copying and data-entry errors.

Subsequent data interpretation can also fall foul of *confirmation bias*. This is the tendency to prioritize evidence that fits well with what we already believe, while ignoring evidence that doesn't. Even highly experienced researchers can fall into this cognitive trap.

Biases toward a positive outcome can also influence report writing and research presentations. In the scientific community similar pressures to succeed exist, such that negative results are less likely to be submitted for publication and, if submitted, are less likely to be accepted than positive results. In consumer research, we've seen obviously negative findings given a ludicrously positive spin in a final research presentation with summary headlines such as: "Five of the 20 people really liked the new concept." Researchers doing this risk their credibility. Business stakes are far too high to risk being misled by a researcher contriving a "feel-good" effect.

This may sound unusual, but you should not care what the outcome of your research is. You should only care that your research design and data are bulletproof and will stand up to the most rigorous scrutiny. Let the chips fall where they may. It's not your job to guarantee a happy ending.

Here are some checks we've found helpful:

- Decide on the data logging procedure ahead of the study. Use a manageable number of data codes to categorize events. Practice using them and document them in a formal test plan.
- Record objective data where possible: for example, task completion rates and time on task.
- Agree any pass/fail criteria ahead of the study, not afterwards.
- It may not be possible to have a "blind" UX researcher, but it may be possible to have "blind" data loggers. Have at least two data loggers (or note-takers) so that you can check for inter-scorer reliability and compare notes.
- Record verbatim what participants say, not what you think they mean.
- Avoid trying to interpret the data during the study.
- Double-check your data coding, data entry and any statistical analysis.
- Ask a research colleague to read your final report, or presentation slides, and give critical feedback.

Sponsorship Biases

Biases toward the company sponsoring the research studies are common. In the pharmaceutical industry, for example, industry-funded trials are about four times more likely to report positive rather than negative results[18]; and studies sponsored by pharmaceutical companies are more likely to have outcomes favoring the sponsor than are studies with other sponsors.[19]

Philip recently witnessed a deliberate example of sponsorship bias, motivated perhaps by a misguided desire for a happy outcome, when he was invited to review a project in which a third party "independent" research company was carrying out long-term in-home trials of a new domestic appliance product. He was astonished to discover that the owner of the research company had planted herself into the study as a test participant, and that for every item on every questionnaire over a three-month period, she gave the product the highest possible five-star positive rating. In her eagerness to please the client, this researcher had clearly lost sight of the purpose of the in-home research, which was to uncover problems so that they could be fixed before the product was launched.

Internal company pressures, often stemming from the ever-escalating collective belief that the project cannot possibly fail (otherwise why are we still doing it?), can create a working environment intolerant of any negative outcomes. Much of this pressure comes from testing or carrying out research too late, and it can be defused by doing research and testing early and often, and by keeping the stakeholders closely involved so that they can make course corrections and mitigate risk before things reach the point of no return.

Again, if a double-blind can be employed, this can effectively put a "firewall" between the funding source and the research team. No one involved in conducting and reporting the study would know who the sponsoring company was. But, as we have noted, in UX research this is nearly impossible, and sometimes you just have to stand by your research data, bite the bullet and break the bad news, sponsor or no sponsor. However, you might be surprised at the reaction you get. Philip once had to present negative UX research data that he knew would deliver a death blow to a $28 million project. To his surprise, the relief in the room was palpable. It was the final piece of evidence that gave the company the confidence to pull the plug and stop wasting more money.

Why You Need to Fix Your Bias Blind Spot

Bias works like a Trojan horse. It hides in our UX research toolbox, slips past our defenses, and operates from the inside. Everyone has a bias blind spot but we are less likely to detect bias in ourselves than in others. Carey Morewedge, associate professor of marketing at Boston University, says[20]: "People seem to have no idea how biased they are. Whether a good decision maker or a bad one, everyone thinks that they are less biased than their peers. This susceptibility to the bias blind spot appears to be pervasive, and is unrelated to people's intelligence, self-esteem, and actual ability to make unbiased judgments and decisions."

Unlike in the academic science community, where research is rigorously peer reviewed and scoured for methodological flaws, even shot down if it cannot pass muster, most UX and market research is seldom subjected to such intense scrutiny. Things are simply moving too fast. Headline findings are often all that most stakeholders see, and findings are largely taken on trust that the results are what they appear to be. Decisions are quickly made and the show moves on down the road.

But false research outcomes can cost a company millions of dollars. In the absence of a double-blind methodology, your strongest weapon against researcher bias may simply be the awareness that it exists.

THINK LIKE A UX RESEARCHER

- Think of the various stages in UX research, from planning a study through to taking action on the findings. What different biases could creep in at each stage? Are some of these stages more vulnerable to researcher bias than others?

- Consider the situation where people from the development team are observing your research. If they discuss their observations with you after the session, are they biasing your recollection of events? Or is this a useful way of highlighting observations you may have missed?

- Do you think the way a UX researcher approaches design experiments meets the standards that a scientist would expect of a "controlled" experiment? Why, or why not? Is UX research a science? Does UX research need to adopt the scientific method to offer value?

- We say that it's nearly impossible to run a double-blind UX research study. But could we come close to a double-blind study if we used remote, unmoderated usability tools?

- Whenever you work with humans, there is a tendency to empathize with some people more deeply than with others. Some participants in your research may be more likable, more articulate, or more needful of a good solution than others. How can you prevent this from biasing the way you interpret and report the results?

4

Analyzing User
Experience Research

Sharpening Your Thinking Tools

Most new products fail within the first few months after launch. We describe 10 critical thinking tools that can be used to flag concerns about the project you are working on. These rules can be used to help save—or in some cases to kill off—struggling projects.

In 1958 Theodore Sturgeon, an American writer and critic of science fiction and horror stories, argued that 90% of everything (he specifically listed science fiction, film, literature and consumer products) is crap.

It seems that Sturgeon was onto something, because working on products that don't succeed is now the rule rather than the exception. It's generally asserted that about 90% (the figure varies between 65% and 95% depending on which book or article you read) of all new products fail in the marketplace within six months of their launch. This means, purely on the balance of probability, that the product, application, device, system, or app that you are working on right now is more likely to be a commercial failure than it is to be a success.

It may even end up in a museum, though maybe not the kind of museum you'd like it to be in. If you want to see some of the sorry 90% take a trip to the offices of market research giant GfK in Ann Arbor, Michigan. It is where products go to die. Among the more than 100,000 clunkers on display in this Museum of Failed Products, you may spot Clairol Touch of Yogurt Shampoo, Gillette For Oily Hair Only, Ben-Gay Aspirin, Colgate TV dinners, and, of course, Crystal Pepsi.

The thing that should strike you is that, once upon a time, these were all active projects in major product companies, with project plans and timelines and launch targets, and with enthusiastic business and project managers, legal experts, accountants, designers, and marketers meeting to debate mission critical decisions, and all convinced they were on to a winner. They were wrong.

"Failure," points out economist, Paul Ormerod, in his book, *Why Most Things Fail*,[1] "is the distinguishing feature of corporate life."

Theodore Sturgeon would have just nodded: "Told you so."

Cheerleaders, Blind Faith and Ideas that Won't Die

It comes as a bit of a surprise, then, to know that company executives and employees, by and large, know quite well why products fail. It's not a mystery. For example, market research resource GreenBook[2] lists these reasons for new product failure:

- Marketers assess the marketing climate inadequately.
- The wrong group was targeted.
- A weak positioning strategy was used.
- A less-than-optimal configuration of attributes and benefits was selected.
- A questionable pricing strategy was implemented.
- The ad campaign generated an insufficient level of awareness.
- Market cannibalization depressed corporate profits.
- Over-optimism about the marketing plan led to an unrealistic forecast.
- Poor implementation of the marketing plan in the real world.
- The new product was pronounced dead and buried too soon.

Clearly, any and all of these factors can contribute to failure, but there's something else going on too, and Isabelle Royer, Professor of Management at Jean Moulin University Lyon 3, nailed it in her Harvard Business Review article entitled "Why Bad Projects Are So Hard to Kill."[3] Analyzing the problem in two French companies, Royer uncovered not incompetence or poor management per se, but a "fervent and widespread belief among managers in the inevitability of their project's ultimate success." This belief surges through an organization and gains momentum as everyone roots for the project like cheerleaders urging on a football team. This produces a "collective belief" that tolerates only positive talk, positive data, and positive outcomes, and it blinds the development team to warning flags and negative feedback.

But it is precisely this kind of unquestioning belief—Royer refers to it as blind faith—that is anathema to scientists and critical thinkers. In science, nothing is taken on belief or blind faith. Everything—every assertion or hypothesis—requires evidence, and every claim and every data point is challenged. In fact, in science it is a prerequisite that a hypothesis must, in principle, be falsifiable, otherwise it is simply dismissed out of hand.

Science is a self-correcting method for discovering the truth about things. But first and foremost *science is a way of thinking*. As part of their training, scientists, irrespective of their specific discipline, acquire a set of techniques or "thinking tools" that are continually sharpened through use.

This raises an interesting question. Can thinking like a scientist, rather than thinking like a cheerleader, help teams and individuals challenge dodgy product ideas, help kill off bad projects, and provide confirmation for potentially good product ideas?

We think it can. Let's take a look at the toolkit.

Thinking Like a Scientist

In his book, *The Demon Haunted World - Science as a Candle in the Dark*,[4] Carl Sagan, scientist, astronomer, astrophysicist, cosmologist, author, and science communicator, presents a tool kit for critical thinking—he calls it his "Baloney Detection Kit." Applying some or all of these "tools for skeptical thinking" is a guaranteed way to uncover errors, flawed thinking, false assertions, hoaxes, frauds, flimflam, pseudoscience, con tricks, scams, myths, superstitions, mysticism, hocus-pocus, outright lies, and general BS. In science, such thinking tools underpin the design of experiments and are used to challenge and test hypotheses—including a scientist's own hypothesis—as well as to debunk spurious claims.

In product design and development we can use these tools to strengthen an idea's claim for support, or to expose flawed assumptions, or to identify projects that should be shut down, and ultimately we can use them to ensure that critical go/no-go decisions are based on verifiable evidence.

Here is Carl Sagan's Baloney Detection Kit with Sagan's thinking tools shown in italics.

Confirm the Facts

"Wherever possible there must be independent confirmation of the facts."

Require evidence. Don't take product mandates or design decisions at face value, or assume that people know what they are doing or that someone else will check the facts. Be a skeptic.

We're not talking here about being negative or cynical, or being a curmudgeon or a naysayer. Thoughtful skepticism is a good thing. It's what stops us from being gullible. Ask yourself: What's driving this decision? What's the evidence for believing that X, Y, or Z is the case?

Evidence supporting a design or marketing decision might be in the form of results from a market research study, a usability test, or observational field research; or it might be an account manager's record of customer requests for a certain product or feature, or a pattern of customer helpline questions. Or the decision to move in a certain direction may be a business decision supported by economic or trends data. Whatever form the evidence takes, confirm its source and its validity and reliability. If your source is the result of secondary desk research, try to follow the references right back to the original source.

As an aside, here's a question we might all ask ourselves: "When was the last time I made a specific design or marketing or (insert your specialty) decision based on actual verifiable evidence, rather than on my gut feel or on my, or someone else's, opinion, or on the outcome of political debating?" Or for that matter, "When was the last time I double-checked the facts about something?"

Encourage Debate

> "Encourage substantive debate on the evidence by knowledgeable proponents of all points of view."

Discuss the evidence as a team. Is the evidence empirical? How were data collected? Does the research method stand up to scrutiny? Do independent sources of evidence converge to support the same decision? Was the evidence interpreted correctly? Do the decisions that resulted flow logically from the evidence? Note that *debating the evidence* is not the same thing as *debating personal opinions and preferences*—there must actually be some evidence on the table.

Remember that Authorities Can Be Wrong

> "Arguments from authority carry little weight. Authorities have made mistakes in the past. They will do so again in the future. Perhaps a better way to say it is that there are no authorities; at most, there are experts."

Don't pull rank in product design or marketing meetings. Instead, present data. Data beats opinion, no matter whose opinion it is. If no one has data, use your position to authorize someone to do the work required to get it.

Develop More than One Idea

"If there is something to be explained, think of all the different ways in which it could be explained. Then think of tests by which you might systematically disprove each of the alternatives. What survives, the hypothesis that resists disproof in this Darwinian selection among 'multiple working hypotheses' has a much better chance of being the right answer than if you had simply run with the first idea that caught your fancy."

Think of all the ways one could solve a user problem or meet a user need. Sketch them as storyboards or mock them up as low fidelity paper prototypes or cardboard models. See which ones fly best. How do you decide which idea to keep? Run experiments. Try to shoot them all down. Don't try to prove them; try to disprove them. This is how science works. Let the data decide. Don't just ask people whether they like your concept. That's a cop out and it does your company a disservice. Instead, design your research to pinpoint the idea that best resists all attempts to discredit it.

Keep an Open Mind

"Try not to get too attached to a hypothesis just because it's yours. It's only a way station in the pursuit of knowledge. Ask yourself why you like the idea. Compare it fairly with the alternatives. See if you can find reasons for rejecting it. If you don't, others will."

Be open to changing direction (Lean UX practitioners call this a pivot). You may think this is odd, but scientists rejoice when a hypothesis is proven wrong. It means they have nudged science forward, have added to the body of human knowledge and have advanced our understanding of the world. Be ready to change direction for the sake of the project. Being wrong is OK. It's how we develop expertise.

Measure Things

> *"Quantify. If whatever it is you're explaining has some measure, some numerical quantity attached to it, you'll be much better able to discriminate among competing hypotheses. What is vague and qualitative is open to many explanations. Of course, there are truths to be sought in many qualitative issues we are obliged to confront, but finding them is more challenging."*

Quantifying things takes the ambiguity and guesswork out of decision making. Whenever possible design your experiments to gather quantitative data, not just people's opinions and comments. Note that Sagan is using the terms "quantitative" and "qualitative" to refer to the kind of data one should collect (precise numerical data v. vague verbal data). He is not using the terms in the way some customer researchers and stakeholders use them, to refer to a study design that has a large or a small number of respondents.

Test Every Link in the Chain

> *"If there's a chain or argument, every link in the chain must work, including the premise, not just most of them."*

Every part of an argument must stand up to scrutiny. Similarly, every element of an idea or product concept must work, or the weak links must be identified so they can be strengthened. In product development we can also apply this thinking to another form of chain. Over the course of a typical product development cycle, bursts of development activity (or sprints in an Agile framework) are strung together like links in a chain, connected by stage gates, or checkpoints, that allow for progress and quality checks. The stage gates are an invitation to apply the thinking tools and to flag any concerns. Applied early they can help confirm or redirect a project; applied late they may still be able to save your company the embarrassment and cost of a failed launch.

Apply Occam's Razor

"This convenient rule of thumb urges us when faced with two hypotheses that explain the data equally well, to choose the simpler."

William of Ockham was a Franciscan friar, logician, and philosopher who lived in the late thirteenth and early fourteenth centuries. He is known for his maxim (his metaphorical razor) that advocates cutting or shaving away unnecessary assumptions. He wrote *Numquam ponenda est pluralitas sine necessitate:* "Plurality must never be posited without necessity." In other words: Opt for the simpler and more parsimonious of available explanations or solutions.

Taking it a step further: Design for simplicity. Don't make your product—or your rationale for it—any more complicated than it needs to be. And kudos in advance to anyone quoting Occam's Razor (in Latin) the next time your team is discussing feature creep.

Test the Hypothesis

"Always ask whether the hypothesis can be, at least in principle, falsified. Propositions that are untestable, unfalsifiable, are not worth much."

It's rather unlikely, in the context of product ideation and development, that we'll encounter truly untestable and unfalsifiable hypotheses of the kind that are sometimes postulated by armchair thinkers (for example, "The universe and everything in it including our memories came into existence just 10 seconds ago."). However, we may still encounter ideas, assertions, or arguments that cannot be tested or falsified for other reasons. Sometimes—especially in large corporations—the origin and rationale for embarking on a certain project can be a mystery to almost everyone on a team; sometimes the mandate has just descended from the higher echelons of the company and so goes unquestioned. Sometimes we build a new product for no other reason than that our competitor is building one. There's a sense in which these directives are untestable—but they can still be questioned. Why are the competitors building the product? What do they know that we don't? How do we know they got it right?

Other times, an idea or hypothesis may be predicated on data that relate to questions we consider to be "untestable," or questions that make no sense, or that respondents cannot reasonably be expected to answer: "What do you think doing laundry will be like 10 years from now?" or "How likely are you to buy this product?"

Always ensure that your ideas are testable and that your research questions can return valid answers.

Conduct Experiments

"The reliance on carefully designed and controlled experiments is key. We will not learn much from mere contemplation."

Sagan rounds out his Baloney Detection Kit by advocating that we carry out experiments. This is not just a general recommendation to "do some research," it is a specific direction to conduct carefully designed experiments in order to decide among competing ideas, solutions, explanations or hypotheses (and is a key principle of Lean UX). This means having control conditions, eliminating sources of error, avoiding biases and, if possible, running double-blind experiments.

Start Using the Thinking Tools

Development teams spend a lot of time and effort debating how to build a product right, but far less time and effort debating whether they are building the right product. The situation described by Professor Royer is not uncommon. Most, if not all, projects, at some point, pass a point of no return, gathering pace like a runaway train until even the product managers have no way of changing course or stopping the momentum.

But it's worth noting that most development teams do have skeptics onboard, people who may have concerns about a project's direction. Some are naturally vocal, some just grumble in the background, and others may not have the confidence to stick their head above the parapet because they are unsure how to critique an idea or challenge an argument.

Sagan's Baloney Detection Kit provides the thinking tools that are needed. Try them out next time you attend a project kick-off meeting or read a research report pertaining to your project. And don't forget to use the Baloney Detection Kit to evaluate your own ideas and arguments before presenting them to others.

We may not be able to change the outcome of Sturgeon's Law, but by applying these thinking tools early in the design lifecycle (ideally during the ideation and concept formation phase) and conducting experiments to test early models, we can increase the probability that our product launch will land safely among the successful 10% rather than in the... well, you know where.

THINK LIKE A UX RESEARCHER

- You may want to master just a few of the thinking tools to begin with. Which of the tools fit your circumstances the best? Do any of the tools resonate with you more strongly than others?
- How do you think your team will react if you apply some of the critical thinking tools discussed here? Consider the kinds of resistance you might encounter and how you might overcome it—and still be friends afterwards.
- Sagan's Baloney Detection Kit prescribes a structured framework for thinking about problems, but nowhere in his kit do we see anything about creativity, intuition, gut feel, or design thinking. Why not? Do you think Sagan's approach stifles or sharpens creativity? How can these different approaches—we can think of them as the art and science of design—complement each other?
- How might you use Occam's Razor to prevent feature creep? Run a team exercise in which you apply it to your current design concept. How much can you "shave" away without compromising your original vision?
- Sagan's Baloney Detection Kit contains 10 thinking tools on how to be a skeptic. Make a credit-card-sized list of the tools and keep it in your wallet. Then, at your next project meeting, check the list as the meeting progresses and think about which tools might usefully challenge the various decisions or claims being made.

UX Research and Strength of Evidence

The concept of "strength of evidence" plays an important role in all fields of research, but is seldom discussed in the context of UX research. We take a closer look at what it means for UX research, and we suggest a taxonomy of research methods based on the strength of the data they return.

Philip once told a project manager that there are no questions in usability. Here's what happened. True story.

Some years ago he was working for a large corporation preparing the test plan for a usability test when the project manager called and asked if he wouldn't mind hurrying up and sending over the list of usability questions because the sponsoring group wanted to vet them.

"There are no questions in usability," he replied.

"What do you mean, there are no questions?" riposted the project manager, momentarily taken aback, "How can there be no questions? How on earth are you going to find out if people like the new design?"

"But I'm not trying to find out if they like it," Philip pointed out, in a manner that he admits in hindsight was a little too testy. "I'm trying to find out if they can use it. I have a list of *tasks* not a list of *questions*."

We might debate long into the night as to whether there really are no questions in usability. But the reason for mentioning this is that it leads to a very useful rule of thumb for UX researchers.

Good and Bad UX Research Data

Requests to shovel explicit, "What do you think?" questions into user experience studies betray the fact that not only do some stakeholders not understand the purpose of a usability test, but also that they believe all user feedback is necessarily valuable. It shows that they are unaware of the concept of *good data* and *bad data*, and, as a result, believe that all user feedback is grist to the mill.

But it isn't. There's good grist and there's useless grist.

Similarly, there are strong data and weak data. This holds true for all fields of research, whether developing a new medicine, discovering a new planet, solving a crime, or evaluating a software interface.

UX research is about observing what people do. It's not about canvassing peoples' opinions. This is because, as data, opinions are worthless. For every

10 people who like your design, 10 others will hate it and 10 more won't care one way or the other. *Opinions are not evidence.*

Behaviors, on the other hand, *are* evidence. This is why a detective would much rather catch someone "red-handed" in the act of committing a crime than depend on hearsay and supposition. Hence the often-repeated UX research advice: "Pay attention to what people do, not to what they say." It's almost become a user experience cliché but it's a good starting point for a discussion about something important: *strength of evidence.* This is the notion that some data provide strong evidence, some provide only moderately strong evidence, and some provide weak evidence. At all costs, we must avoid basing our product development efforts on weak evidence.

Evidence in UX Research

Evidence is what we use to support our claims and our reasoning. It's what gives us credibility when we make decisions about a specific design parameter, about product features, about when to exit an iterative design-test loop, about go/no-go decisions, and about whether to launch a new product, service or website. Evidence is what we present to our development team and what we bring to the table to arbitrate disagreements and disputes. Evidence is what helps us avoid making knee-jerk, seat-of-the-pants decisions. We back our reasoning with evidence based on good data. Data are the stuff of research and investigation.

It may sometimes look as though user experience studies are "method-first" events ("We need a usability test," "I want a contextual inquiry study," "Let's do a card sort,") but the UX researcher, focusing on the underlying research question, thinks "data first": "What kind of data must I collect to provide credible and compelling evidence on this issue?" The method then follows.

What Is Strong Evidence?

Strong evidence results from data that are valid and reliable.

Valid data are data that really do measure the construct that you think they are measuring. In a usability test, valid data measure things like task completion rate and efficiency rather than aesthetic appeal or preference. Reliable data are data that can be replicated if you, or someone else, conducted the research again using the same method but with different test participants.

No matter what the method, research data must be valid and reliable or the data should be discarded.

In UX research, strong data come from task-based studies, from studies that focus on observable user behaviors where the data are objective and unbiased—data that catch the user "red-handed" in the act. Strong data come with a confidence level and assure us that further research is unlikely to change our degree of confidence in our findings.

The following is a brief taxonomy of methods based on levels of evidence—or, more accurately, it's a taxonomy of the types of data that result from the methods. It assumes, in all cases, that the method has been well designed and well conducted. It's not an exhaustive list, but it includes methods the UX researcher is likely to consider in a typical user centered design lifecycle.

Examples of Strong UX Research Evidence

Strong evidence invariably involves target users doing tasks or engaging in some activity that is relevant to the concept being designed or the issue being investigated. It includes data from:

- Contextual research studies (field visits and other ethnography variants that record the behavior of users as they currently do their work and achieve their goals).
- Formative and summative usability tests in which actual users carry out actual tasks using an interface or product.
- Web or search analytics and any kind of automatically collected usage data.
- A/B or multivariate testing.
- Controlled experiments.
- Task analysis.
- Secondary research of behavioral studies, drawing on meta-analyses and peer-reviewed papers, and on previous user experience reports that fully describe the method used.

Examples of Moderately Strong UX Research Evidence

To qualify for this category, data should come from studies that at least include carrying out tasks—either by users or by usability experts, or involve self-reporting of actual behaviors. These methods are often a precursor to methods from the "strong" category. They fall into this category because the data typically have a higher degree of variability or uncertainty. They include:

- Heuristic evaluations.
- Cognitive walkthroughs.
- Feedback from usability experts who have carried out real tasks.
- Interviews or any kind of self-reported behavior like "jobs to be done."

- User journey mapping.
- Diary studies.
- Card sorting.
- Eye tracking.
- Pop-up "guerrilla" research in cafés, libraries, etc.

Examples of Weak UX Research Evidence

Decisions based on weak data can cost companies millions of dollars if they result in bad designs, poor marketing decisions, or false product claims. So the obvious question is: Why would you ever design a study to collect weak data?

You wouldn't.

Data from these methods have no place in UX research. They result from methods that are either badly flawed or are little better than guesswork. If you can choose between spending your UX research budget on one of these methods or donating it to charity—opt for the latter. Weak UX research evidence results from:

- Any kind of faux-usability test: for example, tests that ask people which design they like best; or tests that rely heavily on interviewing for primary data collection.
- Unmoderated, thinking aloud testing that allows users to simply act as if they were expert reviewers while not actually doing the tasks.
- Usability evaluations—even by experts—that are based on "just kicking the tires."
- Focus groups.
- Surveys (you're allowed to disagree but only if you slept through the 2016 US election and its many polling results).
- Intuition, appeal to authorities or personal experience.
- The opinions of friends, family, work colleagues, your boss, company managers, and executives.

How to Judge the Strength of UX Research Evidence from a Study or a Report

Start by asking these questions:

- Why should I believe your claim?
- How good is your evidence?
- Can I depend on these findings?

These are not trick questions: Anyone presenting research findings should be able to answer them.

During a study you can ask yourself:

- Am I observing people working (for example, carrying out tasks with a prototype) rather than listening to what they are saying (such as giving their opinions about a design)?
- Are people in an interview speculating on what they might do in the future? Or are they relating actual events that have happened to them in the past?

We started this essay by promising a rule of thumb. Here it is. Use this as your mantra when evaluating the strength of UX research: *Behavioral data are strong. Opinion data are weak.*

THINK LIKE A UX RESEARCHER

- Think about the UX or market research methods you or your colleagues have used recently. Which level of strength would you assign to the data that were collected?
- Aside from questions you might ask for clarification or to better understand a user action, are there any occasions when a list of usability-based questions could actually be useful? What might these questions be? What would be the pros and cons of such a list?
- Do you agree with our taxonomy of methods? Consider each method and decide if you agree on our classification as strong, moderately strong, or weak. Think of some more research methods and add them to the lists.
- Task-based studies generally return strong data, but the quality of the data still depends on a well designed study. What study design flaws could cause a task-based study to return weak and misleading data?
- Occasionally, colleagues may ask the UX researcher if they can just "tag on" a few direct questions at the end of a usability test— effectively "piggy-backing" their agenda on to a study. As a UX researcher, how would you feel if you were asked this? What reasons might you have to agree or disagree with the request?

Agile Personas

Personas get a mixed reception from development teams, with some questioning their value. A typical criticism is that persona descriptions are superficially elegant but they lack substance. Another criticism is that persona descriptions are too "final" and hard to update with new data. Adopting a lightweight persona description, such as the 2½D sketch, addresses these issues while retaining the strengths of traditional personas.

When we talk to development teams about UX research, none of them has ever said that usability testing is a bad idea. Some will tell us that they do not have the money or inclination to do usability testing, but everyone agrees it has obvious face validity.

The same goes for nearly every UX research method in our toolbox... save one: Personas.

Personas seem to be like Marmite.[5] Some development teams love them and jump in with both feet. But there are other teams that are more sniffy about them. Personas, they say, seem suspiciously definitive. Our audience is too large to be summed up by a handful of personas. Personas seem too shallow. We tried personas and it didn't work. And more recently: "What's the point of wasting time with personas when we can speak to our users directly?"

Before discussing a potential reformulation, it's worth reviewing briefly the history of personas, why they got their bad reputation, and what they are good for.

A Short History of Personas

Personas were invented by Alan Cooper and first described in his book,[6] *The Inmates are Running the Asylum.* Cooper presented them as a way of summarizing the key attributes of different user groups. Their purpose, he said, is to avoid designing for an "elastic" user: a design target that bends and stretches according to the whims of the development team. He writes, "Developing for the elastic user gives the developer license to code as he pleases while paying lip-service to 'the user.' Real users are not elastic." (Cooper, p. 127)

What Are Personas?

In their book,[7] *The Persona Lifecycle*, Pruitt & Adlin describe personas as "detailed descriptions of imaginary people constructed out of well-understood, highly specified data about real people." (Pruitt & Adlin, p. 3) The most common artifact from a persona activity is a *persona description*: a one-page portrayal of a user archetype, describing the persona's goals, motivations and behaviors. To help development teams empathize with users, there is usually a photograph of the persona, some back story and a quotation that summarizes the key user need.

Personas went on to spawn an industry. Cooper's book chapter was followed by website postings, journal articles, conference tracks, and yet more books, all devoted to personas.

Why? What was behind the enthusiasm for this method?

To understand why personas became so popular, we need to understand that, at the time, many development teams had never seen a user. Some didn't even know who their users were. In this situation, personas were like a gift from the gods. A team of researchers from an agency—and it usually was an agency, not an internal team—would go out and find the users, describe them in ways that were useful for design, and then present them to the development team as fully formed characters. The agency took on the role of translator, acting as a go-between to help developers connect with their users. Like a team of Victorian explorers visiting an exotic tribe, the agency journeyed into uncharted territory and returned with pictures and artifacts—personas—to amaze everyone.

What Made Personas Go Sour?

There were three developments that clouded development teams' views on the usefulness of personas.

First: because Agile. "Development" teams morphed into "design" teams. Engaging with users became more of a norm and less of an exception. This is good for user experience, but it's bad news for "traditional" personas. Traditional personas began to look too finished, too final. Teams were savvy enough to know that fully formed, completed descriptions of users are an impossibility at the early stages of design. Instead, they wanted conversation starters. To use the Agile terminology, development teams wanted to get a "shared understanding" of their users and they were suspicious of any attempt to set requirements in concrete.

Second, personas began to parody themselves. Photographs were taken from stock libraries and showed beautiful, happy, lifestyle images of people using… accountancy software. Teams stuck persona descriptions onto squeeze toys (Pruitt & Adlin, p. 317), beer glasses (Pruitt & Adlin, p. 317), packs of candy (Pruitt & Adlin, p. 335), and life-sized sketches (Pruitt & Adlin, p. 320). Even the most conservative personas tended to be shown as a glossy leaflet, implying a robustness and finality to the UX research that was almost certainly unjustified. But above all, none of these artifacts could be easily changed as the team learned new information about users.

And third, in a parallel track, marketers discovered personas and they liked the taste. Marketing teams created versions of personas to represent market segments. Because they used the magic term "personas," development teams were discouraged from developing their own, not realizing that a market segment might contain multiple personas. More cynically, the purpose of marketing personas is primarily to sell more stuff, whereas design personas need to reveal the user behaviors relevant for a product. Development teams couldn't use marketing personas to make design decisions, so they decided personas weren't that useful. (It wasn't helped by the fact that marketers seem fond of giving their personas silly names, such as "Social Butterfly Brenda" or "Value Hunter Valerie," that attempt to collapse nuanced research into a single concept. This trivializes the research, resulting in designers rolling their eyes and shaking their heads.)

Raw Data Is Not a Persona

But if we reject personas, we risk throwing out the baby with the bathwater. This is because we are left with knowledge about individual users who may or may not be representative. Just because you have regular contact with users, it doesn't mean you know who your users are. Let us explain.

One of the great benefits of personas is that they allow you to see the big picture and not get distracted by the raw data. When doing UX research, we start with raw data, but it's messy. Individuals are idiosyncratic. They have rough edges that don't apply to similar users of that type. If we don't analyze and then synthesize our data, we risk getting misled by the user who complains the loudest, or the one that's most helpful, or the one who has an interesting, but isolated, need. Data analysis smooths out these rough edges.

It's great that your team has regular contact with users. But even if you reject personas, you still need to step back, interpret your data, and think about the types of user in your audience: otherwise you'll fall into the "elastic user" trap articulated by Alan Cooper.

New Marmite. Old Bottles

Let us take you on a short detour.

In 1982, David Marr[8] described a computational model of human vision. One of the components of his model was the concept of a 2½D Sketch. Without laboring the details, this idea attempts to capture the notion that the visual system never has enough information to see all sides of an object, so it fills in the gaps. An oft-cited example is to imagine someone with his back turned to you. You make assumptions that this person has a front too and you would be mightily surprised if he turned around and you discovered he had no face. The 2½D Sketch is a metaphor for the fact that our visual system is using data to actively construct the world, based on reasonable assumptions.

We can apply this metaphor to persona descriptions: after all, what the development team are doing is using data to actively construct its view of the user, based on reasonable assumptions. So rather than create a formal persona description with requirements cast in concrete, we can create a 2½D Sketch. This artifact will remind us that we will never have enough information to see all sides of our user: what we have is an approximation. It's a conversation starter, a way to arrive at a shared understanding of our audience. The use of the word "sketch" also reminds us that we don't want to create anything too ostentatious: The medium (which looks unfinished) is the message. We're looking for persona descriptions that are lightweight, disposable, and, well, agile.

Jared Spool captures this ideas when he states,[9] "Personas are to Persona Descriptions as Vacations are to Souvenir Picture Albums." It's the process of UX research that matters, not the beauty of the final artifact.

The best conversation starters are flexible enough to change easily. They shouldn't look like they have been cast in concrete. Here's one approach we've used that meets this criterion.

Creating Your Own 2½D Sketch

Get prepared. You'll need a few sheets of flip chart paper, some Sharpies, and a pack of sticky notes. Call a meeting and get your team to attend.

Begin by coming to a shared understanding of the UX research you have done up to this point. (This is important: You still need to have done the UX research. You're not going to brainstorm a persona out of thin air.) Use this part of the meeting to come to a consensus on the different groups of users in your audience.

The next step is to create one or more 2½D sketches on a sheet of flip chart paper. Arrange the flip chart paper in landscape format, and split it into four quadrants. (See Figure 4.1 for an example).

- Label the top left quadrant with a name for this user type. Draw a sketch showing this user type in a context having some thought that's relevant to your product.
- Label the bottom left quadrant "Facts." Using sticky notes, list the facts you know to be true about this user type (such as gender, age, job title). Put one fact per sticky note.
- Label the top right quadrant, "Behaviors." What does this user type want to do with the product? What do they currently do that's related to usage of the product? Put one behavior per sticky note.

Figure 4.1: An example of a 2½D sketch persona

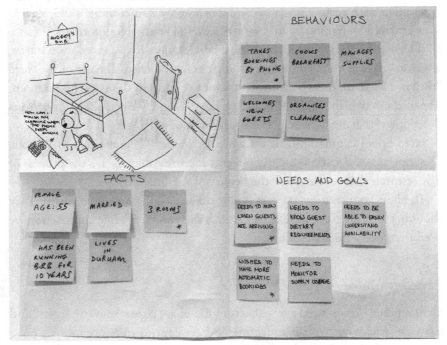

- Label the bottom right quadrant, "Needs and goals." How do users want to feel when using the product? Ultimately, what do users want to achieve with the product? What are this user type's deep drives and motivations? Put one need/goal per sticky note.

Working as a team, complete your 2½D Sketch. Prioritize the stickies in each quadrant. Have a conversation. Work toward a shared understanding.

Above all, *don't* take this away and spend hours turning it into a finished, polished persona. Instead, spend your time speaking to users. Then find some wall space to post your 2½D Sketch and update it with the new information you've collected.

THINK LIKE A UX RESEARCHER

- Pruitt & Adlin describe personas as "detailed descriptions of imaginary people constructed out of well-understood, highly specified data about real people." Jared Spool states that, "Personas are to Persona Descriptions as Vacations are to Souvenir Picture Albums." Are these statements contradictory or can you reconcile them?
- How might you convince a development team who rejected personas in the past to try out the 2½D Sketch? How might you encourage a development team that has never used personas to try them out?
- We argue that a glossy persona description misleads the development team as it implies the UX research is "finished." But do some audiences expect a glossy deliverable? For example, is it appropriate to show a 2½D Sketch to senior stakeholders in your organization? If not, how might you adapt our method to meet the needs of different audiences?
- Personas that include a name and a stock photograph of a user will indirectly define that persona's gender, race, and to some degree their class and status. Some systems (such as public sector services) need to serve a whole population. Should we avoid including demographic data in a persona? And if we do, how might this affect a development team's ability to empathize with their users?
- Having read this essay, do you think critics of personas have a point? Or are their criticisms limited to poor persona descriptions?

How to Prioritize Usability Problems

A typical usability test may return over 100 usability issues. How can you prioritize the issues so that the development team know which ones are the most serious? By asking just three questions of any usability problem, we are able to classify its severity as low, medium, serious, or critical.

Running a usability test has been compared with taking a drink from a fire hydrant: You get swamped with data in the form of usability issues that need to be organized, prioritized, and fixed. Although it's tempting to use your own judgment in determining severity, this causes a difficulty when a developer challenges your decision: "How did you rate that issue as 'critical'? I think it's more of a 'medium' problem."

Having a standard process for defining severity means that you can be consistent in the way you assign severity and means that you provide the transparency needed for people to check your work.

In fact, by asking just three questions, we can classify the severity of any usability problem.

What Is the Impact of the Problem?

Problems that affect completion rate (especially with frequent or critical tasks) are more severe than problems that affect user satisfaction. For example, if the "on-off" button on your newly designed gadget is hard to operate, that's a high-impact problem.

How Many Users Are Affected by the Problem?

A problem that affects several users is more severe than a problem that affects just a few users. For example, if all of the participants in a usability test run into a problem, it's more serious than a problem that just one participant experiences.

Will Users Be Bothered by the Problem Repeatedly?

Persistent problems—problems that keep cropping up—are more severe because they have a bigger impact on time on task and on user satisfaction. Note that "persistent" means that the problem occurs repeatedly, throughout the interface—users come across the problem on multiple screens or pages. An example of a persistent problem is a website that doesn't have underlined hyperlinks. This means users can find the links only by "minesweeping" over the page. This problem is persistent, because even when users know the solution to the problem they still have to experience it. Think of persistence as global v. local: Does it affect one part of a system, or does it affect many parts of the system?

We can put these three questions in a process diagram and use it to define four severity levels (see Figure 4.2).

How Should You Interpret the Severity Levels?

- *Critical*: This usability problem will make some users unwilling or unable to complete a common task. Fix urgently.
- *Serious*: This usability problem will significantly slow down some users when completing a common task and may cause users to find a work-around. Fix as soon as possible.
- *Medium*: This usability problem will make some users feel frustrated or irritated but will not affect task completion. Fix during the next "business as usual" update.
- *Low*: This is a quality problem, for example a cosmetic issue or a spelling error. Note: Although this is a minor issue in isolation, too many "lows" will negatively affect credibility and may damage your brand.

Figure 4.2: Decision tree for classifying the severity of a usability problem

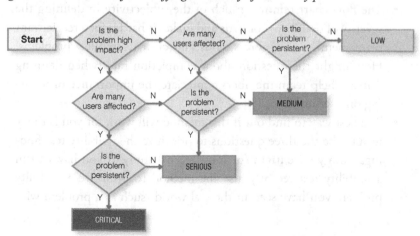

Moving Beyond Intuition

If you currently prioritize usability problems using "gut feel" or intuition, you run the risk of being exposed as a fraud by a developer or manager who asks you to justify your decisions. Instead, deliver more robust findings by using this decision tree.

THINK LIKE A UX RESEARCHER

- Before presenting this approach to your development team, play devil's advocate and think of possible arguments against the three questions and the severity levels we've presented. For example, consider a usability test (with a small sample of participants). A problem experienced by every participant is self-evidently worse than a problem experienced by just one participant. But is a problem that's experienced by two participants that much worse than a problem seen in just one? What if the problem you see in just one participant suggests a deeper issue that you might want to explore (for example, a problem that challenges the very concept of the product)? What does this tell us about prioritizing usability issues?

- Although our flow chart makes it relatively quick to create a semi-objective measure of severity, is it realistic to apply this model to every problem you find in a usability test? Are there quicker, alternative methods you could use to prioritize usability problems that also retain some objectivity?

- The flow chart removes much of the subjectivity in defining the severity of usability problems and makes it harder for a recalcitrant team member to ignore serious and critical usability problems. How might the question about completion rate (when defining impact) help team members appreciate the importance of focusing on user tasks?

- The best way to find out if this method will work for you is to try it out. Use the three questions to prioritize the usability test findings from your current (or most recent) study. If you haven't run a usability test recently, use the method to prioritize a usability problem you have seen in the real world (such as a problem with

(Continued)

THINK LIKE A UX RESEARCHER (Continued)

a car park payment machine or a self-service kiosk). Then ask a colleague to do the same activity and see if their severity rating matches your own.

- Consider a situation where you have run the first ever usability test of a new product. The product has performed badly. You have found over 100 usability problems and more than half of these are serious or critical (according to the flow diagram). Would you report all of the serious or critical problems, given that they can't all be fixed? If not, how would you decide which of the serious or critical problems to share with the development team?

Creating Insights, Hypotheses and Testable Design Ideas

A usability test provides us with a host of observations describing how people interact with a product or service. What it doesn't provide is design solutions. To generate useful design solutions we need to first generate insights to identify the underlying problems and then create testable hypotheses to fix their cause.

You may have heard the gnomic utterance that "a usability test won't improve usability." This is because usability tests are good at finding problems but offer little in the way of solutions. To arrive at a solution, we need to take three further steps:

- *Generate insights:* What is the underlying problem that led to our observations?
- *Develop hypotheses:* What do we think is causing the underlying problem?
- *Create design solutions:* What's the simplest change we can make to fix the underlying problem?

Start with Data

The output from a usability test takes the form of observations. An observation is an objective description of something that you saw or heard during the test. An observation is not your interpretation of what's behind the problem or how you think the problem can be fixed.

An observation could be a direct quotation, a user goal, a user action, a pain point, or anything that surprised you. Here are some examples:

- *Direct quotation*: "I don't know what this 'Subscribe' button means. Will it be a recurring payment?"
- *User goal:* Plans his delivery route around lunch and so wants to be near a bakery or supermarket at noon.
- *User action:* When starting a new expense claim, she retrieves her previous claim and uses it as a template.
- *Pain point:* Working for longer than 30 minutes at a stretch is difficult because of battery life.

In contrast, this is *not* an observation: "We need to change the 'Subscribe' label to 'Sign up'." That's a design solution: our interpretation of what's behind the problem (which may be wrong). We'll return to solutions later, but right now we need to keep our data "clean" by ensuring we focus on objective observations.

Generate Insights: What Is the Underlying Problem?

A usability test can generate a large number of observations. So we need to start by whittling down this number.

Our first step is to remove duplicate observations: situations where you made the same observation with two or more participants. Before discarding the duplicates, make a note of the number of participants where you made this observation as this is useful for later prioritization.

Next, discard observations that aren't important or relevant (although you may want to come back and review these later). An example might be: "User says that she tends to use this website at home when it's more quiet." This is an interesting factoid but it's not going to help us identify usability strengths or weaknesses.

These steps will reduce your initial list of observations but it's still likely you'll have a hundred or so to sort through. To make serious in-roads, you'll need to create an affinity diagram: This entails placing the observations into logical groups.

You can seriously speed up the time it takes to identify logical groups by getting the development team to help you. Write each observation on a sticky note and ask team members to do the affinity sort on a whiteboard. This also helps team members (who may have observed just one or two sessions) get exposed to the range of data you collected during the test.

What makes a "logical group" is up to you, but as a rule of thumb, if you have 100 observations, you should not have 100 groups. We typically find that we end up with somewhere between 10 and 15 groups. For example, we may have one group of observations about "terminology," another about a very specific UI element that made people struggle, and another group about problems navigating the system.

Once you have your groups, start creating insights. An insight captures the thing you've learned from this cluster of observations. You should write each insight as a sentence with a point of view. Think of it as a headline in a newspaper or a conclusion in a report.

Insight statements should be provocative: deliberately causing a strong reaction. One insight might read, "Users don't like the way the search function deletes the search query when it shows the search results." Another might read, "Users don't use the same names for things as we do." A third might read, "Users don't understand the workflow; they want to backtrack."

Creating insight statements is a reminder that part of your role as a UX researcher is to continually act as an irritant to the development team. Harry Brignull makes this point when he writes,[10] "A researcher who is keen to please the design team is useless." You should never let the development team become complacent about your product's user experience; strongly worded insight statements help the team appreciate the work that's still to be done.

At this point, you should step back and look at your affinity diagram. Get the team to dot vote[11] to agree the high priority issues: These are the issues that need to be addressed first in any revised design. It's foolish to try to fix everything, so identify the top three issues and then move on to fix those.

Develop Hypotheses: What's Causing the Problem?

Sometimes, when you look at one of your top three insights, the fix may be obvious. For example, with an insight like, "People struggled to read the light gray text on several screens," the fix is crystal clear. But this is unusual. Most of the insights from our analysis could have several root causes.

For example, we recently ran a usability test of an app that mimicked Google's Material Design guidelines. The app had a vertical ellipsis (a set of three vertical dots) on the top right of the user interface. Clicking the dots opened a "more actions" menu. If you use Chrome, you might be familiar with this kind of control (shown in Figure 4.3). An insight from our usability test was that our users did not interact with this navigation menu within the app.

Here are some possible hypotheses that occurred to us that might explain this observation:

Figure 4.3: An insight from our usability test was that our users did not interact with this navigation menu within the App. What might be behind this?

- People don't realize it's a control. They think it's branding or a visual design conceit.
- The control is hard to see. It's on the far right of the screen. People read left to right and don't look there.
- People see the control, but they assume it does something else, like expand the page. It doesn't look like a menu control.
- People don't need the menu: They can do everything they need to with the existing navigation options.

We don't know which of these, if any, is correct. We may have a gut feeling that one of them is more likely than another, but without data it's precisely that: a gut feeling. How can we turn hypotheses into testable design changes?

Create Design Solutions: What's the Simplest Change We Can Make to Fix the Problem?

In his book, *Rocket Surgery Made Easy*,[12] Steve Krug argues that when fixing usability problems, you should try to do the least you can. He argues for a "tweaking" approach where you ask: "What's the smallest, simplest change we can make that's likely to keep people from having the problem we observed?"

We like this approach because it avoids the major redesign and it fits well with the rapid, iterative approach used by most Scrum teams. The point is that there's almost always something you can do to mitigate the impact of a usability problem on users.

Another benefit is that with this approach, you can often fix a problem in a few days. This compares with weeks or months for a complete redesign.

Table 4.1 shows how we can use this approach to generate testable design ideas from our initial list of hypotheses. Notice that each hypothesis would lead to a different change to the design.

As a UX Researcher You Are a Fully Paid Up Member of the Development Team

UX researchers are sometimes reluctant to take these steps, believing that "design" isn't their job. More than one UX researcher has told us that they are simply told to report the observations from a test to the development team and not provide recommendations for improvement. Failing to provide design solutions risks signaling that you are only useful as a critic and not

Table 4.1: Generating hypotheses and testable design ideas from the usability test insight "Users did not interact with the ellipsis navigation menu"

Hypothesis	Simplest Change to Prevent People from Having This Problem
People don't realize it's a control. They think it's branding or a visual design conceit.	Make it more clickable, for example draw an outline around it and have a drop shadow.
The control is hard to see. It's on the far right of the screen. People read left to right and don't look there.	Place the control on the left-hand side.
People see the control but they assume it does something else, like reload the page. It doesn't look like a menu control.	Replace the three dots with a word like "MENU."
People don't need the menu: they can do everything they need to on the main screen.	Ask people to do tasks that require use of the menu, or remove some options from the main screen and re-test.

as a problem solver. Conversely, offering realistic and actionable solutions increases your credibility and helps position you as a design partner.

Although you may not have "design" in your job title, as a UX researcher you are as much a part of the development team as an interaction designer, a visual designer, and a front-end developer. This is because you have the kind of insight that can be gained only by sitting next to users as they struggle with the product.

Often the development team knows there is something wrong with a design. But they don't know how to proceed; or they have got stuck on a solution that's sub-optimal; or they are thinking of it only from an engineering or visual design point of view; or they risk implementing a solution that creates a worse problem. Get them using your knowledge about users to uncover the ideas that could really fix it.

THINK LIKE A UX RESEARCHER

- To arrive at a design solution to a usability problem, we argue that you need to first generate a design insight and then create testable hypotheses that might account for the participant's behavior. Why not simply observe a usability test and write down a design solution?
- What makes a design hypothesis "testable"? Assuming you had a list of potential changes (as in Table 4.1), how would you decide which one to test first?

(Continued)

THINK LIKE A UX RESEARCHER   (Continued)

- We argue that as a UX researcher you have special insight into user behavior because you have empathy from observing participants in a usability test. But could this backfire? Is it possible to be unduly swayed by certain participants (such as the ones who complain the loudest, or who we find most interesting) and as a consequence over-prioritize insights that apply only to that participant?
- Consider Harry Brignull's point that a researcher who is keen to please the development team is useless. Is there a risk in pushing too hard in fighting for your (UX's) corner? How can you use usability test data to help you manage the fine line between being too strident and simply rolling over?
- Having observed test participants, you have the advantage of understanding both *how* and *why* users struggle with a usability problem. This puts you in a strong position to anticipate any new usability problems that might be introduced in a redesign. If you find yourself in a situation where the development team excludes you from contributing to design fixes, how would you phrase this argument to persuade them to include you?

How to Manage Design Projects with User Experience Metrics

UX metrics are measures that help you assess how your design stacks up against the needs of your users and the needs of your business. Lab-based methods of collecting user experience metrics can often be too slow and expensive to be part of most design projects, especially those using Agile methodologies. But with online usability testing tools, regular user experience benchmarking is now cheap and quick to carry out.

We all agree that it's important to create a "good" user experience, but when you're in the heat of a design project, how do you know if you're on track?

Traditional, lab-based usability testing is a good way to find usability issues that need to be fixed—but they're not the best way to monitor the progress of a design over time. A sample size of five participants—typical in a lab-based usability test—is quick to run but has too few participants to give you the kind of robust data you need to make critical business decisions.

You can increase reliability by testing larger participant samples, but this slows down development as teams wait for your results. Participants need to be recruited and scheduled, lab space needs to be reserved, participants need to be tested, and data need to be analyzed. As well as taking time, it makes usability testing a real drain on the project manager's budget.

This has led Jakob Nielsen to claim that, "Metrics are expensive and are a poor use of typically scarce usability resources."[13]

But this causes a problem for people who manage design and development projects.

If project managers can't measure it, it can't be monitored. And if it's not monitored, it gets ignored. This is one reason why many usability tests get delayed until the end of development—but by that time, it's too late to make any significant changes to enhance the users' experience.

Surely there's a better way.

Indeed there is. We can satisfy the needs of the project manager, the budget holder, and the statistician by using remote usability testing tools to run a metrics-based test. With these tools we'll also be able to run several usability tests throughout the project, and we'll find it's cheaper than running a large, lab-based test at the end of design.

But we're getting ahead of ourselves. First, let's take a look at some of the benefits of collecting user experience metrics. Then we'll discuss how to create bullet-proof measures you can use on your own projects. Finally, we'll return to the issue of how you collect the data.

Why User Experience Metrics?

UX metrics provide a way for you to see how your current design measures up to what your users (and the business) needs. In practice, we characterize user experience by measuring the user performance on a basket of test tasks.

UX metrics help you:

- *Make design decisions*: When you are guided by a clear set of user experience metrics, decisions about features, functionality and resource allocation can be made more quickly, consistently, and rationally. User experience metrics prevent feature creep because they help your team resist diversions and keep everyone focused on user and business priorities.
- *Measure progress*: User experience metrics provide an objective way to track your progress on Agile projects and help you decide if your system is ready to move from one sprint to the next. They can also be used in traditional waterfall development methods to judge if a design is ready to move from one lifecycle phase to the next.
- *Communicate with the project team and senior management*: User experience metrics create a framework for communicating progress toward the project's goals.

Creating User Experience Metrics

There are five steps to creating a solid user experience metric:

1. Identify the critical tasks.
2. Create a user story.
3. Define success and how you'll measure it.
4. Assign values to the criteria.
5. Monitor throughout development.

Let's look at each of these steps with a worked example.

Identify the Critical Tasks

UX metrics need to focus on the most critical user journeys with the system. Most systems, even quite complex ones, usually have only a handful of critical tasks. This doesn't mean that the system will support only those tasks: It simply means that these tasks are the essential ones for the business and for users. So it makes sense to use these tasks to track progress.

There are many ways to identify the most critical tasks for a system. For example, for a website, you could:

- *Examine competitor sites*: What tasks are commonly supported on similar sites to yours?
- *Identify the top 20 most-visited pages*: What are most people doing?
- *Analyze top search terms*: What are people looking for in your site?
- *Speak to support staff*: What are the most common requests for help?
- Brainstorm a potential (long) list of tasks and survey users to find the top five.
- Use an intercept survey on your website ("Why did you visit the site today?")

For example, let's say that we're developing a car satnav system. Our initial long list of tasks might include:

- Plan an itinerary.
- Get live traffic information.
- Find an alternative route.
- Plan a route.
- Advanced lane guidance.
- Change the voice.
- Navigate home.
- Add a favorite location.
- Set up voice commands.
- Change the map colors.
- Speak street names.
- Change the display brightness.

We're looking for tasks that are carried out by most or all of the people most or all of the time. This helps us prioritize the list and arrive at a smaller set of critical tasks. For example, these might be:

- Plan a route.
- Navigate home.
- Find an alternative route.
- Add a favorite.

Create a User Story

Our next step is to create a user story so we can think about the context of the task.

User stories are a key component of Agile development, but you don't need to be using Agile to benefit from them. User stories have a particular structure:

"As a user, I want to ___ so that I can ___"

Traditionally, these are written on index cards, so you'll hear people in Agile teams talk about "story cards."

We like Anders Ramsay's take on user stories where the persona "narrates" the story, because this ensures the scenario is fully grounded.[14] Now, instead of thinking of generic segments (like "holiday maker" or "sales rep" as users of a satnav system), we're thinking of the needs and goals of a specific persona. So for example, for the "Find an alternative route" task we might write:

Justin says, "I want to find an alternative route so that I can avoid motorways,"

...where Justin is a 50-year-old who uses his satnav intermittently and has low technology experience.

Define Success and How You'll Measure It

In this step, we need to define what success means on this task. This is where our previous hard work, thinking of the most critical tasks, and user stories, becomes vital.

Without those earlier steps, if you try to define a successful user experience, the chances are that you'll come up with generic statements like "easy to use," "enjoyable" or "quick to learn." It's not that these aren't worthy design goals, it's that they are simply too abstract to help you measure user experience.

But with our earlier investment in critical tasks and user stories, we can now decide what success means for those specific tasks. So for example, we can now talk about task-specific measures, such as task success, time taken and overall satisfaction. For our specific example, we might define success as the percentage of people who successfully manage to calculate a motorway-free route, measured by usability testing.

Note that although we've been talking about a single user experience metric for simplicity, a typical system is likely to have a handful of user experience metrics. These will cover each of the most critical tasks for the system.

Assign Values to the Criteria

Deciding on the precise criteria to use for the user experience metric requires you to have some benchmark to compare it with. This could be a competitor system or it could be the performance of the previous product. Without these data you can't say if the current design is an improvement over the previous one.

If your system is truly novel, then try thinking about that ultimate business metric: revenue. How much money do you expect to make from this product? What difference in revenue might arise from a success rate of (say) 70% versus 80%?

When setting these values, it's useful to consider both "target" values and "minimum" values. So for example, if competitor systems are scoring at 70%, we may set our target value at 80% with a minimum acceptable value of 70%.

Monitor Throughout Development

The final step is to monitor progress throughout development, but we need to achieve this without the expense of large sample, lab-based usability testing.

For tracking metrics, remote on-line usability tests are ideal because they're cheap to run and quick to set up. For example, at the beginning of the project, a simple web-based usability test, such as "first click" testing on a screen shot, may be sufficient. In the past, we've used one of the many web-based companies offering this kind of remote testing.

You'll find that a test can be set up in less than an hour, with results often available in a day or less—quicker, in fact, than holding a meeting to discuss the design with the team (with the added benefit that any design changes that result will be based on data rather than opinion). Sample sizes of over 100 participants are easy to achieve and will ensure that the data you collect can be generalized. (Be sure to preface your test with a short screener to make sure participants will be actual users of the product you are testing.)

Table 4.2: Example of a user experience metric

Critical User Task	User Story	Measure	Metric	Status as of Sprint 3
Plan a route	Justin says: "I want to find an alternative route so that I can avoid motorways."	Percentage of people who successfully manage to calculate a motorway-free route, measured by usability testing	Min: 70% Target: 80%	73% (below target)

As you move toward a more fleshed-out system, you can monitor progress with other remote testing tools, such as benchmark tests, where participants complete an end-to-end task with a design that's more functionally rich. The important thing is to test early and often, ideally within each sprint, to measure progress.

For your management report, we're again looking for something light-weight with the minimum of documentation, so a simple table (see Table 4.2) or graphic (see the essay, "Creating a User Experience Dashboard" in Chapter 5) works fine.

This is the strength of metrics-based testing: it gives us the "what" of usability.

But to discover how get the score up to 80%, we need to understand *why* participants are struggling. And that leads us to an important final point.

Metrics-Based versus Lab-Based Usability Tests

Metrics-based usability tests aren't an alternative to traditional lab-based tests: They just answer different questions. Like an A/B test that can prove one design is better than another but can't say why, it's often hard to find out why a participant has failed on a metrics-based test. You could ask your online participants why, with a post-test survey, but there's little benefit because people are poor at introspecting into their own behavior (see the essay "Applying psychology to UX research" in Chapter 1).

In our experience, working with a range of companies who use a variety of development methods, the most successful teams combine large sample, unmoderated usability tests to capture the "what" and use small sample usability tests to understand the "why."

Until now, metrics-based testing has played a minor role in user centered design projects when compared with lab-based testing. But the current avalanche of cheap, quick, and reliable online tools will surely reverse that trend.

THINK LIKE A UX RESEARCHER

- Nielsen's observation that, "Metrics are expensive and are a poor use of typically scarce usability resources" identifies two potentially limiting factors often encountered by UX researchers: Lack of budget and lack of user experience people to do the work. Imagine you have taken over leadership of a small and inexperienced user experience team with a modest budget. How would you weigh the benefits of carrying out summative (measuring usability) tests versus formative (finding usability problems) tests? What trade-offs would you aim for, and what arguments would you use to support your decisions?
- What are the possible disadvantages of remote, unmoderated usability testing?
- How can user experience metrics help your development team avoid feature creep?
- If the user experience metrics fall short, it is not unheard of for development teams to change their minimum acceptance criteria once they see the results. How can you prevent stakeholders "moving the goal posts" and rationalizing their way out of making design improvements?
- Establishing critical tasks and user stories is important but it's also the case that new product features are frequently decided by marketing or derived from earlier product versions or from competitor products. These features are then handed to the development team as a *fait accompli*. How would you handle a situation where the planned features of a product did not support your research-based list of critical user tasks?

Two Measures that Will Justify Any Design Change

Two measures commonly taken in a usability test—success rate and time on task—are the critical numbers you need to prove the benefits of almost any potential design change. These values can be re-expressed in the language that managers understand: the expected financial benefit.

We've known for some time that usability improvements can have a massive effect on the bottom line, so what stops usability professionals from actually measuring the return on investment of their work?

Is it because they think the benefit of a usability-induced change is obvious, so there's no need to measure anything?

If so, then they're taking a risk. The development team is unlikely to share their vision of "obviousness." The project manager may push back, claiming that the change is too difficult to implement, that it will need to wait for the next release, or that "user satisfaction" isn't as important as selling more product.

Or is it that they can't be bothered? Perhaps because return on investment calculations aren't the only way to sell usability to your manager.

Again, they are missing an opportunity. There is something uniquely persuasive about being able to prove that a design change can make or save the company money.

Or is it simply because people think the computations are too difficult?

In fact, using two common measures from usability tests, the calculations are easy enough to do with a paper and pencil.

When a 5% Improvement in Completion Rate Is Worth $7 Million

Success rate is the most important usability measure with any website: How many users can complete the task?

Let's say you carry out a large sample, benchmark usability test of a website. You find that 70% of your sample manages to complete the task successfully.

By making design changes to the website, we should be able to improve this figure. Usability improvements invariably have a dramatic effect on improving success rates, but for argument's sake, let's assume we can improve the success rate by a measly 5%, making the new success rate 75%. Most usability professionals would bet their house that they could make at least that improvement.

How Much Is that 5% Improvement Worth?

We can do a simple calculation using this equation:

$$Sales = Success\ Rate \times Potential\ Sales$$

- "Sales" is the actual turnover of the website. "Success Rate" is the figure we're about to improve.
- "Potential Sales" is the amount of sales we would make if every user could complete the task.

At this point, we need to know the sales of the website. Let's assume it's $100 million per annum. (For most serious businesses this is a conservative figure. A top high street chain will take $100 million per week. And Jared Spool describes a design change to a business website that was worth $300 million per annum[15]).

So at the moment, 70% of people manage to check out and the sales figure is $100 million. In other words:

- $100,000,000 = 70\% \times$ Potential Sales.

The Potential Sales is, therefore, $100,000,000/70\% = \$142,857,142$.

We think we can increase the success rate to 75%, so:

- Sales = Success Rate × Potential Sales.

- Sales = 75% × $142,857,142.

Which comes to $107,142,857. The difference between this figure and our original $100 million is over $7 million. This is how much our 5% improvement in success rate is worth.

When Improving Time on Task by 15 Seconds Is Worth $1.3 Million

An important measure for an intranet is time on task: How long do people take to complete a task?

A good example for an intranet would be looking up a colleague using the people directory. This is something that most intranet users do most days, often more than once per day. What would be the cost savings of reducing the amount of time people spent on this task?

Let's assume that we've measured the time it takes an employee to find someone's email address in the intranet address book and begin an email message with that person's name in the "To:" field. Assume it takes 60 seconds. We reckon we can reduce the time on task to 45 seconds by displaying a clickable email address alongside the employee's name in the search results.

What's the Financial Benefit of 15 Seconds?

To do this calculation properly, we need to know how many times per day people carry out this task. Let's make the conservative assumption that people do this task once per working day on average. If your organization employs 100,000 people who do this task and the average loaded salary is $15/hour (again, a conservative figure), we can calculate that:

- Current time on task = 45 seconds = 45/60 minutes = 45/(60 × 60) hours = 0.0125 hours.
- Daily cost of task per employee = 0.0125 hours × $15/hour = $0.1875
- Daily cost of task for all employees = $0.1875 × 100,000 employees = $18,750.
- Most people work an average of 220 days per year, so the yearly cost is = $18,750 × 220 days = $4,125,000.

Now let's work out what the cost would be if we reduced the time from 45 seconds to 30 seconds. Working through the same calculations as above, we get:

- New time on task = 30 seconds = 30/60 minutes = 30/(60 × 60) hours = 0.0083 hours.
- Daily cost of task per employee = 0.0083 hours × $15 = $0.125.
- Daily cost of task for all employees = $0.125 × 100,000 employees = $12,500.
- The new yearly cost is = $12,500 × 220 days = $2,750,000.

The difference between the before and after figures is over $1.3 million.

The Easy Way to Make Sure Design Changes Happen

These kinds of calculation are very simple to make, so long as you have the kind of robust usability measures you get from a well executed, large sample usability test. But when computing your own numbers, here's the golden rule: *Err on the conservative side.* So for example, if you're not sure if all employees use the people directory on your intranet, reduce the number of users to a more persuasive value.

The fact is that virtually any improvement in usability will have a knock-on improvement in your organization's bottom line—but to make sure your voice is heard, you'll need to collect the data and crunch the numbers.

THINK LIKE A UX RESEARCHER

- Calculate the financial benefits of UX research for your current (or recent) project, using the two measures we have discussed. Use best estimates if you don't yet have real financial figures.
- Find out who in your organization can give you the real financial figures you'll need for future calculations. Introduce yourself and share with him or her the examples we've discussed. Get feedback on this approach—and get the cost/time/employee numbers that you can work with.
- We discussed just two measures—both based on user performance criteria—that you can use to calculate the financial benefits of UX research. Looking at your company's own development process can also reveal inefficiencies that can be reduced by UX research. List two or three ways UX research can help improve your development cycle while also saving costs, and think about the best measures to quantify these.
- How would you use these kinds of analyses to argue for greater investment in your user experience team?
- Why is it important to err on the conservative side when calculating the financial benefits of your UX research?

Your Web Survey Is a Lot Less Reliable than You Think

Because surveys usually involve hundreds of respondents, many development teams value the findings from a survey more highly than the results from small sample usability tests, user interviews and field visits. But the results of most web surveys are biased by coverage error and non-response error. This means surveys, like most UX research findings, should be triangulated with other sources of data.

In a recent academic study,[16] some researchers asked people to examine products available on Amazon. The researchers wanted to answer a very specific question: How do people use review and rating information when choosing products?

In one experiment, the researchers asked participants to choose which of two phone cases they would buy. Both phone cases had the same (mediocre) average rating but one of the cases had many more reviews than the other.

In this experiment, the participants should choose the product with fewer reviews. This is because, with just a few reviews, the average rating is more likely to be a statistical glitch. The participants should not choose the product with a large number of ratings, because that just makes it more certain that the product really is poor quality.

It turned out that participants did exactly what they shouldn't. People chose the product that had more reviews over the product that had fewer reviews. The researchers reasoned that this is because people use the number of reviews as an indicator of a product's popularity—and their behavior is then influenced by the crowd. Interestingly, the authors titled their paper "The Love of Large Numbers."

This love of large numbers is frequently seen in the field of UX research. It's one of the reasons people are more likely to believe the results of a survey of 10,000 people than a usability test of just five. Surely, having such a large sample size must make the data more robust and reliable? In fact, as Caroline Jarrett has pointed out, asking one person the right question is better than asking 10,000 people the wrong question.[17]

The problem lies with two obvious, and two less obvious, sources of error in web surveys.

Two Obvious Sources of Error in Web Surveys

Asking the Wrong Questions

Most researchers are aware of the importance of asking the right questions. Many surveys are ruined because the respondent doesn't understand the question, or understands it differently to the intention of the researcher, or doesn't have an answer to the question (and there's not an "other" or "not applicable" option). There are also surveys where the question asked by the researcher doesn't match the purpose of the survey, and therefore the validity of the survey is in question.

Sampling Error

Sampling error is a second obvious source of error in surveys. When we sample, we select a proportion of people from the total population and we hope that their views are representative of the whole population.

As an example, imagine we have one million users and we want to find out their opinion on paying for software by subscription versus owning the software outright. Rather than ask all one million, we can take a sample. Remarkably, with a sample size of just 384, we can achieve a margin of error of just 5%. So if 60% of our sample say they would prefer to own software outright rather than pay for it on subscription, we can be confident that the actual number would be somewhere between 55% and 65%.[18]

You reduce sampling error by increasing the size of your sample. In the previous example, if we increase our sample size to 1,066 then our margin of error would be 3%. Ultimately, when your sample is the same size as the whole population (that is to say, you have a census) then you no longer have any sampling error.

Most people who commission web surveys know about sampling error. And because it's quite common to get thousands of people responding to a survey, people often think that any errors in their data are small.

Sadly, this isn't the case. This is because *sampling is valid only if the sample you take is random.* "Random" means that everybody in your population has an *equal likelihood* of being in the sample. For example, you might sample every 1,000th person in your population of one million and continue to pester them until they respond.

To understand what prevents us getting a truly random sample, we need to examine two further types of error that are less well understood: coverage error and non-response error.

Two Less Obvious Sources of Error in Web Surveys

Coverage Error

This type of error occurs when the research method you have chosen excludes certain people. For example, carrying out a telephone survey with respondents sampled from a directory of landline telephone numbers will exclude people who use a mobile phone exclusively (as well as people who don't have a phone at all).

Similarly, a web survey will exclude people who don't have access to the internet such as lower socio-economic groups, the homeless and people who just don't use digital channels (currently around 8% of the population in the UK[19] and 11% of the population in the United States[20]).

But what if you are interested only in sampling from people who visit your website today: Surely you won't suffer from coverage error then? That depends how you go about asking. Typically, websites give users a cookie with each survey invitation to prevent the same user being repeatedly bothered by survey invites. Think of this in the context of a website that provides information about train times. Frequent travelers are likely to use the website more than people who travel infrequently. This means many of the frequent travelers will have been given a cookie and so taken out of the sampling frame. In contrast, all of the infrequent travelers who are using the site for the first time will be included in the sampling frame. This has created a coverage error by skewing the sample toward less frequent travelers.

Non-response Error

To understand non-response error, imagine we devised a survey to measure people's experience with the internet. Imagine that the survey invitation appears as a pop-up when people land on a web page. It might be the case that advanced users of the internet have installed software to block pop-ups. And even those advanced users who allow pop-ups will be more familiar than novice users with finding the "no thanks" link (often rendered in a small, low contrast font). In contrast, novice users of the internet may think they need to accept the pop-up to proceed. Factors like these bias the sample because experienced internet users will be less likely to take part.

This isn't coverage error because both advanced and novice users are equally likely to be in the sampling frame. This is non-response error: Non-respondents (advanced internet users) are different from respondents in a way that matters to the research question.

Non-response error is a serious source of error with web surveys. This is because researchers tend to blast the survey to everyone as it's so easy to do: Getting a sample size of one million doesn't cost any more than getting a sample size of 1,000 (it just takes a little longer). But imagine you send the survey to one million people and find that 10,000 (1%) respond (we're being generous here: You're more likely to get a 0.1% response rate from a pop-up survey). Although the sampling error may be small, the fact that you have such a large non-response error (99%) is a serious source of bias. Those people who responded may not be representative of the total population: They may like taking surveys, or they may feel well disposed to your brand or they may just have been sucked in by a pop-up dark pattern.

What's a UX Researcher to Do?

There are a number of ways you can control these two, less obvious, sources of bias.

First, you should start creating proper samples. Rather than ask everyone to take part and hope for a good response rate, sample around 1,500 people from your user base and aim for a response rate of around 70% (this will give you a sample size close to 1,066—a magic number for a population of one million). It's true that even with a 70% response rate you could still suffer from non-response error, but it's also true that a 70% response rate from a sample is better than a 10% response rate from everyone. *Remember that the key is to select from your population randomly.*

Second, control coverage error by making sure that you give everyone in your population an equal likelihood of being asked to take part: This means not using cookies to exclude frequent visitors.

Third, to control non-response error, look at ways of encouraging more of your sample to take part in your survey.

- Tell people how the results will be used and how this will benefit them.
- Offer a valuable incentive.
- Ask as few questions as possible and make those questions easy to answer.
- Use persuasion techniques like social proof ("Over 60% of people have already responded!"), reciprocation ("We hope you find our content useful. Here's something you can do for us."), and scarcity ("There's only five days left to make your views known!").
- Follow up non-responders by email, phone, and even by post to make them realize you're genuinely interested in their answers.

Fighting Against the Love of Large Numbers

If this sounds like a lot of hard work, you're right. Doing a good survey is about more than buying a subscription to a survey tool and mass mailing your user base.

But there's an alternative.

For many questions in UX research, we're happy with a fair degree of error. It's not always necessary to have results that are statistically significant. Many times we just want to know which way the wind is blowing. So an easy alternative is to accept that your sample isn't representative of your total population. Then use your survey as an indicator that you can triangulate with other UX research data, like field visits, user interviews and usability tests.

This approach has an added benefit. It will help you avoid thinking that your survey results are somehow more credible because you have a larger sample.

THINK LIKE A UX RESEARCHER

- We once encountered a survey, from a major U.S. corporation, that expected its customers to make 596 separate responses to complete the survey! Apart from respondents simply bailing out, what are some of the data quality risks from surveys that have too many questions? What is a reasonable number of questions to ask in an online survey? How did you arrive at this number?
- Many senior managers in organizations suffer from the "love of large numbers" that we talk about in this essay. As a consequence, organizations tend to value shallow, large sample, quantitative data from surveys over deep, small sample, qualitative data from field research and usability tests. How might you adapt the points raised in this essay to raise the profile of qualitative research?
- Research works best when it is triangulated. Quantitative data tell us *what* people are doing. Qualitative data tell us *why* people are doing it. How might you combine survey data with field research or usability testing so that the methodologies were complementary?
- You have probably taken at least one online survey in the past. Think back to your experience. What motivated you to take the survey? How motivated were you to complete it? Did you feel

(Continued)

THINK LIKE A UX RESEARCHER (Continued)

your responses would make a difference to anything? Were you expected to complete the survey for free? Would a monetary incentive have made any difference to how thoroughly you thought about your responses, and how much time you spent on the survey?

- Find out a bit more about your own company's use of surveys. How do your customer-facing departments go about creating and conducting online surveys? Do stakeholders favor surveys over other research methods? How much confidence do stakeholders have in the resulting survey findings?

5

Persuading People to Take Action on the Results of User Experience Research

Evangelizing UX Research

UX professionals often complain that development teams fail to take action on the findings from UX research. But researchers need to shoulder some of the blame: research reports are often too wordy, arrive too late, and fail to engage teams with the data. User journey maps, photo-ethnographies, affinity diagramming, screen-shot forensics, and hallway evangelism provide five alternatives.

Jill spent weeks shadowing her users. She carried out field visits, ran user interviews, and moderated usability tests. She observed the way people used similar products day-to-day and she felt she really understood the struggles that people faced when achieving their goals.

With lots of data to analyze and present, she gave herself a full week to prepare the report. She analyzed the data. She typed up comments from users. She told stories about the way people lived. As she attached the report to her email and hit the Send button, she congratulated herself on a job well done. Any outsider would agree: This was truly an excellent piece of work.

Over the following week, she waited for the comments to come in. There was just one. "Thanks for the report, Jill" said the email from the lead developer. "I'll get back to you."

But he never did.

The Problem

In an Agile world, development teams don't have the time or inclination to read research reports—especially when they cover material that would have been useful three months ago but that is now so far back in sprint-land that it may well have been another project. UX researchers often misinterpret this behavior, instead thinking that development teams aren't interested in UX research. In reality, the development team is hungry for practical knowledge about users. The problem is that we're now in a world of just-in-time UX research—and three months ago is not just-in-time.

What could Jill have done differently?

The Fundamental Principle

We'll describe five techniques for engaging Agile teams in the results of UX research: two techniques for user needs research, and three techniques for usability testing. But before describing the techniques, there's a fundamental principle about presenting the results back to development teams that is worth bearing in mind: *UX research is a team sport.*

The whole concept of presenting the results of UX research to development teams is predicated on the assumption that the development team don't experience the UX research first-hand. But what if members of the development team *were* present when the research takes place?

Jared Spool has pointed out[1] that the most effective development teams have a two-hour dose of exposure to users every six weeks. So what if teams worked together to plan the research (to ensure it will answer the right questions), to observe the research sessions as they happen and to analyze the data? In such a world, the whole need for reporting is moot, since the development team has seen the research first-hand.

It may sound like Nirvana, but it's not as hard to achieve as you might think. One way you can encourage this behavior in development teams is by creating and maintaining a simple dashboard to help the team appreciate this requirement. Here's an example of such a dashboard from a project that David worked on recently.

That number on the right of Figure 5.1 (95%) shows the proportion of the team who has observed a user session in the last six weeks. This makes sure people are getting their exposure hours.

The other metrics show the number of users tested since inception (this makes sure that there is a continual focus on users) and the number of days elapsed since the last usability test (this ensures that the project is practicing iterative design).

But what if you're in Jill's position and, for whatever reason, you didn't get the development team engaged in the research? In that case, the next best thing is to get the team arguing over real data instead of what they think users want. Developers like to solve problems: It's what they do best. In the absence of data, Agile teams will solve the problem that's been formulated in the team's shared consciousness. To prevent this, expose people to the raw data and get them analyzing it.

And that's where our five techniques come in.

Figure 5.1: A UX research dashboard showing the number of participants involved since the start of the project (136), the time elapsed since the last usability test (4 days) and the proportion of the Scrum team that has observed a user session in the recent past (95% in the previous six weeks)

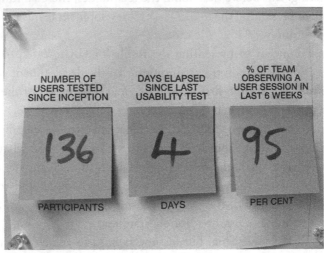

Two Techniques for Engaging the Design Team in User Needs Research

In this section, we'll review two methods for engaging the development team with the data from user needs research, such as field visits and user interviews. These methods are the user journey map and photo-ethnographies.

User Journey Map

A user journey map shows the user's steps from the beginning of the process to the end of the process. "Process" here means the meaningful activity that people carry out to achieve their goals, so this method works well to characterize the results of a field visit.

To create your own user journey map, start with a set of sticky notes that contain the observations you made during the field visit. Each sticky note contains a single observation (see Figure 5.2).

Working as a team, group the observations into common tasks that people carry out (see Figure 5.3).

Figure 5.2: A whiteboard with a number of sticky notes. Each of the sticky notes contains an observation from a contextual inquiry or field visit

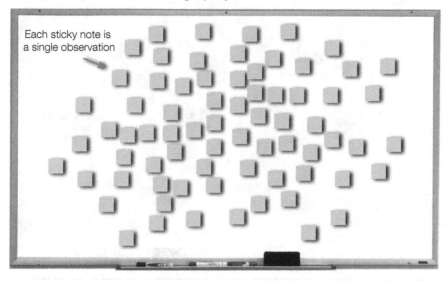

Figure 5.3: This shows the same whiteboard, but now the sticky notes with the observations have been placed into 13 groups, where each group relates to a common task

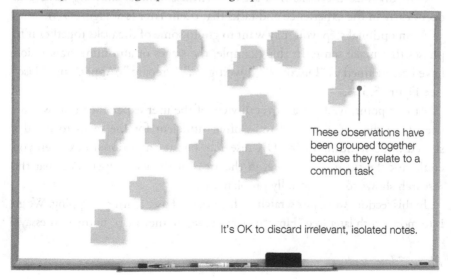

Figure 5.4: Each of the groups has now been given a group title using a darker sticky note. The group title is simply the working name for this task

The darker sticky note shows your working name for this task

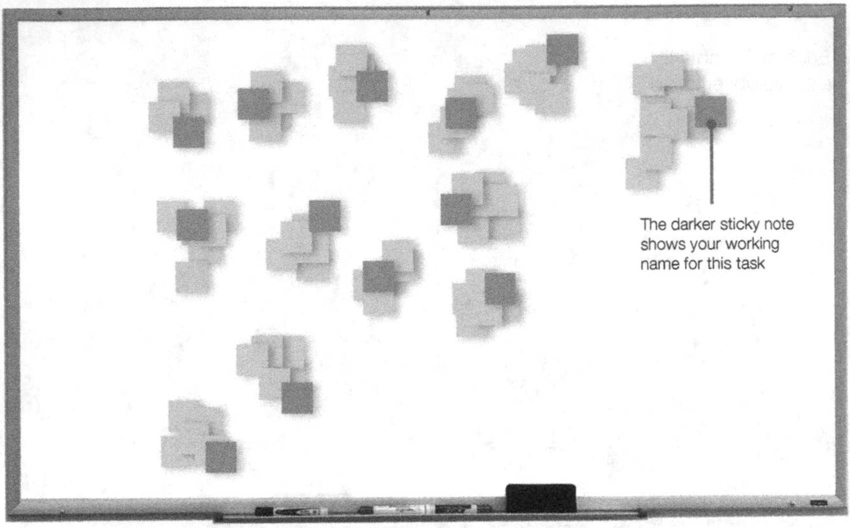

Next, label each of the tasks with a shorthand name. This doesn't need to be the term that users use to describe the task as it's just your own shorthand (see Figure 5.4).

Now organize the tasks in a set of vertical columns, showing tasks that occur early in the experience and tasks that occur later (see Figure 5.5).

As an optional step, you may want to group some of the tasks together into phases that make sense. In this example, the stages of an online transaction have been defined as "Discover," "Investigate," "Prepare," "Apply," and "Use" (see Figure 5.6).

At this point, we have an overall view of the user experience that we can use to see the big picture. This is often sufficient for the team to build a shared understanding of the UX research, but as an optional next step you could ask the team to dot-vote on the areas of the user experience that the research shows to be especially problematic.

In this section, we've just scratched the surface of user journey mapping. We go into more depth later (see "How to create a user journey map" in the next essay).

Photo-Ethnographies

Whenever we speak with someone who has just returned from a field visit, the first comment we usually hear is that the user's environment was very

Figure 5.5: At this point, the sticky notes are arranged into a sequence of vertical columns from tasks that appear early in the process to tasks that appear later in the process. The darker note (with the task title) is placed at the top of each column and each of the sticky notes that relate to that task are placed below it

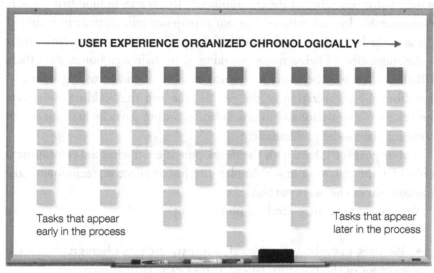

Figure 5.6: The user experience has been divided into five sequential areas, such as "discover" and "investigate." Each of these broad areas contains one or more sub-tasks

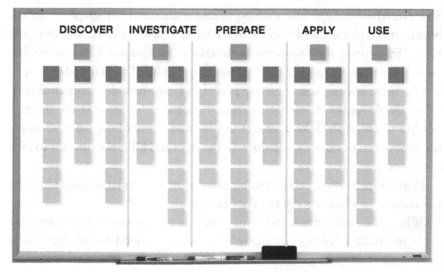

different to what the researcher expected. We all have assumptions about the user's context and one of the great benefits of carrying out a field visit is that it usually challenges those assumptions.

One way you can share these experiences with the development team is to make a video recording of the environment. This is a technique that's widely recommended by researchers—but our experience tells us that, in reality, it can actually be quite difficult to do. If the person we're visiting isn't aghast at the suggestion of being filmed working or in their own home, then there will almost certainly be a very long form we need to complete to get permission from the organization or the people who run the building. Whatever the reason, we've personally found video recording participants (outside of a usability lab) to be problematic.

If your goal is to share with the development team what the environment looks like, then there's a much simpler, and just as effective, technique: Take photographs of the user's context.

You should take three kinds of photograph:

- Pictures that show the overall context, such as photographs of the exterior of the building and pictures of the entire office.
- Pictures that show the participant alongside other people and objects in the environment.
- Close-up photographs of the participant interacting with specific objects in his or her environment.

Shy researchers struggle when asking to take someone's photograph. The trick here is to normalize your behavior. You'll recall that we touched on this in the essay, "Structuring the Ethnographic Interview" in Chapter 3. When we first meet the person we're interviewing, we'll say, "While I'm here today, I need to take some photographs with my phone so I can share the experience with other people on the development team. Here's a list of some of the things I need to photograph. Take a look at this list and if any of them are off-limits for any reason, just draw a line through the item and I'll make sure not to take photos of it."

Photographs provide an incredible amount of additional insight. Don't be the researcher who's too shy to take photographs.

When you return from the visit, print the photos you've taken and use them to create a "photo ethnography", a kind of mood board that shows users in their environment. People enjoy looking at photographs, so this is a simple and effective way to get your team engaged in the context of the user.

Three Techniques for Engaging the Design Team in the Results from Usability Testing

In this section, we'll review three methods for getting the development team engaged with the results from usability testing. These methods are affinity diagramming, screenshot forensics, and hallway evangelism.

Affinity Diagramming

The process of affinity diagramming is very similar to the process of creating a user journey map. The difference is that instead of trying to build up a picture of the total user experience, you use the technique to group together usability issues experienced by different participants in a usability test.

One of the most effective implementations of this technique is to encourage the development team to observe usability test sessions and to ask each observer to note down usability problems as they occur, on sticky notes. As the test sessions progress, the whiteboard gradually fills with observations. At the end of the day, the observers engage in a group affinity sort and together identify the key usability issues.

One problem with this method is that a day's usability testing can be quite long. This means people are reluctant to stay into the early evening to do the analysis. Because this reaching of consensus is so important, it's worth running shorter usability testing sessions, or even sacrificing the last participant session of the day, to make sure there is sufficient time left for people to do the analysis. The development team is much more likely to engage with the affinity sort if it takes place at 3 p.m. than if it takes place at 5 p.m.

Screenshot Forensics

But what about people who were unable to attend a usability test session? How can you quickly feedback the results to this audience and avoid death by PowerPoint?

Here's a quick and effective technique that we call "Screenshot forensics" (see Figure 5.7).

Figure 5.7: Screenshot forensics. This example shows the first three screens in a task. To the right of each screen, a series of differently-colored sticky notes show user quotes and actions, findings, questions and actions

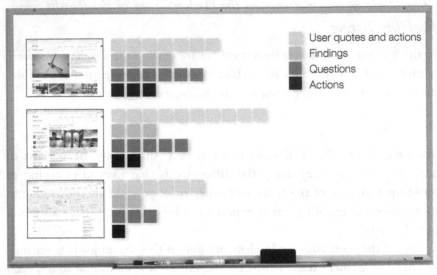

For each of the tasks in your usability test, take a screen shot of each step in the task. Stick these to a noticeboard or a wall area in a vertical sequence, with the first screenshot at the top of the board, the second screenshot below it and so on. To the right of the screenshot, place sticky notes in one of four categories:

- *User quotes and actions*: These are the key observations that you made in the usability test: things that the test participants said or did.
- *Findings*: These are conclusions and interpretations that you've drawn from the data.
- *Questions*: These are issues that have come up as a result of the usability test that require the development team or the business to provide answers.
- *Actions*: These are specific design or business process changes that need to be implemented.

This kind of artifact is an information radiator that ensures everyone in the development team is made aware of what happened in the usability test.

Hallway Evangelism

We can build on the notion of information radiators with the concept of hallway evangelism. This technique works well when you are at the point where you have a reasonable amount of conclusive data from your discovery phase.

The idea is to summarize the key points of the UX research in a poster that you can print large and place on the wall somewhere in the building. The poster, which could take the form of an infographic, briefly summarizes the key research you've carried out: For example, it could describe five facts about your users, five findings from usability testing or five ways people use your product in the wild. There's nothing magic about the number five: Just don't drown people with your data.

Once you've designed your poster, you need to find a suitable hallway in which to place it. Look for high traffic areas (such as the route to the canteen). In her book, *The User Experience Team of One*, Leah Buley[2] suggests placing posters on the inside of the doors in the ladies and gents bathrooms. This will certainly give you a captive audience!

Wrapping Up

If you ever find yourself in Jill's position, first examine how you can engage the development team in the research itself. Jill's mistake was to fall for what Caroline Jarrett has termed the User Researcher's Fallacy[2]:

> *"User researcher's fallacy: 'My job is to learn about users'. Truth: 'My job is to help my team learn about users'."*

Remember: *No presentation will be more persuasive than having the development team observe users as they do their tasks.*

Then, engage the development team with the data by using user journey maps, photo-ethnographies, affinity diagramming, screenshot forensics, and hallway evangelism.[3]

THINK LIKE A UX RESEARCHER

- Bite-sized research summaries are a powerful way to help your research results travel through an organization. But could the brevity also trivialize research, reduce it to soundbites, or ignore nuance? How might you reduce this risk?

- Whenever you focus on numbers as a metric (as in Figure 5.1) there is a possibility that people will try to improve the numbers but ignore their underlying motivation. Which UX research related metrics are harder to "game"?

- Which one of the five techniques described in this essay do you think would work best with your development team? What needs to happen for you to be able to apply it to your current project?

- How would you deal with a situation where a senior stakeholder in your organization *insisted* on long reports or time-consuming deliverables "to maintain an audit trail"? How might you encourage your organization to adopt leaner ways of reporting?

- The photo-ethnographies technique may reveal the identities of the research participants since the photographs will show their home or work environment. How could you adapt this UX research technique to protect your participants' privacy yet at the same time still help the development team empathize with users?

How to Create a User Journey Map

A user journey map describes the entire user experience when people are achieving their goals. It's the first step in coming up with design solutions that are truly innovative.

Some people are confused by the difference between "usability" and "user experience." If you find someone in this position, introduce them to the user journey map. If there's a better way of helping someone understand the difference, we have yet to see it.

A user journey map gives us an overview of the entire user experience. It makes it clear that what users are trying to achieve is much bigger than our app, or website, or service. This helps prevent the team thinking in terms of functions and instead helps the team think in terms of user goals.

A user journey map also helps us identify the good parts of the experience and the poor parts that we can then improve.

To explain this, let's take an example. In this example we'll be using the Mail Merge feature from Microsoft Word.

Let's map out the user experience of someone using this feature. In this case, that would be David. He uses Mail Merge to print address labels for his Christmas card envelopes. (Nothing says "I care" like receiving a Christmas card addressed with a pre-printed label.)

Let's look at the user experience. We've written the actions David takes when preparing, printing and using the labels. There are about 14 actions:

- In early January, before recycling his Christmas cards, he notes down who they came from. That's because next Christmas, David wants to send cards only to those people who sent him a card this year.
- He then creates a "Christmas Card" group in his Mac address book.
- Fast forward to December. He opens his Mac address book and exports the "Christmas Card" group of contacts to a file.
- He then finds some cheap labels in a stationery shop.
- He opens Microsoft Word and starts the Mail Merge, which requires him to select the label type that corresponds to the ones he bought.
- He imports the addresses from the exported file.
- Then he needs to map the fields properly (for example, he needs to identify each contact's first and last name and their post code).

- David then lays out the labels in Word.
- Next, he previews the results to check that they will print OK.
- He then prints the labels.
- His next step is to pour some mulled wine, play Nat King Cole's Christmas album and write the cards.
- He then sticks the labels on the envelopes.
- He puts stamps on the envelopes.
- And finally, he posts the cards.

Notice that the "user experience" of writing Christmas cards is bigger than simply creating labels. Although the boffins at Microsoft may see "label creation" as an end in itself, it will never be the beginning and end of the process for a user. The user experience also includes creating a list of contacts and posting the cards.

Let's see how we create a user journey map from these data.

Our first step is to write each of the steps onto stickies (see Figure 5.8).

Figure 5.8: Each of the steps has been written onto stickies

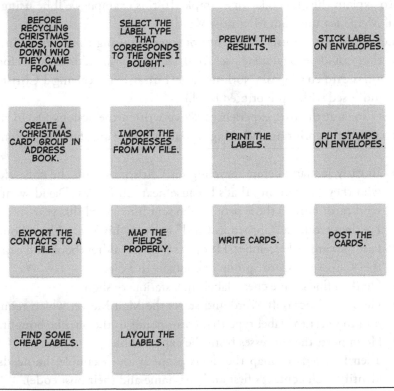

Figure 5.9: Actions are organized into groups that make sense

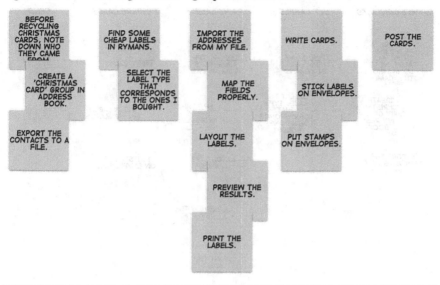

The next step is to arrange these actions into groups that make sense. For example, the actions where David notes down who sent him a card, creates a "Christmas Card" list and exports the list could be seen as part of a common group of steps (even though they happen nearly a year apart). In our analysis, we've created five groups, as shown in Figure 5.9.

Now we label the groups. For example, the actions where David writes cards, sticks labels on envelopes, and puts stamps on the envelopes are all part of a "Prepare cards" group (see Figure 5.10).

Pause for a second and take a look at the high-level groups in Figure 5.10, like "Update contacts" and "Get labels." These are the key tasks, the important user goals that people need to achieve with your system. By defining key tasks for your system you are taking your first step in identifying and eliminating the usability obstacles on these key user journeys.

Let's examine the key tasks and identify the actions that work well—happy moments—and the actions that could be improved (see Figure 5.11). For example, finding cheap labels is a relatively painless process but selecting the labels in Microsoft Word that correspond to the ones you have bought can be a problem. Sometimes the label type doesn't exist, so you have to create a unique label (which requires measuring the dimensions of the label).

Figure 5.10: The groups are labeled

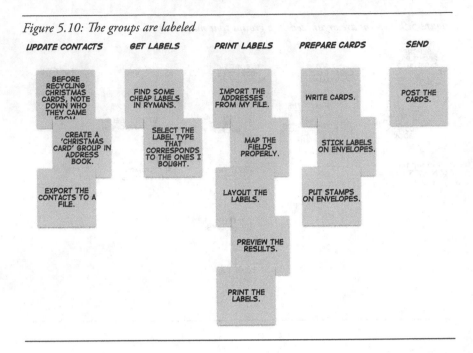

Figure 5.11: The actions are divided into "Happy Moments" and "Pain Points"

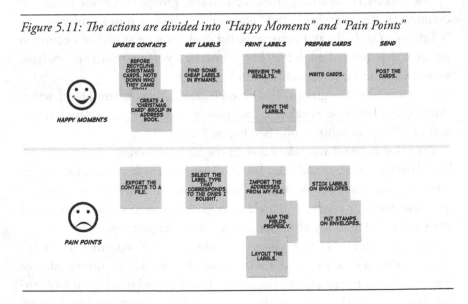

We can also discover what kinds of question people have at each of these steps (see Figures 5.12 through 5.14). For example, in the "Update contacts" step, David needs to remind himself how to create a group of contacts in his Mac address book and how to export the contacts in the right format for Word.

Figure 5.12: Questions the user has during the "Update Contacts" step

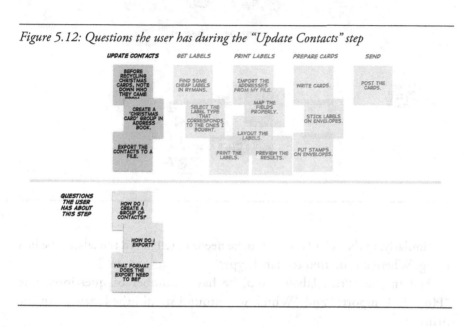

Figure 5.13: Questions the user has during the "Get Labels" step

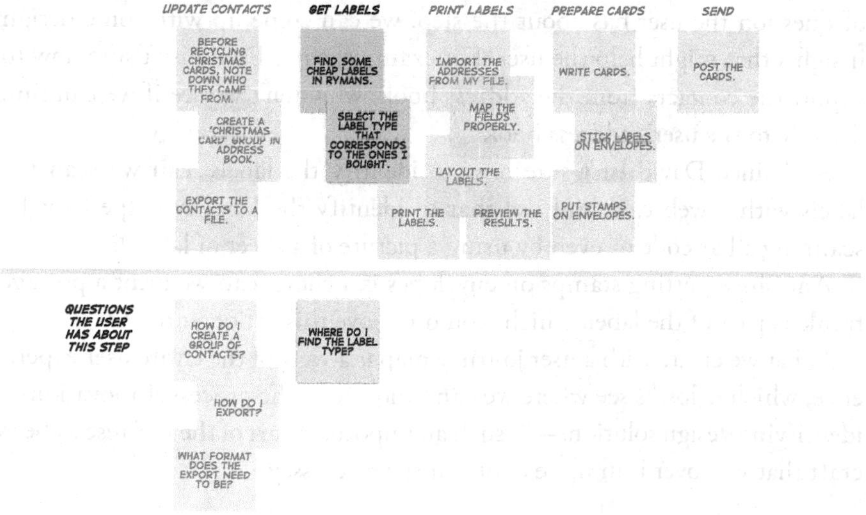

Figure 5.14: Questions the user has during the "Print Labels" step

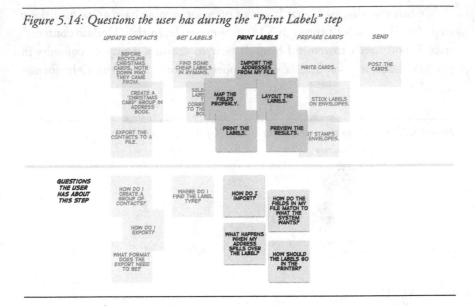

Similarly, in the "Get labels" step, he needs to tell Word the label type he's using. Where do you find the label type?

And in the "Print labels" step, he has a number of questions, like "How do I import?" and "Which way around should the labels go in the printer?"

We can also turn to the user journey map to identify design opportunities (see Figures 5.15 through 5.17). Considering the pain points and the kinds of question the user has about the step, we can come up with some design insights that might help the user. For example, since David isn't sure how to export the contacts from the address book, why don't we see if we can link directly to the user's address book?

And since David isn't sure how to identify the labels, can we scan the labels with a web cam and use that to identify the label type (perhaps by scanning a bar code or even by using a picture of a sheet of labels)?

And since putting stamps on envelopes is a chore, can we print a postage frank as part of the label, which would remove this action entirely?

What we create with a user journey map is a view of the entire user experience, which helps us see where we can innovate in the process. Innovation—identifying design solutions—is such an important part of the UX researcher's craft that we cover it in more depth in the next essay.

Figure 5.15: Design opportunities for the "Update Contacts" step

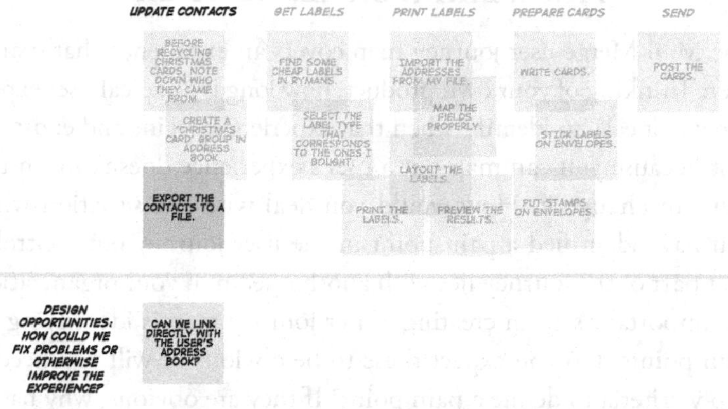

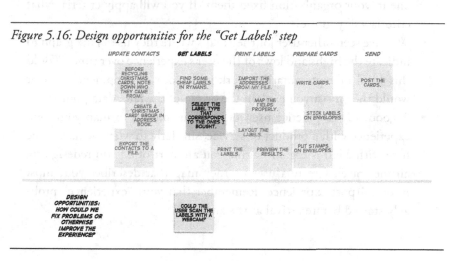

Figure 5.16: Design opportunities for the "Get Labels" step

Figure 5.17: Design opportunities for the "Prepare Cards" step

THINK LIKE A UX RESEARCHER

- The Mail Merge user journey map covers an experience that spans a year. Thinking of your own product, how long is a typical user experience? Is it easy to identify when that experience begins and ends?

- Just because you can map out a user's experience doesn't mean that you can change it. How would you deal with the situation where you have identified a pain point in the user journey but control of that part of the journey lies with another team in your organization?

- An important step in creating a user journey map is identifying the pain points. Do you expect these to be obvious or will you need to apply criteria to define a pain point? If they are obvious, why has no one in your organization fixed them? If you will apply criteria, what criteria will you use?

- We have seen other user journey maps where they use a faux graph to indicate the highs and lows of the user's experience over time. Would this kind of representation work with your development team or would they insist you explain the origin of the faux data points?

- A good way to practice user journey mapping is to map your own experience with a product or service, similarly to what we have done here with Mail Merge. Imagine you are part of a team redesigning airline travel. Create a user journey map that describes your most recent airport experience. Remember that your "experience" probably started before arrival at the airport.

Generating Solutions to Usability Problems

It's sometimes said that usability professionals are good at finding problems, but not quite as good at coming up with creative solutions. This essay describes a creativity technique called SCAMPER that will help you effortlessly generate dozens of design solutions to any usability problem you identify.

There is no shortage of people willing to pass judgment on what they see as the weaknesses of a user interface. But it takes more than design opinions to make a user experience professional. What distinguishes good practitioners is that they also come up with design solutions to the problems they find.

There are several techniques for finding usability problems, such as expert reviews and usability tests. But there is no standard technique we know of to help you come up with suggested fixes. For that, we can turn to a particular creativity technique that will help you come up with many design solutions to the problems you find.

Generating Design Ideas

SCAMPER is a checklist of questions you can ask yourself to generate design ideas. We first came across this creativity technique in Michael Michalko's book,[4] *Thinkertoys*. The basic idea is that you pose questions at each step of a process or idea and see if the question makes new ideas emerge. Michalko writes that asking the questions "is like tapping all over the challenge with a hammer to see where the hollow spots are."

SCAMPER is an acronym for these techniques:

- Substitute something.
- Combine it with something else.
- Adapt something to it.
- Modify, magnify, or minify it.
- Put it to some other use.
- Eliminate something.
- Reverse or rearrange it.

Although you can use these questions to generate ideas to any problem, we want to show how we can apply the techniques to solving usability problems specifically.

Substitute Something

The aim of these questions is to generate ideas for replacing something in the design. You would phrase your suggested usability change as: "Instead of... the interface could..."

As you "tap" your design problem, you ask questions like, "What can be substituted?" "Can we use another approach?" and "What other UI control can we use in place of this?"

For example, imagine this usability problem: You observe that during a task where participants need to change their account details, few people choose the navigation link that the designers have titled "Update." Reviewing the substitute questions, we might suggest that the term "Update" is replaced with something more meaningful, like "My Account." Or we might substitute the approach and argue that an address change should be carried out during the next order completion. Or we might change the location of the navigation item and place the "Update" button in the body of the page.

Combine It with Something Else

The aim of these questions is to generate ideas for amalgamating things in the design. You would phrase your suggested design change as: "The interface could bring... and... together to..."

Questions you can ask to generate ideas to combine things in the design include, "Can we create an assortment?", "Can we combine UI controls or labels?" and "What other control could be merged with this?"

For example, imagine we have observed the following usability problem: When completing an insurance application form, participants encounter problems selecting from a long list of potential titles (such as Mr., Miss, Dr., Rev., etc.). Reviewing the combine questions, we might suggest that we provide an assortment of titles: Perhaps we could have just four or so titles and ask users to choose using radio buttons. Or we could combine the title, first name, and surname fields into one field, with a label like, "How do you want to be addressed?"

Adapt Something to It

The aim of these questions is to generate ideas for adjusting things in the design. You would phrase your suggested usability change as: "The development team could adapt... in this way... to..."

Questions you can ask to generate ideas for adapting the design include, "What can we adapt for use as a solution?", "What could we copy?" and "What other process could be adapted?"

For example, imagine we have observed the following usability problem: Participants are reluctant to add comments to a blog post because they don't want to create an account at this website. Reviewing the "adapt" questions, we might suggest that we adapt the interface to allow users to use a social media identity to sign in and add a comment. Or we could treat it like a traditional newspaper's Letters to the Editor page and allow people to submit comments by email.

Modify, Magnify or Minify It

The aim of these questions is to generate ideas for transforming things in the design, for example by making them bigger or smaller. You would phrase your suggested usability change as: "The development team could transform... in this way... to..."

Good questions to ask include, "What can be altered for the better?", "What can be magnified, made larger, or extended?" and "Can we make it smaller or more streamlined?"

For example, imagine we have observed the following usability problem: On a form with an Address Finder button, some participants miss the button and complete all of the fields manually. Reviewing the "modify, magnify, and minify" questions, we might suggest making the Address Finder button larger or changing its color to create a stronger call to action. Or we might suggest removing the address fields and showing them only after someone has clicked on the address finder button.

Put It to Some Other Use

The aim of these questions is to generate ideas for changing the functionality of things in the design. You would phrase your suggested usability change as: "The interface could re-use... in this way... by..."

Questions you can ask to generate ideas for putting things to some other use include, "What else could be made from this?", "Are there other extensions?" and "Are there other uses if we modify it?"

For example, imagine we have observed the following usability problem: The registration form has placeholder text in the fields, but the placeholder text simply repeats the label (Enter First Name). Reviewing the "put it to some other use" questions, we might suggest changing the text so it is more helpful, or moving the text outside the field so that it is permanently on screen and not overwritten.

Eliminate Something

The aim of these questions is to generate ideas for removing things from the design. You would phrase your suggested usability change as: "The design could eliminate... by..."

Questions you can ask to generate ideas for eliminating things from the design include, "Can we divide it up, split it up or separate it into different parts?", "What's not necessary?" and "Can we reduce time or reduce effort?"

Simplification via elimination is the bread and butter of usability professionals, so it hardly needs an example. But let's try one anyway. Imagine we have observed the following usability problem: Users seem reluctant to scroll the page. Reviewing the "eliminate" questions, we might suggest removing the advertising banner to allow more task-oriented items to appear above the fold or removing the horizontal rule at the bottom of the first screenful that acts like a scroll stopper.

Reverse or Rearrange It

The aim of these questions is to generate ideas for reorganizing items in the design. You would phrase your suggested usability change as: "The development team could rearrange... like this... such that..."

Questions you can ask to generate ideas for reversing or rearranging items in the design include, "Can we use another pattern or another layout?", "Can we use another sequence or change the order?" and "Can we change pace or change schedule?"

For example, imagine we have observed the following usability problem: When users attempt to access content that is for registered users only, a Register pop-up form appears. Participants appear surprised by this, and it appears to be a jolt to the user experience. Reviewing the "reverse" questions, we may come up with ideas like changing the order in which we solicit information for the form or even do away with registration completely (so-called lazy registration).

Applying the Techniques

The obvious time to try this technique is the next time you're facing a usability problem and just can't formulate a good solution. But you should also consider it for those usability problems where an obvious solution presents itself. In this situation, the SCAMPER method can still help you because it will prevent you getting fixated on only one solution. After all, there is more than one way to skin an interface.

THINK LIKE A UX RESEARCHER

- A problem we often observe in usability tests is that an important control is hidden (for example, it may be buried in a tab or require the user to click on a "More options..." link). Use the SCAMPER technique to generate five potential design solutions to this problem.
- In answer to the question, "How do you manage to have so many good ideas?" Linus Pauling famously said,[5] "Oh, I just have lots of ideas, and throw away the bad ones." Why do many development teams generate one or two design solutions and then stop?
- The SCAMPER technique may generate unconventional ideas. Rather than dismiss these ideas as impractical, how could you refine them to become more workable?
- How could you apply the SCAMPER technique to other areas of your work, for example in generating ideas to convince the development team to take action on your findings or to convince stakeholders to invest in UX research?
- What other creativity boosters have you tried in the past? Could you adapt those to help generate solutions to usability problems?

Building UX Research Into the Design Studio Methodology

A Design Studio is a wonderful methodology to encourage multidisciplinary design but, in practice, teams often create design concepts that aren't grounded in UX research. We can bake UX research findings into every design concept that emerges by using the context of use (users, goals, and environments) as a constraint. As an added bonus, this approach helps teams create many more solutions to a design problem.

A Design Studio is an intense ideation session used by development teams to generate a range of potential design solutions to a problem. By bringing together a multidisciplinary team, a Design Studio ensures that all voices and disciplines are heard in the design process instead of relegating design to a single, genius designer.

If you participated in a well-run Design Studio, you would first hear a summary of the UX research that had been done up to that point and arrive at a shared understanding of the user needs and the business constraints. Next, you would work alone or with a partner to sketch many potential design solutions. (The focus is on quantity rather than quality.) After 30 minutes or so, you place your designs on the wall and present them to the group for critique, describing how each of your sketches solves the design problem. Once all the designs have been presented, the sketching process repeats with teams iterating on the most promising ideas.

That's the theory, anyway.

Having observed more than a few Scrum teams take part in Design Studios, our overriding impression is that most of the resulting designs pay lip service at best to UX research.

In some cases, this is because the team members simply ignore the research. This sometimes stems from the fact that, in the past, team members have experienced sloppy, non-actionable research that isn't helpful for design, so they mentally switch off during the research briefing and roll their eyes.

And in other cases, we suspect teams get caught up in the frenetic atmosphere of a Design Studio, feel under pressure to create many design ideas quickly, and simply forget to ground their designs in research.

Whatever the cause, we've seen participants frequently fall back on stale ideas that have been rejected in the past, submit design concepts based on invalidated assumptions, and create sketches that reflect design concepts that they personally like. The end result is that in a poorly run Design Studio, even one where the personas have been proudly stuck to the walls, teams can very quickly end up designing for themselves.

The end result is the same: The UX research ends up making a minor contribution to the design ideas.

Baking UX Research Into the Design Ideas

We decided to change things up in a recent Design Studio that we joint-facilitated. This time, we wanted to ensure that UX research was baked into every design idea by presenting the research as a constraint.

It's tempting to believe that to come up with creative ideas, we should ignore all constraints. Ignore what's possible! Imagine you had infinite time and money! We can do anything! However, that belief is wrong: creativity is helped, not hindered, by constraints. For example, when asked to design a house with no constraints, architect Frank Gehry said,[6] "I had a horrible time with it. I had to look in the mirror a lot. Who am I? Why am I doing this? What is this all about? It's better to have some problem to work on. I think we turn those constraints into action."

The Most Important Constraint in User Experience

The most important constraint in user experience is the context of use: the user, the user's tasks, and the environment where the action takes place. To this, we could add other constraints to encourage our thinking, such as the emotional intent, a UI design pattern, a user experience design principle, a usability objective or a behavioral nudge. But by ensuring that every design idea is grounded in the context of use, we can be sure that research is at the heart of every design idea.

How this Works in Practice

To make this work in practice, we used another creativity booster from Michael Michalko's creativity book, *ThinkerToys.*[7] This idea is called Selection Box. Here's how to include this in your own Design Studio.

Step 1: Find Some Whiteboard Space

Find a whiteboard or a wall. If you need to, take some flip chart paper and attach it to the wall.

Draw five columns on the whiteboard and label the first three columns: User, Environment, and Goal. Then decide on a couple of other constraints for the other two columns. In the example shown in Figure 5.18, we've added Design pattern and Emotional intent.

Step 2: Create a Sticky Note Grid

Place five sticky notes in each column. This will form the skeleton of your selection box (see Figure 5.19).

Step 3: Identify the Constraints

In this step, you list five specific examples of each constraint. For example, for User, you would probably list your personas. In the example shown in Figure 5.20, we've used examples of user types, such as Tech novice, Intermediate, and so on. For Environment, you would list the relevant

Figure 5.18: A whiteboard is divided into five columns labeled "User," "Environment," "Goal," "Design Pattern," and "Emotional Intent"

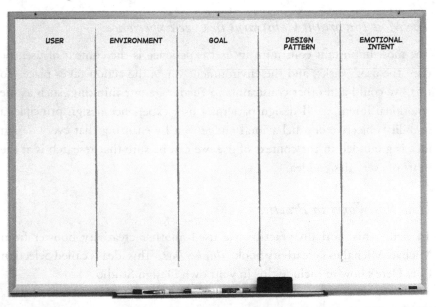

Figure 5.19: The whiteboard contains a grid of 25 blank sticky notes, with five notes in each column

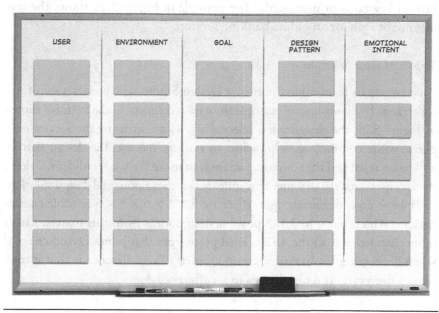

Figure 5.20: Each of the sticky notes in each column now has written on it an example of each constraint

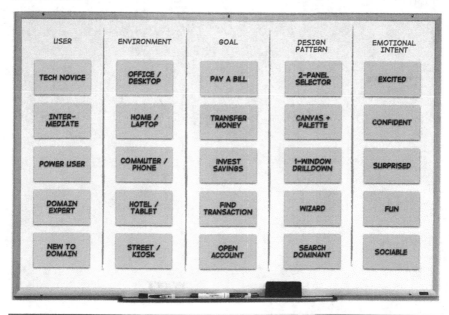

aspects of the users' environments that you have seen in your field research, such as Office/Desktop or Commuter/Phone. For Goals, you would list the various key tasks or user needs. The example in Figure 5.20 shows the way this might look for an online banking service.

Step 4: Make a Selection

Each person or team taking part in a Design Studio now creates a set of five constraints by choosing one example from each column. In the example shown in Figure 5.21, the designer has selected a novice user using the service on a phone while commuting, who wants to transfer money. The design pattern will be a wizard and the emotional intent is to make the user confident. Taking these constraints, the designer now quickly sketches a potential design solution.

If we've done our math right, there are $5 \times 5 \times 5 \times 5 \times 5$ possible combinations, which result in 3,125 possible design ideas from this matrix. That's more than halfway to the 5,127 failed prototypes that James Dyson created[8] when developing his bagless vacuum cleaner! (The difference is that it took Dyson five years. You can do this in an afternoon.)

Figure 5.21: One sticky note in each column is highlighted. In this example, the highlighted sticky notes are "Tech Novice," "Commuter/Phone," "Transfer Money," "Wizard," and "Confident"

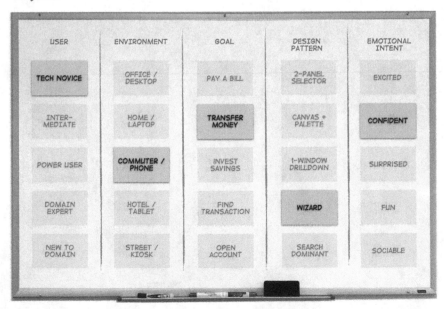

Step 5: Build on the Selection

To generate more ideas, take each of the selected constraints and "turn it up to 11" (with apologies to Spinal Tap). For example, to turn a persona up to 11, take one of the persona's important characteristics and magnify it. In the example shown in Figure 5.22, a tech novice becomes someone who has never even used an ATM.

Then take each item and reverse your assumption. For example, instead of a wizard design pattern, how could we design a system that showed all of the options?

If you need yet more ideas, return to Step 3 and replace the two end columns with alternative constraints.

Here's some alternative constraints that we've found useful:

- *UX design principles*: Use your own project's design principles, or adopt someone else's.
- *Usability objectives*: List usability objectives such as decreasing time on task, reducing errors or improving learnability.

Figure 5.22: Each of the selected constraints shown in Figure 5.21 has Been "turned Up to 11" and "Reversed" to create more design ideas

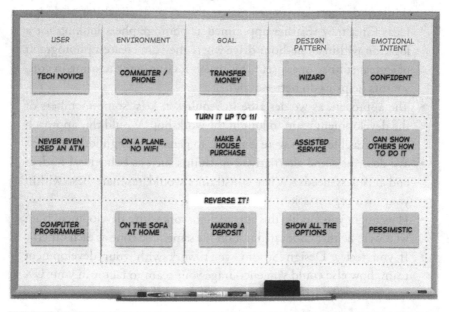

- *Behavioral nudges*: Ask how could you use cognitive biases like reciprocation, social proof, and framing to achieve your goals.
- *Business constraints*: Common ones include time to market, project cost, and product quality.

It's wise to keep the first three columns focused on the context of use since that's how you'll bake your research findings into every design concept. We've also found it works best when we have 4–5 constraints in total: Fewer than that fails to tell a story and more than that makes it a little too complex.

The approach has at least two benefits.

- It ensures that every design idea is linked to a specific user, doing a specific task in a specific context. This guarantees that the UX research will be considered as part of every design concept.
- It helps teams generate a large number of design alternatives. By combining items from the various columns, people find it much easier to come up with novel ideas.

THINK LIKE A UX RESEARCHER

- We argue that constraints help, not hinder, creativity but if you would like to check our assertion here's a quick design activity. First, think of design ideas for a new weather app. Then, think of design ideas for a new weather app aimed at photographers looking for a location within a one-hour drive where they can create a photograph of a great sunrise or sunset. This makes it clear how factoring in constraints helps us do better design.
- The approach, as we describe it, requires at least some members of the development team to join in the workshop. Would this approach still be feasible if you were expected to generate design ideas alone?
- We describe some alternative constraints such as behavioral nudges and business needs. What constraints would resonate best within your own organization?
- How might you modify this approach to work with a development team who were neither co-located nor on the same time zone as each other?
- If you feel a Design Studio won't work with your development team, how else could you encourage your team to factor in your UX research results when making design decisions?

Dealing with Common Objections to UX Research

Heard these before? "Market research uses hundreds of people. How come you can get answers with just 5?" "Our product is aimed at everyone, so we can use ourselves as users." "Users don't know what they want" "Apple doesn't do UX research, so why should we?" "Our agency does all of this for us." Here's how to successfully counter each of these objections.

David was meeting with a potential client who wanted a usability test. "Tell me about your users," he asked, hoping that he could then use this information as the basis for a recruitment screener.

"Well, it's aimed at everyone really, so you don't need to recruit any special kind of user," came the reply.

Red flag. David was just formulating a response when the client said: "Anyway, that's good news for you as you'll need quite a few users!"

David put on his best actually-you'll-be-surprised-by-this face and said, "Often, we find we can get lots of insight with as few as five people."

He laughed. "Five! Our marketing department uses hundreds. How do you seriously expect to get decent results with a handful?"

It turned into a long meeting.

Just Sprinkle Some User Experience Magic on It

Has this happened to you? With user experience being such a growth field, we find we're increasingly meeting with people who claim to want some user experience magic sprinkled on their user interface but appear not to know many of the basic tenets of user experience. Sometimes these people are senior managers in an organization. Other times they may be project managers.

The problem with these kinds of discussion is that, if you're not careful, you end up giving your internal or external client *what they ask for* rather than *what they need.* And when what they've asked for doesn't give them the results they want, they don't come back for any future work.

Here's some of the common objections we've heard, along with some tactful ways to help you convince managers—whether they're inside or outside your organization—to see the light.

Market Research Uses Hundreds of People. How Come You Can Get Answers with Just Five?

Market research is based on opinions. Opinions vary from person to person. It would be ludicrous for a political pollster to sample five people in an attempt to predict an election. And even if we take a single person, his or her opinions will change over time, depending on what's in the news, the other experiences they have and how we phrase the question.

To reduce the inherent variability in opinion data, we need to sample a large group of people. For example, if there are 10,000 people who use our product and we want to know how many of them think it is easy to use, we'll need to randomly sample 370 to achieve a sampling error within 5%.

In contrast, UX research is based on behavior. Behavior turns out to be remarkably consistent from person to person. For example, if you watch five people approach a door and four of them attempt to pull it when the door needs to be pushed, you know there's something wrong with the design. You don't need to randomly sample 370 people to draw this conclusion. You observe that the door has a pull handle and it's probably that's causing the problem. So you replace the pull handle with a push panel and see if you've fixed the problem.

UX researchers can get away with small samples because they are looking for behavioral insights, not opinions.

Our Product Is Aimed at Everyone, So We Can Use Ourselves as Users

This one contains so many flawed assumptions that you'll need to take a deep breath before answering it.

First up, we have the "aimed at everyone" assumption. Just because everyone can use your product doesn't mean that everyone will. The downside of a product with "something for everyone" is that it has "everything for no one." Even if your product will be used by a wide variety of users, focusing on a small group of users first will result in a product that's much more likely to be successful.

The best evidence for this comes from Geoffrey Moore's *Crossing the Chasm*,[9] a marketing book published in 1991 but now enjoying a renaissance as part of the Lean Startup movement. Moore shows that whenever truly innovative high-tech products are first brought to market, they initially have some success in an early market made up of technology enthusiasts and visionaries. But most then fall into a chasm, during which sales falter and often plummet. To cross the chasm, high-tech products must first be adopted by niche customers who find the product a total solution to their specific needs. He calls this niche a "beachhead segment" and this is the group of customers you should aim to satisfy first (for example, by developing personas).

The second assumption—that you can use the person at the next desk as your user—is equally flawed. With the exception of intranets, it's very rare that internal staff are the target market for the product you're designing. Real users are almost certainly less tech-savvy, much less knowledgeable about the product domain, and a lot less tolerant of the product's shortcomings than internal users will be.

Here's an interesting story we came across that shows the value of listening to, and observing, users.[10] Leo Fender, the American inventor, was not a guitarist. So when he started building guitars and amplifiers in the 1950s, he turned to Dick Dale, the "King of the Surf Guitar", to test his designs and help him work out the bugs.

But Dale's playing style pushed the limits of the equipment and he kept breaking Fender's low-power amplifiers. As quickly as Fender modified the amplifiers, Dale blew them up.

Fifty amplifiers later, Fender decided to see for himself what was going on. He drove to a Dick Dale concert at the Rendezvous Ballroom in Balboa, California along with guitar designer Freddie Tavares.

It didn't take them long to spot the problem: The noise from four thousand screaming, shouting and dancing Dick Dale fans was deafening. The amplifier couldn't keep up. Leo turned to Freddie and yelled, "OK, now I know what Dick Dale is trying to tell me!"

They went back to the drawing board and created the Fender Showman amplifier. The amplifier could peak at 100 watts and later at 180 watts, and Dale finally had an amplifier that he couldn't blow up.

This makes us wonder if the real inventor of UX research was Leo Fender.

When managers ask you to design in isolation from users, it's rather like being asked to buy a book for someone else to enjoy reading on holiday. Just because you like a certain author doesn't mean someone else will enjoy reading the book. You'll only be able to get the right book if you know something about the person, either by spending some time with them or by asking questions.

Users Don't Know What They Want

Perhaps you've been in a meeting with someone who repeats the famous Henry Ford quotation: "If I had asked people what they wanted, they would have said a faster horse." This is normally said with a dismissive wave of the hand, indicating that this is conclusive proof that speaking to users in the early stages of design has no value.

If you want to get fired, you could just respond that there's no evidence that Henry Ford ever actually said this.[11] On the other hand, if you want to keep your job and do the research, you should agree. "You're right," you should say, "users don't know what they want. So instead of asking them, I plan to transport them to the future and see what we can learn by watching them use our new concept."

UX research isn't about finding out what people like or dislike. And it's not about asking users to design your interface. It's about seeing the difficulties users face when trying to use the design you've invented.

By their very nature, project managers are often focused on solutions. They are often preoccupied with making decisions on what to build, how to build it, and what new features it should have. An unintended consequence of this is that they sometimes fail to take the long view and consider the problems they are solving. One role of the user experience practitioner is to help project managers take this long view.

Apple Doesn't Do Market Research So Why Should We?

This is closely related to the previous objection. Steve Jobs famously said[12] that Apple "does no market research," and Sir Jonathan Ive has said,[13] "We don't do focus groups—that is the job of the designer. It's unfair to ask people who don't have a sense of the opportunities of tomorrow from the context of today to design."

There's nothing new here of course. The problem is that people conflate *market* research with UX research. Apple has found *market* research methods, like focus groups, to be ineffective ways of finding out what people want from technology or how they'll use it.

But this doesn't mean Apple passes up UX research. In an interview[14] in 1985, Jobs said, "We've done studies that prove the mouse is faster than traditional ways of moving through data or applications," and there's lots of evidence of usability testing being carried out in the early development of the Mac.

One of our favorite examples[15] comes from Apple's User Interface Group. They needed to prototype a portable computer for architects, and the first design questions centered on the size and weight of the device. So they stuffed a pizza box with bricks to match the expected weight of the computer and asked an architect to carry it about. They then used techniques from UX research to observe how the architect carried the "computer," noted down the other things he carried, and identified the tasks he carried out.

Our Agency Does All of This for Us

By "agency" here, we're referring to the company that designs and implements your website or product. An agency will typically provide an all-in-one design service that also includes UX research. It's understandable that managers expect their design agency to have the user experience base covered because that's one of the things they're paying for.

Now, there are good and bad agencies and we don't want to tar them all with the same brush. But in our experience, there are some flaws behind this assumption.

An agency doesn't get paid to please users: it gets paid to please the client. By the time the client has discovered the system isn't delivering the business benefits expected, the agency has cashed the check.

Clients are often deluded into thinking they know their users well. Agencies are sometimes complicit in this and can get swayed by the client's view of the user, rather than doing their own research. It's difficult to tell clients they're wrong—and even more difficult to ask them for the money to pay for the research to prove it.

Clients are usually unwilling to pay for multiple iterations of a design, arguing that the agency should get it right first time. Similarly, few clients will pay for follow up research to check that the final design is, in fact, better than the one it replaced.

Get Prepared

These five objections aren't exhaustive. There are other objections and misconceptions we have heard, including:

- "Rather than test with users, we want you to spend only an hour or two and give us some quick feedback."
- "We can do an online survey and ask people how they work. We'll get more people for less money than doing field research (and we can include Poland and Germany without having to travel)."

- "Our market researchers already go into homes and interview people, so we can do contextual inquiry ourselves."
- "We already do UX research: we recently had five teachers in a room and we demonstrated our product and then asked them to talk about it."
- "We can't let usability needs dictate the aesthetics."

There are many misconceptions about user experience and as a result some project managers still do not fully embrace it. Why not try preparing your own set of responses to these kinds of objections and start to better educate your clients?

THINK LIKE A UX RESEARCHER

- One passive-aggressive way we've found to deal with objections to UX research is to write each one down in a notebook titled, "Silly things clients say" (maybe you can think of a snappier title). In quiet moments, we'll review the notebook and write a cogent argument to deal with the objection. Why not start creating your own notebook (either real or electronic) and start compiling objections and responses?
- This chapter of the book is about persuading teams to take action on your results. Do you think logical arguments (like the ones we present here) are the best way of persuading teams to take action? How might you move people emotionally instead?
- If you worked in an agency, how would you deal with the situation where your client was unwilling to pay for multiple iterations of a design because they expect you to get it right first time?
- In the final part of this essay, we list some additional objections and misconceptions. Choose one of those that you have heard in the past and prepare a suitable response.
- Has Apple made it easier or harder to argue the case for UX research? Why?

The User Experience Debrief Meeting

UX debrief meetings are sometimes viewed as little more than a way to wrap-up a project. This is a mistake. A debrief meeting can accomplish much more than just tying a bow on the project. But it's easier to get a debrief meeting wrong than it is to get it right. We list some practitioner takeaways to make UX debrief meetings more effective.

To debrief someone is to question that person about a mission or an undertaking that they've completed, or about some experience they've been through. A user experience debrief has this component too, because it's an opportunity for development team members to ask you questions about the work you've done. But if that's all you achieve in a debrief meeting, you haven't moved the project, or the development team, forward—so it's a missed opportunity.

An effective user experience debrief meeting has to accomplish much more than just clarify the things people don't understand. To warrant having conducted UX research in the first place, your research findings must connect with the product design process—and the debrief meeting is an opportunity to make sure that happens. What the development team learns from the debrief of a user experience study must in some way effect change:

- Change to the design of the product or service.
- Change to the design process itself.
- Change in the way the development team (and the organization) thinks about its users.
- Change in people's attitudes toward the value of user experience.

So you're failing your client and your development team if you think a user experience debrief meeting is merely a way of wrapping up the job. Experienced researchers know that the debrief meeting is a golden opportunity to answer the most important question a development team can ask at the end of a study: "What do we do next?"

Philip held two user experience debrief meetings recently. The first bore less resemblance to an effective meeting than it did to the Gunfight at the O.K. Corral. The second debrief meeting ran perfectly smoothly.

What makes this all the more surprising was that both meetings were with the same client.

Debrief 1: Getting It Wrong

As a UX researcher, every now and again you will find yourself trying to accommodate a request from the development team that, somewhere deep down, goes against your better judgment. You may find yourself agreeing to a plan that you should have questioned. Sometimes when you do this, the project still works out OK and you live to research another day. But sometimes things go wrong.

Things went wrong.

Corners got cut during a study due to client pressure on the timeline and budget. As a result, no members of the development team observed the study. In fact, Philip's primary contact in the company (we'll just call him "Alan"—not his real name, which was Jeff) had, for reasons known only to himself, worked to create an invisible wall or barrier between Philip on the one side and the development team on the other.

As a result, the designers and engineers had little awareness of the study—until, that is, they got invited to the user experience debrief meeting. We don't need to say much more. You can already sense this is not going to end well.

Suffice to say, one way or another, Philip managed to encounter all of the following potential hazards in one meeting. (No mean feat, we might add.)

- No one in the meeting (other than Alan) knew who Philip was.
- No one had read the report (Alan had distributed it only a few minutes before the meeting started).
- The development team was on the other end of a phone line.
- The main decision makers did not turn up.
- The meeting could not be postponed due to deadline demands.
- The meeting lasted about 59 minutes and 30 seconds longer than the Gunfight at the O.K. Corral (which, for the record, lasted just 30 seconds).

Because no one had read the report or had time to think about the findings or discuss them in advance, the meeting pretty much amounted to "some guy on the other end of the phone" telling the designers and engineers where they had screwed up. No useful discussion could take place until everyone had at least some common grasp on the findings, so the meeting degenerated into little more than a monologue describing the study and its results. Each finding was either summarily disputed (if there was any question about its interpretation) or was met with deafening silence (if its interpretation was undeniable).

Figure 5.23: A debrief meeting that only a masochist could love

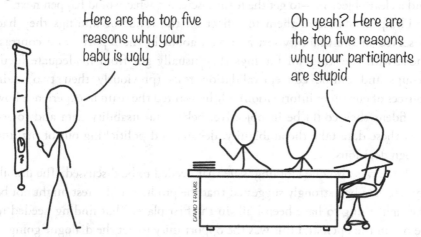

Because the team was encountering the usability problems for the first time, the tone of the meeting was characterized by their honest (and sometimes brutal) first reactions. A cartoonist might have captured it like Figure 5.23.

The debrief meeting should probably not have taken place. And, on reflection, the study should not have taken place either—at least not under those particular circumstances. Much was learned by all concerned.

Happily, Philip was able to have a follow-up meeting afterwards with Alan (who had been curiously silent throughout the entire team debrief), and they worked through the problems together and the invisible wall came down and Philip was able to build a proper relationship with the designers, the engineers, and the marketers. And that led to another user experience project and that led to a second debrief meeting.

Debrief 2: Getting It Right

The second debrief worked well. The foundations were in place this time to ensure that the development team was engaged and on board from the beginning. They had attended the kick-off meeting, provided the participant screening criteria and the core tasks, reviewed the usability test plan, and signed off on it. Most important of all, they had all attended at least one of the usability test sessions and shared their thoughts at the end of each test day.

What a transformation!

Now, rather than being hidden behind an invisible wall, Philip was working with a team that was actively seeking user experience guidance. But he was leaving nothing to chance when it came to the debrief meeting. He had a plan and a clear objective—to get the team discussing what would happen next.

Philip also wanted them to reflect on the kinds of findings they had observed in the usability test and read about in the report—and contrast those with the kinds of findings they usually got from inadequate focus groups and online concept-validation tests (previously their two main sources of customer information). Philip wanted the team to experience how confident they could be in objective, behavioral usability data and to see how these data take the ambiguity, debate, and politicking out of making design decisions.

There was also one looming issue that needed to be discussed. The usability test data had strongly suggested that the product under test might not be the right thing to have been built in the first place. That finding needed to be out in the open and this was the opportunity to get the dialogue going.

In contrast to the first meeting, the second meeting was characterized by:

- Attendees who knew the study and its findings, who had all read the report, who had time to think about it, and who came prepared with questions and comments.
- The presence of the main project leaders and decision makers.
- A genuine eagerness, on the part of the team, for guidance about achieving optimal usability (fueled mainly by having observed participants struggling with basic tasks that the team had assumed were easy).
- A clearly defined three-step agenda to: (a) Get all team reactions and feedback on the table—the surprises, the confirmations, the learnings, and the "Aha!" moments; (b) Reach consensus on the main five "buckets" of usability problems that needed to be addressed; (c) Confirm which issues could realistically be fixed.
- No slideshow presentation and no page-by-page re-reading of the report. Instead, an open discussion of the usability issues following only a brief summary introduction.
- A discussion—initiated by the team members themselves—about the "big issue" of whether the concept we had tested was the right thing to be building and whether it even made sense to customers.
- Ownership of the usability problems by the designers, the engineers, and the marketing leaders.

This time Philip made sure to co-chair the meeting with Alan and that helped overcome any sense of us v. them. Ahead of the meeting, Philip had made it clear that this was not going to be a slideshow presentation and that he was assuming everyone would come prepared having read the report. This seemed a reasonable request, given that they had commissioned the research and the report took only 30 minutes to read.

It worked.

Philip knew that he now had grounds for a common starting point and that he would not be derailed by people attributing the usability problems to "stupid users," as had happened in the first meeting.

But just in case, Philip had prepared a usability test highlights video proving that it was the interface that was stupid.

After just 10 minutes of listening to what the team had learned from the study, it was clear that there would be no disputing the findings this time. It was easy to flow from their list of critical issues into prioritizing the most important usability problems they would have to fix and what process they would use to manage the design changes. Within 30 minutes of starting the meeting four different disciplines, as well as an overseas satellite group, were all singing from the same song sheet.

Then, as the meeting neared its close, something unexpected happened. The attendees started asking strategic questions. Questions like:

- In the future, how can we discover usability problems earlier?
- Can we usability test without building out the whole system next time?
- How can we mitigate the risk of conceiving the wrong product offering in the future?
- How can we get better at discovering genuine user needs?

We extended the meeting just long enough for a thumbnail introduction to field research techniques, paper prototyping, user personas, and Lean UX.

And that was one happy, and rather excited, development team.

So here are our 10 practitioner takeaways for running an effective user experience debrief meeting. We recommend you read them here rather than learn them the hard way. Take it from us: Learning them the hard way is a lot less fun.

10 Practitioner Takeaways for an Effective UX Debrief Meeting

1. Don't wing it. Prepare thoroughly. Have a plan.
2. Don't think of the debrief as a wrap-up meeting—think of it as a spring-board to the next step. And make sure user experience is part of that next step.
3. Co-chair the meeting with the product owner or product manager.
4. Make sure the main decision-makers attend.
5. Don't give a PowerPoint presentation and don't rehash the report. If you have 60 minutes, talk for 15 minutes, then discuss for 45 minutes.
6. Keep the report brief but insist that attendees read the report and come armed with comments and questions.
7. Before you summarize the study findings, ask the team to share what they had learned from the study, what surprised them, and what usability issues they feel are most important or most serious.
8. Simplify your message. Focus on just the five most severe usability problems. Don't overwhelm the team by trying to cover everything (they can check the report for those details).
9. Get consensus on the problems rather than argue over solutions.
10. Don't expect or insist that everything must be fixed. Focus next steps on the important problems that can be realistically changed within the budget and timeline.

THINK LIKE A UX RESEARCHER

- Imagine you are in the first situation that Philip describes: No one knows who you are; no one has read your report or skimmed your slide deck; the development team is on the other end of a phone line; and the main decision makers have not turned up. The meeting needs to go ahead because of deadline demands. What could you have done or said to avoid the situation from happening in the first place? What can you do or say during the meeting to minimize its impact?
- Philip's story describes his experiences working as an external consultant. Do you think the practitioner takeaways listed at the end of the essay would also work for internal UX researchers?

(Continued)

THINK LIKE A UX RESEARCHER (Continued)

- How would you approach a formal report back to stakeholders compared to an informal "show and tell" with the development team? What might need to be included in the stakeholder meeting that you could skip in the development team meeting, and vice versa?
- Rather than a presentation at the end of a round of research, some UX researchers release results before the analysis is complete. For example, they may send an email to the team immediately after a usability test session describing an interesting finding. What are the risks and rewards of this approach?
- Is there any way of telling a development team that their baby is ugly without them becoming defensive and shooting the messenger?

Creating a User Experience Dashboard

We're often told that senior managers don't have the time to read a detailed report describing the findings from a usability test. This means our thoroughly argued, carefully analyzed and clearly presented 60-page report could have no effect on improving the product or changing the culture. How can we better engage managers with our data?

There is no point in creating a report that nobody wants to read. A lengthy report will probably end up gathering dust in a manager's in-box or lost for eternity in the bowels of a company's intranet. But just because stakeholders aren't interested in a comprehensive report doesn't mean that they are not interested in the findings from UX research.

All managers are interested in Business Intelligence: What you get when you analyze raw data and turn it into knowledge. One good example of this is web analytics. With web analytics we risk being drowned by data, but companies such as Google have devised creative ways to present the data in the form of a dashboard—a short report that delivers business intelligence in graphical form.

When we run UX benchmarking studies—where we directly compare the usability of one product with another—we know that collecting the data is only half the battle. We know that companies don't act on UX research data unless senior management are swayed by the findings. So we set to work devising a way to present the data in a format to help managers engage with the data.

To illustrate our thinking, we'll be presenting data from a study we carried out comparing the usability of two Valentine's Day web florists: bunches.co.uk and interflora.co.uk. (The actual websites aren't important here; we simply use the data to show how you can create metrics for a dashboard.) We carried out this benchmark study with over 100 participants. Half the participants used the Bunches website and the other half used the Interflora website. Each participant carried out four tasks, and for each task we measured success rate, time on task, and a subjective rating of task difficulty. Participants also commented on the ease or difficulty of the task by writing one or two sentences describing their experience.

Our challenge was to compress these data into a concise graphical summary—a user experience dashboard.

A sensible starting point for any user experience dashboard report would be the ISO definition of usability. ISO 9241-11[16] defines usability as the "Extent to which a product can be used by specified users to achieve specified goals with effectiveness, efficiency, and satisfaction in a specified context of use." This gives us three areas to focus on: effectiveness, efficiency, and satisfaction. Within these areas we want to find *emblematic measures*: Metrics that everyone (from the CEO on down) gets immediately and can judge if they are good or bad.

How Effective Is the Design?

An obvious emblematic measure for effectiveness is success rate: The number of participants who manage to complete the task successfully. This should certainly resonate with our senior managers since this has clear face validity: If users can't complete a task, you can't make money from it. We can make the data more informative by including not just the number of successful users but also the number of unsuccessful users and the number of users who abandoned the task. A bar chart becomes the obvious choice for representing these data. Figure 5.24 shows the results from the usability test of bunches.co.uk.

We also need to supply the underlying numbers behind this graph. In this task, the success rate was 60%. But this number on its own isn't sufficient. Along with our estimate of success rate we need to provide an estimate of our confidence in this number—our margin of error. For this

Figure 5.24: Stacked bar chart showing the number of successful and unsuccessful participants and the number of participants who abandoned the task

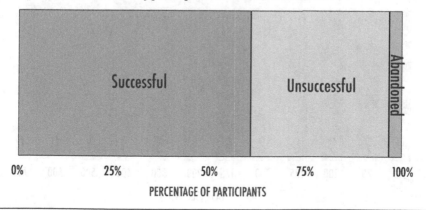

study, the 95% upper and lower confidence intervals were 47% and 72% respectively. Our dashboard will need to include these numbers alongside the graph.

How Efficient Is the Design?

There are various ways of measuring efficiency but again a measure that most senior managers would understand is the time taken to complete a task. Unlike success rate, there will be a wide distribution of task times. Some people will be able to complete the task quickly and others will take longer. So rather than simply present the mean value, we could show the distribution of task times for all the participants. Figure 5.25 shows the way this looks for our sample study. The bars show the number of participants whose time to complete the task fell within the appropriate "bin." Each bin shows a range of times; for example, three participants completed the task in 126–150 seconds.

Again, we need to provide the core measure, which is the average time taken to complete the task. Because task times are not normally distributed, we use the geometric mean. In this study, the average time on task was 1 m 54 s, 95% CI (1 m 37 s, 2 m 14 s).

How Satisfying Is the Design?

Most usability tests include some kind of survey or questionnaire, and this lends itself to creating the kind of chart shown in Figure 5.26. This chart

Figure 5.25: Bar chart showing the distribution of task times in a usability test

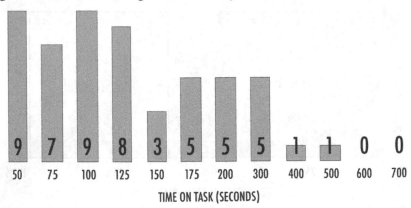

Figure 5.26: Bar chart showing the distribution of participant ratings

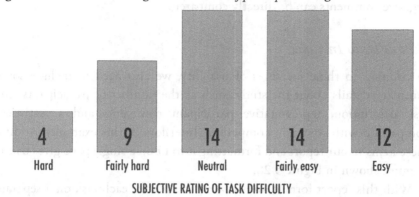

shows the number of participants who rated the task difficulty as Hard through to Easy. For example, the graph shows that four people though the task was Hard.

Again, there needs to be a summary measure indicating the average rating. In this study, the average rating was 60%, 95% CI (51%, 68%).

Survey results are not our only insight into user satisfaction. Another measure of satisfaction that would resonate with senior managers is the ratio of positive to negative comments made by participants. Since some proportion of these will be neutral, a split area chart (see Figure 5.27) is a logical way to

Figure 5.27: Area chart showing the distribution of positive, negative and neutral participant comments

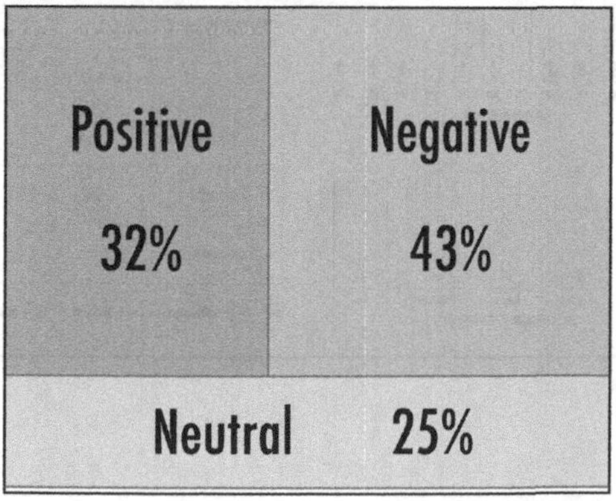

present the data in our dashboard since then the proportion of positive and negative comments can be directly compared.

What Else to Include?

In addition to these measures of usability, we also need to include some summary details about the study, such as the number of participants, the task description, representative participant comments and a statistical comparison with the main competitor (Interflora in this example). Adding these items to our report and formatting it to fit on a single page gives us the example shown in Figure 5.28.

With this report format, we show the results for each task on a separate page. Our senior manager now has a lot less paper to shuffle through and at-a-glance can assess the performance of the product using robust measures of usability.

Figure 5.28: Benchmark report on one page

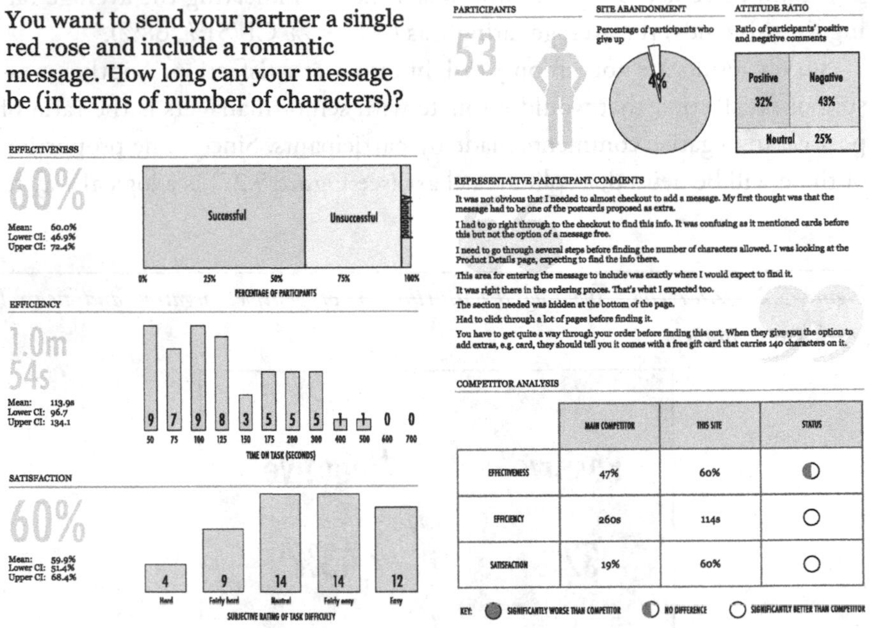

THINK LIKE A UX RESEARCHER

- The ISO definition of usability requires us to measure effectiveness, efficiency, and satisfaction. Do you think these are sufficient for a user experience dashboard? If not, what do you think is missing and how would you measure it?
- We created the graphs in this essay using a spreadsheet (Numbers on a Mac). This makes it easy to create new reports quickly: When we carry out a new benchmark test, we simply replace the raw data with the data from a new study. Try creating your own basic version of this dashboard using your favorite spreadsheet package.
- Dashboards like the kind in this essay may be useful for stakeholders, but would they have the same impact or usefulness for people on the development team? If you needed to create an alternative, short report for the development team describing your UX research results, what would it include? How short would you need to make it to ensure that it got read?
- The impetus for creating a dashboard is to simplify the reporting of UX research results. The ultimate short report would be a single number that captures the user experience of a product. Would such a report be meaningful or should a report, no matter how short, also include some kind of qualitative description of the user's experience?
- The margin of error on success rates can be quite large, especially when the sample size is small (in our example, the success rate was 60% but the margin of error provides a range of 47%–72%). Does including the margin of error in your report undermine quantitative user experience metrics? Or does it show readers of your report that you know how to account for behavioral variability?

Achieving Boardroom Influence

We're seeing a sea-change in our industry as firms scramble to build fledgling user experience teams. While this is a sure sign of a maturing discipline, it is not without its teething problems. In particular, the voice of the user experience team can sometimes sound more like a whisper. Why do some user experience teams fail to achieve the impact expected of them? Here are six mistakes we've seen that prevent user experience teams from having boardroom influence.

There are risks in launching a new user experience team. Over the years we've seen a pattern of mistakes that are pretty much guaranteed to get things off on the wrong foot.

Here are six mistakes that user experience teams frequently make:

- Not doing proper UX research.
- Trying to build user experience from the bottom up.
- Falling into the "cargo cult usability" trap.
- Being too academic.
- Being too insular.
- Failing to educate the organization about user experience.

Let's look at each in turn and then we'll provide some possible solutions.

Not Doing Proper UX Research

We've noticed something rather curious about some user experience teams: They don't seem to be doing any UX research. They *claim* to be doing UX research in theory, but that's not what they do in practice. Instead they seem to be engaged in a mishmash of homegrown activities that fail to meet even the most basic standards of UX research. Some of the work might be called preference testing and amounts to asking people what they think about things; some of it seems focused on measuring product parameters; some bears a closer resemblance to market research than to UX research; some is clearly quality assurance work or user acceptance testing; and some just seems like made up stuff that may or may not involve red, yellow and green checkboxes.

Trying to Build User Experience from the Bottom Up

You can't build a user experience team by starting at the lowest level and working upward. Don't expect to succeed if you start out by hiring inexperienced or junior staff, or by converting web designers simply by putting "User Experience" on their business cards (we've seen this happen).

You have to start at the top with the two most critical roles:

- The user experience team leader (this is likely to be a new hire).
- An executive-level user experience champion (this should be an existing VP-level sponsor who will blaze a trail through the highest levels of the company).

We describe the skills of the user experience team leader in the next essay ("Hiring a User Experience Leader") so here we'd like to expand on the executive-level champion role.

Most companies assume this role can be filled by anyone with "Manager" in their job title, or by someone at Director level. We've seen sponsors at this level, already too busy with other responsibilities, just give the nod at the outset and pay lip service to the value of user experience, playing no meaningful role as user experience flounders or grinds to a halt. In our experience, this vitally important role only works if it is operating at VP level. We're talking about a major mover and shaker here, someone with clout who can open doors, create strategy and loosen the purse-strings.

Falling Into the Cargo Cult Usability Trap

"Cargo cult" thinking is predicated on the mistaken belief that the most important requirement for achieving your goals and aspirations is having the right equipment and paraphernalia. The term originated with the people of Melanesia and the culture shock they experienced, particularly during WWII, on the arrival of "magical" technology (ships, aircraft, and radio) and the unimaginable wealth brought in by the army of friendly King Rusefel (Roosevelt). Their own subsequent attempts at building aircraft out of palm trees, and a radio by wrapping copper wire around a woman who then spoke gibberish and made whistling noises, failed to produce the riches they desired.[17]

When Philip was eight years old he desperately wanted a horse—preferably a white one with a long mane like the Lone Ranger used to ride. Instead of a horse (which obviously was never going to fit in his parents' coal shed) his mother bought him a leather riding crop. It was all she could afford. That was Philip's horse-riding experience. Cargo cult horse riding.

Alas, buying an expensive Stratocaster doesn't turn you into Eric Clapton, and you're never going to win the Triple Crown if all you have is a riding crop.

Cargo cult usability is what happens when a company mistakes having a state of the art usability lab for actually doing UX research. Thousands of dollars spent on studio-quality cameras, microphones and half-silvered windows is no guarantee of success in UX research. A quiet room is all that's needed. Pencil and paper are fine. A digital video camera and a tripod can be useful. But don't blow your budget on unnecessary equipment. Invest in good UX researchers instead.

Being Too Academic

UX teams are sometimes accused of being too academic and of being out of touch with the cut and thrust of real-life business and product development.

We hear stakeholders complain, "I just needed a best guess answer but I got a full usability study that took weeks," or "The user experience team always wants to get the 100% perfect answer, when 80% is good enough," or "Instead of a quick response I get a 30-page report in a week's time."

Avoid this kind of criticism by being pragmatic, adaptable, and lean. Find out exactly what your team needs and understand why they need it. Then tailor your methods to the timeline, set expectations, and report back in an appropriate and effective way whether that's a written report or not. Don't take weeks writing a dissertation-length report if a face-to-face chat over coffee is all that's needed.

Being Too Insular

The one thing a new user experience team absolutely cannot afford to do is to become isolated and detached from the main action. Yet many of the embryonic or failing teams we've seen manage to do just this.

Newly formed user experience teams have a tendency to quickly turn inward and focus heavily on their own practices, tools, and methods: heads down, working in a vacuum, doing work that doesn't actually influence anything. As a result, we hear frustrated stakeholders say things like, "I don't involve the user experience team because they always seem too busy." We've even heard user experience team members themselves complain that, "We're so busy and so mired in the day-to-day that we don't have time to work alongside the development team."

This reminds us of the (hilarious but true) story of the Staffordshire (UK) bus company. In 1976 it was reported that the buses on the Hanley to Bagnall route were not stopping to pick up passengers. People complained that buses were driving right past long lines of waiting passengers. The complaints prompted Councillor Arthur Cholerton to make transport history by stating that if the buses stopped to pick up passengers it would disrupt the timetable!

We've said it before and we'll say it again: UX is a team sport. If you're following the design process in ISO 9241-210[18] (and if you're not, you should), you'll know that one of the key principles is "The design team includes multidisciplinary skills and perspectives."

UX teams can't afford to be self-serving, or introverted, or become obsessed with whatever is the user experience equivalent of not disrupting the bus timetable. There's no point just beavering away in the background. If you don't want to be excluded, don't start out by excluding yourself. Stop and pick up the passengers.

Failing to Educate the Organization about User Experience

Let's be honest: Most people in your organization probably don't know what user experience is about. They just know "UX" as a buzzword and want some of that secret sauce. You are about to introduce a concept that, although seemingly obvious, usually catches people off guard: the concept of *user* centered rather than *product* centered design thinking. We frequently encounter development teams who, no matter how many times they agree about putting the user first, simply cannot do it. They seem unable to think beyond the product or service they are currently working on, couching everything (including user experience questions) in terms of product parameters rather than in terms of user needs.

Part of the user experience team's role is to educate people to help them make this subtle but vital shift in thinking.

Solving the Problem

First, don't try to wing it. It's far too important to play this by the seat of your pants. You may only get one real shot at creating an effective user experience team. Any one of these six mistakes (and there are many others just waiting to trip you up) can derail your hard work.

Here are some ideas to get back on track.

Get Agile

The days of isolated user experience teams are numbered. Team members should be working (and sitting) alongside the development team who are designing the product. It's really hard to do good user experience work when you are parachuted in to solve a specific problem (like run a usability test) and then afterward you just return to base. Each user experience person should be a fully paid-up member of the development team they are supporting, helping to answer their day-to-day research and design questions.

Help Team Members See Where They Fit

Some newly formed user experience teams are an assembly of people with quite disparate backgrounds and skill sets. Multidisciplinary design is important, but without good user experience leadership and training, team members tend to fall back on the disciplines they know well and try to apply the methods they are comfortable with.

This can account for an over-emphasis on statistical, psychology, engineering, or design-biased work, at the expense of actual UX research. "I know about stats so I'm going to focus on stats." "I trained as an engineer or designer so I'm going to focus on the product components." By all means, hire people with a range of skills, but make sure they understand that although they may have got the job because they have a background in psychology, statistics, design, or whatever, you're not hiring them to be a psychologist, statistician, or designer. You want them to apply the principles of their specialist disciplines to improving the user experience.

Say No to Dishwasherology

It's not uncommon for user experience teams lacking in direction and without a user experience champion to find themselves being appropriated by other groups who just need "some customer research." This can result in user experience teams being asked to do market research, quality assurance evaluations, craftsmanship reviews (though involving actual craftsmen appears not to be a requisite), and generally faffing around with odd things that have low validity and low credibility. For example, when Philip worked in an internal user experience team, he was once asked by marketing to conjure up something called "Dishwasherology." Marketing didn't know what they meant by this, but they were pretty sure that an -ology of some kind backed by a PhD psychologist could get some marketing mileage.

Never lose sight of the fact that your user experience team has been set up to bring something new to the company—not to just roll over and help propagate the same old methods that weren't working in the first place or to make up silly stuff that no one understands. Avoid this trap. Just say No (Philip said No to Dishwasherology). Say Yes and you'll get sucked into a black hole that you may never get out of again.

Get Your Team Trained

Think of UX training as providing your team with a compass direction. Unless your new hires are already very experienced, without training your team will become at best aimless and at worst a liability. Sometimes, a team needs re-orienting around the user experience equivalent of magnetic north.

Some of your internal partners may also want to join the training classes so that they know what to expect from your team and know how to apply the output of your work. We've found in house UX training to be particularly effective, and a great way to unite everyone, giving them a shared user experience vocabulary and a shared user experience vision.

THINK LIKE A UX RESEARCHER

- Read over the six mistakes that we see user experience teams make. Which of these have you seen in your own organization?
- We claim that the UX research done by some user experience teams fails to meet even the most basic standards of UX research. How would you rate the quality of UX research carried out by your user experience team? How are you making this judgment? How would you know if the quality of your UX research was improving or getting worse?
- Most organizations build their user experience competency using one of two approaches. In one approach, the user experience team is its own function with UX researchers working as consultants to the development team. In the other approach, development teams have a dedicated UX researcher who is permanently located with them. What are the advantages and disadvantages of these approaches? Which would you personally prefer?

(Continued)

THINK LIKE A UX RESEARCHER (Continued)

- Is "UX" a buzzword in your organization? Does your manager understand what user experience entails? How about your manager's manager? How might you educate people in your organization to understand what user experience is really about?
- We describe user experience training as a way of providing your team with a compass direction. How else might you help your user experience team, or your development team, understand best practice in user experience?

6

Building a Career in
User Experience

❧

Hiring a User Experience Leader

We're frequently asked by organizations for guidance on building a user experience competency. Our advice is to start at the top and hire the right person for that first user experience leadership role. But what qualities should that person have? And what hiring mistakes should you avoid?

You're the Design VP of a sizable company. You just got the green light to build a new user experience team, and right now you're sitting with your head in your hands.

You just spent 15 minutes staring at job titles on a user experience careers website. What a mess. UX Designer, UX Developer, UX Researcher, Usability Specialist, Insights Designer, UX Digital Analyst, User Researcher, Usability Analyst, Software UX Designer, UX Architect, Content Designer, Human Factors Engineer, UX/UI Designer, UX Marketer, UI Artist, Interaction Designer, Information Architect. Your head is spinning. You already called in HR but now they are sitting across the desk with their heads in their hands, too.

This muddle of seemingly made up words feels like so much gobbledygook, and it has you worried because you know that confusing job titles are a symptom of companies that don't know the discipline well and don't know what a user experience team should look like. You worry that the strongest candidates will be turned off while the weaker ones will change their identity faster than Clark Kent in a phone booth.

What should you do?

Engage a User Experience Expert

Catch-22. If you don't know user experience well and if your hiring managers don't know the field, how can you know how to find good user experience candidates? You can't. So get someone who can. Engage a seasoned user experience consultant for the duration of the job search— someone who has built user experience teams and hired user experience staff before. He or she will build rigor into your job search and will guide you through the hiring process, helping you to write the job posting, screen applicants, design the selection process, attend interviews and make recommendations.

Hire the User Experience Leader First

Building a team, observed Sir Winston Churchill, is not like building a house. You don't start from the bottom and work upwards and then add the leader on top like a chimney pot. You build a team from the top down. Hire your user experience team leader first. He or she will be the most important user experience hire you make. Don't start by hiring inexperienced people. Doing so risks user experience becoming marginalized before you ever get out of the starting blocks. Starting with the team leader means that he or she can establish the operational framework, plan strategy, evangelize user experience, and make subsequent hiring decisions to build the team.

Hire a User Experience Leader with Vision

There are certain characteristics that all good leaders share: confidence, the ability to communicate well, to motivate and inspire, to think strategically and see the bigger picture, to persuade and influence, to manage complexity, to be able to go toe-to-toe with upper management if necessary. You can add to this list. These are qualities all leaders need to have—in addition to the technical skills relevant to user experience. But these are not sufficient to lead a user experience team.

The one "must have" characteristic we've seen in great user experience leaders is *vision*, which translates to the ability to conceive and articulate a future state for user experience for the product, for the team and for the company, coupled with the ability to motivate people to get behind the vision.

Leadership requires movement, progress, and change. A leader has to actually lead the team to somewhere (some goal or quest) that is not where it's currently at. Some leaders never get started on their journey because they don't know what the destination is, and some just get busy running on the spot. If your user experience team is doing the same thing this year that it was doing last year, then no leadership is taking place. A good leader provides the destination, the map, and the compass bearings for the team.

Hire a Researcher

The foundation of a good user experience is research. So hire a researcher. Preferably one with experience researching human behavior. This still allows for a wide range of disciplines that might include, among others, cognitive science, human factors, anthropology, sociology, ergonomics, and psychology. The discipline that takes a scientific approach to studying human behavior is called Experimental Psychology, and this is a good indicator of what to look for in your first user experience hire. Look for someone with a demonstrable track record of designing and conducting behavioral research that they have personally carried out.

Other disciplines may seem like viable starting points, but they do not guarantee experience in the science of human behavior or in the rigors of user centered research and data analysis which are the foundations of user experience.

Hire a User Experience Leader with a Working Knowledge of Related Disciplines

Leaders want to inspire their team members, and to do this they must understand their values and interests. This means having a working knowledge and understanding of a wide range of user experience-related disciplines. In addition to UX research, the leader will build and lead a team made up of interaction designers, visual designers, and software programmers and prototypers; and people with different views, levels of experience and training.

In addition, a user experience leader will understand how the business makes money and how user experience can help grow the business. He or she will be able to speak the language of business. This will include being able to calculate and communicate the return on investment for user experience, secure and manage a user experience budget, and build bridges into the financial and marketing divisions of the company.

Make a VP Level Appointment

This is a position with company-wide influence. Your user experience leader can transform the way your company thinks about its customers and users, and the way it develops products and services. Appoint this person at an organizational level that carries authority. We strongly recommend hiring at VP level, or at least director level, to ensure the user experience leader can have influence. Without a senior role in the organization, the user experience vision can be derailed at any time by a senior manager who decides to change direction.

Budget can be an obstacle, of course. So if you were hoping to start by hiring two or three lower level user experience practitioners, we recommend sacrificing one or two of these and hiring at a higher level. You can't influence thinking, innovation, ideas, culture and brand if user experience becomes a commodity and you just end up cranking out usability tests. Aim high. You may only get one chance. If you need more money ask for it.

Three Common Hiring Mistakes

These are the three most common user experience leader hiring mistakes we encounter:

The Accidental Manager

Let's be clear, it's not a mistake to hire a user experience manager. Your user experience manager should be your second hire. But it is a mistake to hire a user experience manager when you're supposed to be hiring a user experience leader. These are two different roles. Leadership and management are almost certainly orthogonal to one another, and may even be opposites. Think of your user experience leader as looking outwards towards the business and your user experience manager as looking inwards towards the team. Good leadership is about vision; good management is about developing your team. The leader's focus is on the impact of user experience on the business and the company culture; the manager's focus is on day-to-day operations, on the technical aspects of user experience, and on mentoring and developing user experience team members. Rather like a ship's captain, it's difficult for a leader to chart a course and steer the ship and at the same time be down in the engine room checking the oil levels.

The One-Man Band

A well-balanced user experience team will include a range of research and design disciplines and skills (more on this in the next essay), but you won't find all these in one person and it's a mistake to try. Don't expect your first user experience hire to be both a researcher and also a visual designer and also a content author. These disciplines may seem interchangeable on a job-posting website, but they are very different and very specialized. Your candidate will have awareness and knowledge of these areas but beware of trying to hire a one-man band. We may find the one-man band entertaining, but his music is usually pretty awful. Avoiding this mistake means writing job postings that are specific and avoiding the temptation to shovel in every role and responsibility you can think of just to sound impressive. You're hiring a specialist, so be specific.

The Lateral Arabesque

It's not uncommon, especially in larger corporations, for a designer to be allocated the role of user experience leader with the aim of heading up a new user experience competency. Sometimes it's an engineer and sometimes a marketer. We've seen all three. We've even seen a customer service agent put into this position. We've yet to see it work out very well.

This sideways pseudo-promotion comes close to what Lawrence Peter and Raymond Hull call the Lateral Arabesque—a variant of the Peter Principle.[1] The Lateral Arabesque involves giving someone a longer job title and somewhere else to work. Note that we're not talking here about people who, of their own volition, move into user experience because they find the discipline fascinating and see user experience as a career move. User experience practitioners tend to arrive in the field from a variety of backgrounds and, with training and coaching, become important contributors—though we would still not advocate putting such a person straight into a user experience leadership position. No, here we are talking about people who have been moved by management out of their own discipline and into user experience because they were not cutting it in design, engineering, marketing, or some other part of the corporation.

We also see a variant of this—yes, a variant of a variant—in what we've taken to calling the "Andy Capp" model of team building. Comic strip character, Andy Capp applies for a job as a "handy man" but then admits he has no experience or skills for any of the required work. "In what way are you a handy man then?" asks the foreman. "I just live round the corner," replies Andy.

In this model, user experience teams end up staffed with internal people who do not have the skills or experience but who just need a "home." These are sometimes former admin people, or people whose current job has been eliminated, or sometimes just people who have been around a long time but who don't easily fit in anywhere else. In our experience these "willing but unable" candidates usually have little to zero user experience background and so cannot personally do the work. When handed the user experience reins they typically call in outside help, further reinforcing the redundant nature of their role.

Both of these approaches to user experience staffing devalue user experience and, frankly, devalue the skills that these people do have. Such user experience teams usually struggle to do good work or to have any influence and are frequently ignored by development teams.

Ruthless Though It May Seem…

Leadership is a bit like user experience itself: It's noticeable by its absence. You know good leadership when the team is excited about its work, everyone on the team has a sense of purpose and people are happy in their jobs. Admittedly, these are hard things to measure and it's even harder to pin down the leadership behaviors that create this atmosphere. But it comes back to the idea of vision: the best user experience leaders we've come across have an unerring vision for what "good" looks like. They are happy to discuss this vision and help you understand it, but the vision isn't set by any committee. Ruthless though it may seem, either you buy into their vision or you get shipped out.

THINK LIKE A UX RESEARCHER

- Write a job advertisement for hiring a user experience leader in your organization. What job title did you use? Why did you choose that title? How would changing the job title change the candidates who apply? Be sure to include the user experience leader's first year objectives. Describe the needs of the projects they'll work on and the challenges they'll need to overcome.
- What if, rather than being able to build a team, you are able to hire just one user experience expert? What background, experience and qualities would you look for? What role would you see this person playing in your company?
- Consider a situation where you've been told that your user experience hire must be recruited at a lower level but with a training budget to help them climb the ladder to a leadership position in time. What are the pros and cons of this "grow your own" approach to user experience leadership?
- You've talked to your boss about the challenges of finding the right candidate for your user experience leadership position. He tells you to use a professional recruiting agency. What are the advantages of doing this and what are the risks?
- Imagine you wanted to apply for a user experience leadership role yourself. What would you emphasize on your CV to present yourself as a user experience *leader* rather than as a user experience *manager*?

A Tool for Assessing and Developing the Technical Skills of User Experience Practitioners

A user experience practitioner demonstrates eight core competencies. By assessing each team member's "signature" in these eight areas, managers can build a fully rounded user experience team. This approach also helps identify the roles for which each team member is most suited alongside areas for individual development.

We are often asked, "What skills does a user experience practitioner need?" It's true that the term "UX practitioner" (and its variants) can be problematic but that doesn't mean we should avoid identifying the competences in which an individual needs to be accomplished to work in the field of user experience. Managers still need to identify the gaps in their user experience team and HR departments still need to set proper criteria for hiring and writing job postings (instead of just scanning CVs and résumés for keywords that they may not understand).

Key Competencies

The key competences required by a user experience practitioner fall into eight areas:

- User needs research.
- Usability evaluation.
- Information architecture.
- Interaction design.
- Visual design.
- Technical writing.
- User interface prototyping.
- User experience leadership.

These are "competencies" but to properly understand them we need to identify the behaviors that underlie them. What behaviors describe the knowledge, skills, and actions shown by the best performers in each of these competency areas?

In the following sections, we describe the behaviors behind each of these competences along with a star chart that you can use to create a "signature" for each member of your team. Then we review the canonical signatures for a range of different practitioners so you can build a fully rounded user experience team.

User Needs Research

This competence is defined by the following behaviors:

- Articulate the importance of user research, not just before the system is designed but also during design and after deployment.
- Identify the potential users of the system.
- Plan field visits to users, including deciding who to sample.
- Structure an effective interview that gets beyond the surface opinions (what users say) to reveal user goals (what users want).
- Keep appropriate records of each observation.
- Analyze qualitative data from a field visit.
- Present the data from a field visit in ways that can be used to drive design: for example, personas, user stories, user journey maps.
- Analyze and interpret existing data (for example web analytics, user surveys, customer support calls).
- Critically evaluate previous user research.

Usability Evaluation

This competence is defined by the following behaviors:

- Choose the most appropriate evaluation method (for example, formative v. summative test, moderated v. unmoderated test, lab v. remote test, usability testing v. expert review, usability testing v. A/B test, usability testing v. survey).
- Interpret usability principles and guidelines and use them to identify likely problems in user interfaces.
- Understand how to design an experiment, and how to control and measure variables.
- Plan and administer different types of usability evaluation.
- Log the data from usability evaluations.
- Analyze the data from usability evaluations.
- Measure usability.

- Prioritize usability problems.
- Choose the most appropriate format for sharing findings and recommendations: for example, a report, a presentation, a daily stand-up or a highlights video.
- Persuade the development team to take action on the results.

Information Architecture

This competence is defined by the following behaviors:

- Establish the flow between a person and a product or service (also known as service design).
- Uncover and describe users' models of the work domain.
- Organize, structure, and label content, functions and features.
- Choose between different design patterns for organizing content (such as faceted navigation, tagging, and hub and spoke).
- Develop a controlled vocabulary.
- Articulate the importance and use of metadata.
- Analyze search logs.
- Run online and offline card sorting sessions.

Interaction Design

This competence is defined by the following behaviors:

- Choose between different user interface patterns (for example, Wizards, Organizer Workspaces, and Coach Marks).
- Use the correct user interface "grammar" (for example, choosing the correct control in an interface, such as checkbox v. radio button).
- Describe how a specific user interface interaction will behave (for example, pinch to zoom).
- Create user interface animations.
- Create affordances within a user interface.
- Create design ideas toward a solution.
- Sketch and tell user centered stories about the way an interaction should work.

Visual Design

This competence is defined by the following behaviors:

- Use fundamental principles of visual design (like contrast, alignment, repetition and proximity) to de-clutter user interfaces.
- Choose appropriate typography.
- Devise grids.
- Lay out pages.
- Choose color palettes.
- Develop icons.
- Articulate the importance of following a common brand style.

Technical Writing

This competence is defined by the following behaviors:

- Write content in plain English.
- Phrase content from the user's perspective (rather than the system's perspective).
- Create content that helps users complete tasks and transactions.
- Express complex ideas concisely.
- Create and edit macro- and micro-copy.
- Write content in the tone of voice that matches the organization's identity or brand.
- Choose the right kind of help for the situation: tutorials v. manuals v. contextual help v. micro-copy.

User Interface Prototyping

This competence is defined by the following behaviors:

- Translate ideas into interactions by developing prototypes and simulations.
- Choose the appropriate fidelity of prototype for the phase of design.
- Articulate the benefits of fast iteration.
- Create paper prototypes.
- Properly explore the design space before deciding on a solution.
- Create interactive electronic prototypes.

User Experience Leadership

This competence is defined by the following behaviors:

- Plan and schedule user experience work.
- Argue the cost-benefit of user experience activities.
- Lead a multidisciplinary team.
- Assemble team members for a project.
- Promote ongoing professional development of the team.
- Liaise with stakeholders.
- Manage client expectations.
- Measure and monitor the effect of user experience on the company's success.
- Evangelize user experience throughout the company.

How to Assess the Competence of Your User Experience Team

When coaching people in these competences, we've found it useful to formalize the discussion around a simple star chart (Figure 6.1). The purpose of the star chart is simply to provide a framework for our conversation, although people tell us they find it a useful reference that they can return to and assess their progress over time.

You'll notice that the star chart contains the eight competences that we've reviewed in this essay along with a five-point scale for each one. This five-point scale is to frame a discussion only; it's there to help people identify their strengths and weaknesses.

Unless you have worked with each of your team members for several years, we recommend that you ask team members to assess their own competency. We usually give people the following instructions:

Pick one of the competency areas on this star chart that you are most familiar with. Read over the behavioral descriptions for this competency area and then rate your own competency between 0 and 5, using the following scale:

> 0—I don't understand this competence or it is non-existent
> 1—Novice: I have a basic understanding of this competence
> 2—Advanced beginner: I can demonstrate this competence under supervision
> 3—Competent: I can demonstrate this competence independently
> 4—Proficient: I can supervise other people in this competence
> 5—Expert: I develop new ways of applying this competence

Then move onto the other competency areas and complete the diagram.

Figure 6.1: A template to assess your own competence

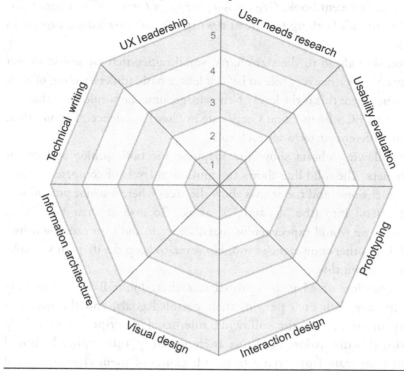

There are problems when you ask people to rate their own competence. The Dunning-Kruger effect[2] tells us that novices tend to overestimate their competence and experts tend to underestimate their competence. For example, a novice who should rate themselves a "1" may over-rate themselves as a 2 or 3 whereas an expert that should rate themselves a "5" may under-rate themselves as a 3 or 4. To counteract this bias, we recommend that you either (a) ignore the absolute ratings and instead look at a team member's general pattern across the eight competencies; or (b) you follow up each chart with an interview where you ask team members to provide specific examples of behaviors to justify their rating.

Mapping the Competences to User Experience Practitioner Roles

We've noted earlier that the field of user experience has a bewildering array of job titles. So to map these competencies onto different user experience roles, we've taken some of the practitioner roles from Merholz and Skinner's recent book, *Org Design for Design Orgs*.[3] We've chosen this book because it's both up to date and written by acknowledged experts in the field.

If you skip ahead to the star charts, you'll notice that we would expect every practitioner in every role to have at least a basic understanding of each competence area: this is the level of knowledge someone would have that has acquired the BCS Foundation Certificate in User Experience.[4] Beyond that, there are different patterns for each role.

The following charts show the mapping for both junior and senior practitioners. The solid line shows the minimum levels of competence for a junior practitioner and the arrows show the areas where a senior practitioner should extend into (the "4" and "5" areas). Because of their breadth of experience, we would expect senior practitioners to show an expansion into 2s and 3s in other competencies too. However, to keep the diagrams simple, we've not shown this.

The question of what an optimal star chart looks like is ultimately going to vary with each person, their personal goals, and the needs of the organization. But the following role-based descriptions may help you with this discussion. And just as importantly, this approach should prevent your team from trying to recruit clones of themselves. It should help everyone realize the range of competencies needed by a fully rounded user experience team.

UX Researcher

Merholz and Skinner describe the UX researcher as responsible for generative and evaluative research. Generative research means field research to generate "insights for framing problems in new ways" and evaluative research means testing the "efficacy of designed solutions, through observing use and seeing where people have problems." The competence signature we would expect to see of someone in this role would show expertise in user needs research and usability evaluation (Figure 6.2).

Figure 6.2: The solid line shows the minimum competence levels for a junior UX researcher. The arrows show the levels that senior practitioners should attain (usually 4s and 5s). Because of their breadth of experience, senior practitioners should also display a broader signature (2s and 3s) in other areas of the star chart (this will be individual-specific and not role-specific)

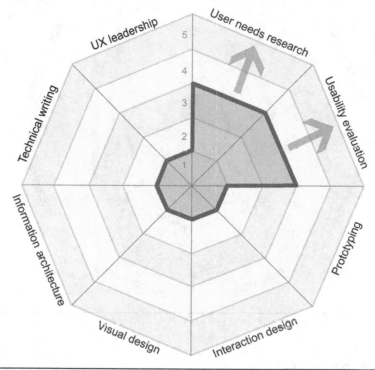

Product Designer

Merholz and Skinner describe the Product Designer as "responsible for the interaction design, the visual design and sometimes even front-end development." The competence signature we would expect to see of someone in this role would show expertise in visual design and interaction design and to a lesser extent, prototyping (Figure 6.3).

Figure 6.3: The solid line shows the minimum competence levels for a junior product designer. See the legend of Figure 6.2 for more detail

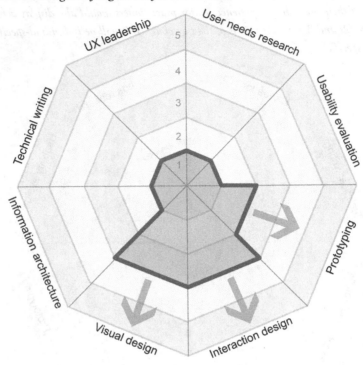

Creative Technologist

Merholz and Skinner describe the Creative Technologist as someone who helps the development team explore design solutions through interactive prototyping. This role is distinct from front-end development: "The Creative Technologist is less concerned about delivery than possibility." The competence signature we would expect to see of someone in this role would show expertise in prototyping and to a lesser extent, visual design and interaction design (Figure 6.4).

Figure 6.4: The solid line shows the minimum competence levels for a junior creative technologist. See the legend of Figure 6.2 for more detail

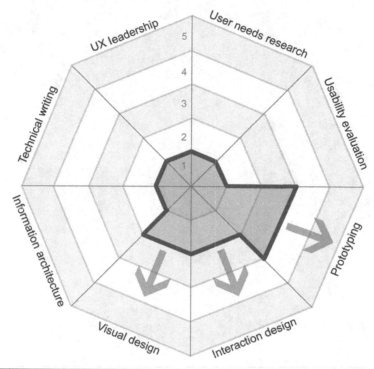

Content Strategist

Merholz and Skinner describe the Content Strategist as someone who "develops content models and navigation design" and who "write[s] the words, whether it's the labels in the user interface, or the copy that helps people accomplish their tasks." The competence signature we would expect to see of someone in this role would show expertise in technical writing and information architecture (Figure 6.5).

Figure 6.5: The solid line shows the minimum competence levels for a junior content strategist. See the legend of Figure 6.2 for more detail

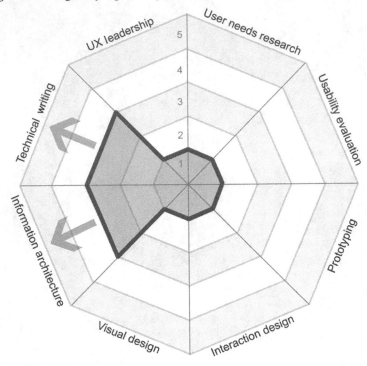

Communication Designer

Merholz and Skinner describe the Communication Designer as someone with a background in the visual arts and graphic design and is aware of "core concepts such as layout, color, composition, typography, and use of imagery." The competence signature we would expect to see of someone in this role would show expertise in visual design (Figure 6.6).

If you are a user experience manager, reproduce Figure 6.2 and ask each member of your team to complete the star chart as a self-reflection exercise. Discuss the results as a group and use the discussion to identify the competency areas where your team thinks it needs support.

Figure 6.6: The solid line shows the minimum competence levels for a junior communication designer. See the legend of Figure 6.2 for more detail

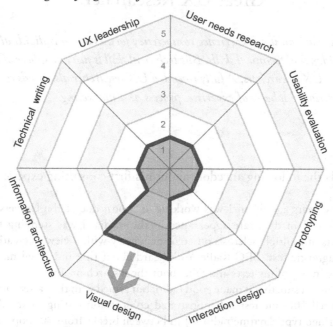

THINK LIKE A UX RESEARCHER

- If you are a manager, discuss the results individually with each team member in a 1–1 to objectively identify areas where your rating of their competence differs from their rating. What behaviors do you expect them to demonstrate to prove they actually are a 3, 4 or 5?
- If you are a practitioner who works in the field, use the template to sketch out your own competence signature. Use the diagram as a benchmark (current state) to identify areas for improvement.
- Compare your signature with the ones in this essay to discover if you are in the role you want—and if not, see what competencies you need to develop to move into a different role.
- Use the diagram to set performance goals for evaluation and professional development purposes.
- If you do not work in the field but are responsible for recruiting people to user experience teams, use the competency descriptions in this essay to set behavioral-based criteria for hiring and writing job postings.

Going Beyond Technical Skills: What Makes a Great UX Researcher?

Most of the work on user experience competency focuses on an individual's ability to show evidence of technical skills. But technical skill is just one sphere of expertise required by UX researchers. A fully rounded UX researcher also needs competence in two additional spheres of expertise: process and marketing.

David tells the following anecdote about his first consulting experience:

Many years ago when I was working as a post doc at the University of York, I made a rare appearance in the media. I was studying the effects of multiple sclerosis on color deficiency with a view to creating a diagnostic test. BBC Radio York heard about this and asked me to bring in one of my tests and talk about the research on air.

I'm not sure that it made good radio, but armed with the Farnsworth-Munsell 100-hue test I demonstrated color vision testing to an Alan Partridge-type daytime radio DJ in between breaks from 80s pop hits.

After my 5-minutes of fame, a local businessman contacted me and asked if I would visit him to discuss the color-coding used on fire extinguishers in his company. I'd always harbored an interest in consultancy and thought this might be a great way to supplement a meager academic salary. I attended my first sales meeting with a certain amount of trepidation but the meeting must have gone well as I won my first consultancy project.

It may have been just two days of work, but I learned an important lesson from this assignment.

Lesson 1: It's a lot easier to sell consultancy to clients if they have a personal interest in your work. Because it turned out that my first client was color blind—and I suspect he was more interested in me assessing his color vision on company time than in the detailed report I wrote on color-coding in fire extinguishers.

A few years later, I learned a second important lesson about consultancy.

I had started my career in human factors proper at BT Labs in Ipswich. During that period, I remember coming across various "one-man band" consultants. I was impressed that these consultants were providing practical, human factors advice to large UK companies and even more impressed that the companies appeared to be acting on their advice.

But if I'm honest, I was also indignant.

I felt that a lot of these consultants had simply pulled the wool over the eyes of their clients because they didn't have a PhD like I did.

I felt that their technical skills were rudimentary at best.

I felt envious because I thought I knew much more about human factors than they did, yet they were the ones making a go of it as consultants.

Until then, I had thought that consultancy was about big companies asking bright people to distill their knowledge into simple words that the company could then act on and exploit. In this view of consultancy, technical competence is everything.

But my experience was telling me something different. Although it took me a few more years to articulate it, I learned Lesson 2: Technical expertise is a small component in making user experience happen. Technical expertise is what gets you in the door, but it's not what makes a great practitioner.

To make the point more directly, I like to use a consultancy activity with which we're all familiar: a visit to a medical professional. Clearly, when you visit medics you want to know that they have passed all their exams and are competent to dispense advice on illness. This is what gets a medic in the door (or you in the consulting room).

Now think back over the medical professionals you've met in your life and work out which one you think was best. The chances are that your decision won't be based on the technical expertise or qualifications of the individual. My favorite was a very amenable GP: He seemed to take time to explain stuff to me, and he spoke to me as an individual, not as a patient. He had a great bedside manner, if you like.

User experience professionals have a bedside manner, too. And it's the bedside manner that's missing from most of the current discussions around user experience competency. Technical expertise, although important, is not enough. We need to consider three spheres of user experience practice:

- Technical skills.
- Process skills.
- Marketing skills.

The First Sphere of Practice: Technical

Any professional person needs a core set of technical skills, and the field of user experience is no exception. In the previous essay, "A tool for assessing and developing the technical skills of user experience practitioners," we listed these competencies:

- User needs research.
- Usability evaluation.
- Information architecture.

- Interaction design.
- Visual design.
- Technical writing.
- User interface prototyping.
- User experience leadership.

Although we might argue over the details, this sphere of user experience is well served by university courses and by the various short courses available in user experience. But user experience training providers do not address the two other spheres of user experience practice: process and marketing.

The Second Sphere of Practice: Process

Process skills are the activities a practitioner uses when managing clients and managing projects. This includes:

- Active listening.
- Helping teams implement change.
- Making appropriate ethical choices.
- Project management.

Active Listening

Active listening means really seeking to understand the client's problem and providing a solution that will fix it—rather than selling the client an off-the-shelf user experience activity like eye tracking that may look impressive but that doesn't address the underlying problem. This sounds easy, but when you're put on the spot as a practitioner it's tempting to simply pull out one of the tools in your box and tell the client this is what he or she needs. It's much harder to admit that you haven't understood the problem and you need to ask more questions. As part of this, it's important to understand the development world that your client really lives in—how things really work inside that company or design group. You need this information to establish the practical constraints for design change.

Helping Teams Implement Change

Helping clients implement your research insights is important because in many user experience activities, the real work begins when the activity is finished. Running a usability test will never make a website usable. Systems get improved not by reports or by presentations but by the development team changing the interface. So the next step after a user experience activity is to express the findings in a way that will encourage the team to take action. This doesn't mean deciding to present the results in a slide deck rather than in a 40-page written report. There is a skill in showing a development team how to fix problems, captured neatly in Steve Krug's aphorism,[5] "When fixing problems, try to do the least you can do." Rather than redesign the interface, his suggestion is to make the simplest change that solves the problem for most people. That's the difference between an experienced consultant talking and someone taking their first steps in the field.

Making Appropriate Ethical Choices

A good consultant needs to make the right ethical choices. From some clients, the pressure to do your research a particular way can be overwhelming. In some cases, the changes may be minor: for example, the client may want you to recruit participants for a user experience activity according to strict marketing demographics, like geographical location or age ranges. As we point out in Chapter 2 ("Arguments against a representative sample"), we know that demographic groupings are rarely important in UX research— and even when they are important the small sample sizes used in usability research render segment-related conclusions meaningless. But since the final impact on the research will be negligible, there's no need to argue every little point. The ethical issue arises when the client insists on more fundamental methodological changes that will affect the outcome of your research, such as running a focus group in place of a usability test. At this point, the good practitioner will resist the change or walk away.

Project Management

Good practitioners know how to manage their time and manage the projects on which they work. It's not important to know the difference between a Gantt chart and a PERT chart, but you do need to know how to estimate how long a project will take and keep the client informed if the schedule looks like it's going to slip.

The Third Sphere of Practice: Marketing

We've yet to meet a UX practitioner who thinks of him or herself as working in sales. But we are, whether we like it or not. Typical marketing activities that user experience practitioners need to master include:

- Explaining the cost-benefit of usability activities.
- Formulating a proposal.
- Generating new work.
- Leaving a legacy.

Explaining the Cost-Benefit of Usability Activities

We can probably all rehearse the main benefits of a focus on user experience. But a good user experience practitioner will be able to ground these examples in the client's domain. This means talking with the client to understand how success is measured and then collecting the data, or providing good estimates, to evaluate the outcomes.

Formulating a Proposal

New user experience practitioners tend to confuse writing a *proposal* with creating a *research plan*. A research plan simply lists the steps in the project, calculates how long each one will take and then provides an overall cost. Although this is an inevitable part of any research program, a good practitioner realizes that a proposal needs much more than this because it is a sales tool. It needs to include a section that gives your client confidence that you really understand the problem to be solved and it needs to list explicitly the benefits that the client will receive as a result of the work. Formulating a proposal also includes revising your proposal based on feedback, negotiating with the client on what can and can't be changed and, when there are several bidders, pitching to the client.

Generating New Work

Generating new work is a necessary evil for both external and internal practitioners. To keep their business afloat, external consultants need to find new clients and sell more to existing clients. Similarly, internal consultants need to identify the next big enterprise project and ensure that the user experience flag gets flown on the project. There's no point having expertise if clients don't get to hear about it. Inevitably, this involves selling your skills. The notion of selling carries a lot of negative baggage, with clients wary of being "sold" to and practitioners worrying that they won't make the sale.

But by being truly client-centered and by behaving authentically, you can overcome this situation (see the essay, "Conducting an effective stakeholder interview" in Chapter 2 for some suggestions).

Leaving a Legacy

Practitioners need to build the business: this means growing a company (or the team you work in) and the industry as a whole. One way to achieve this is to use and contribute to the field's body of knowledge. For example, there are many good resources on the internet that you can use to demonstrate the benefits of UX research to clients. Good practitioners add to these resources by writing online articles, publishing presentations and encouraging people to reuse what they have created. Ultimately, you should be trying to build a legacy: to leave your company, your team and anyone you manage, stronger.

What Are the Implications of the Three Spheres of Practice?

Adopting a model based on broad spheres of practice, rather than a narrow focus on technical competencies, raises a number of implications for ensuring competence in "process" and "marketing" skills.

These skills:

- Are not really amenable to the "chalk and talk" style of teaching found in many university courses. So how will inexperienced practitioners develop them?
- Are harder to measure than technical skills. So how can we incorporate them in any certification scheme?
- May seem soft and woolly. So how can we persuade managers to train their staff in these areas of practice?
- Are not part of existing appraisal and reward systems for user experience practitioners. This means practitioners may be reluctant to develop them, favoring technical skills that can be more easily traded.

Given that these skills require experience and practice, university courses could include a requirement that students spend a certain amount of time in practice before they can graduate. This requirement already exists in some other postgraduate courses; for example, university courses in counseling require students to accrue a certain number of hours in counseling practice ("flying hours" acquired during their course) before they can graduate.

Another alternative is for a professional body like the User Experience Professionals' Association (UXPA) to develop a "practitioner in training" scheme to ensure that graduates in user experience develop these skills post-qualification. Although this requires a significant investment in infrastructure—including supervisors, log books and CPD monitoring—let's hope the appetite exists to make this happen.

THINK LIKE A UX RESEARCHER

- In his anecdote, David says that, "Technical expertise is a small component in making user experience happen." Think back to a project that you have worked on where the team was especially engaged in UX research. Was this solely because of the technical contribution you made or something else? What was that "something else?"
- This essay describes three spheres of expertise: technical skills, process skills, and marketing skills. If you were asked to assess an experienced practitioner in these three areas, how would you weight them? Are they equally important or is one more important than the others? Why?
- Larger organizations are beginning to introduce processes to plan, deliver and integrate UX research with other disciplines (giving us a new term: "ResearchOps"). The purpose behind this is to deliver consistent quality research at scale. What operational inefficiencies are you aware of in your organization's research workflow? Assume you've been asked to re-design the UX research function in your organization: what changes would you make?
- Think about how you are assessed in your job, perhaps at an annual performance review. Are process and marketing skills included in your review (perhaps with different names)? If they're not, how could you persuade your manager to allow you to build these skills?
- Do you keep a blog or publish articles somewhere? What else could you do to "leave a legacy?"

How to Wow People with Your UX Research Portfolio

If you work in user experience, the portfolio has replaced your CV. This is fine if you are a visual designer but for people who specialize in UX research, the portfolio poses a particular challenge. Here are some suggestions on ways to create a winning UX research portfolio.

Portfolios are common in visual arts, like design and photography. Picasso, we're fairly sure, had a portfolio. But they are uncommon to the point of being unheard of in scientific fields, like research and technology. Einstein, we're fairly sure, didn't have a portfolio.

Where did the concept of the user experience portfolio come from? We think that at some point over the last decade, a clueless recruiter or employer asked a UX researcher for their portfolio. In a panic, the job candidate pulled something together, and now it's just seen as a given that a UX researcher will have a portfolio that illustrates their work—even if they don't create visual designs.

So if your work involves voice recordings from field visits, bits of paper prototype, and formulae in spreadsheets—these days, you're still expected to create a portfolio.

The Problem with UX Research Portfolios

Most weeks, one of us receives an email from a prospective employee. The email nearly always has their CV as an attachment; sometimes the prospective employee will also attach their portfolio (or provide a link to it).

It's rare that we see a portfolio that impresses us. If we were the judging types, most of them would, at best, get a C grade.

You're not going to get an interview if that's the best you can do. Almost always, we see the same set of problems. Here are those problems along with some suggestions on how to fix them.

Stop Pretending You're a Visual Designer

Visual designers are in the business of creating interfaces that look good. Depending on the research (or lack of it) that went into the designs, the interfaces may actually not be that easy to use—but the first impression will have impact. First impressions do matter and that's probably why so many researchers try to pad their portfolios with examples of user interfaces.

But this is the worst thing you can do.

If you're a UX researcher, you don't design *screens*. You design *experiences*.

Instead of creating amateurish mock-ups in PowerPoint or—even worse—presenting someone else's design as your own, use your portfolio to showcase the research work that underpins the designs you've been involved with. What were the business objectives? How did you ensure they were met? At what points in the process did you involve users?

Research projects can still be presented visually. Do an internet search for "usability testing infographic" and you'll see what we mean. And there are many deliverables in UX research that are inherently visual: Personas, user journey mapping, and usability expert reviews are three that jump immediately to mind.

Show the Journey, Not Just the Destination

A second common mistake we see in portfolios is that they focus on the deliverables and not the journey.

For example, a research portfolio case study on personas might show the final personas, perfectly formatted, ready for a magazine.

But that's not the challenge.

The challenge when developing personas is doing the field research, analyzing the data, and helping the development team use the personas to create better designs. Creating the personas themselves is the icing on the cake. So although it's less photogenic, you need to explain the research behind the deliverable. (You can still show the deliverable—just make sure to show your working, as a math teacher might say).

Another reason to show the journey is that it keeps you honest. David saw a portfolio once that described how the candidate had designed a successful smartphone app. What the candidate forgot to mention was that he was part of a team of eight, and his main contribution was to run a usability test of a prototype.

Claiming other people's work as your own is a surefire way to lose out at interview.

To make sure you show the journey, *tell the story* of your involvement:

- Explain the business problem you were trying to solve. Just one or two sentences will do. If you struggle with this, try to remember how the project started: How did your internal or external client articulate the problem? In the context of a story, this is the trigger that starts us off.

- Describe your approach. Of the universe of possible research methods, why did you pick that one? Remember that research takes place in a business context and your approach doesn't need to be some mythical, ideal approach; it needs to be an approach that offers the best value. In a story, this phase is known as the quest.

- Present your results. Be brief, but show enough detail to make it clear that you know what you're talking about. Describe one of the major problems you encountered with the study and how you solved it. In any good story, the hero always has to overcome difficulties, and this is the place to show you are a problem solver.

- Describe the impact of your work. Relate your findings back to the business problem. Did you solve it? If not, what did you learn that you will apply to your next project? Show how you moved the needle on an important business metric or at least how you improved effectiveness, efficiency and/ or satisfaction. A good case study will also include descriptions of what went wrong or what you would do differently next time (this demonstrates you are a reflective practitioner). This is the resolution to your story where you, and your client, both became a little wiser.

Assume You Have One Minute to Land Your Dream Job

You spend hours on your portfolio. Sadly, a potential employer will spend one minute looking at it. After one minute, he or she will decide to spend another five minutes on it—or send a rejection letter. We know, it's brutal.

But it's not dissimilar to the way you behave when you land on a web page. You scan it and then quickly make a decision to invest more time or hit the Back button. You can be brutal, too.

This means you must design your portfolio like a web page, for skim reading: headings, bulleted lists, bold text for key points. Don't assume people will read the whole page, even if it's short. Imagine you have

10 seconds of attention per page. Not only does this mean it's more likely to get looked at, it also demonstrates your skills in user experience by showing you know how people read. It's a great example of the medium being the message.

(And if you don't know how people read, why not usability test your portfolio with friends and family?)

In terms of overall size, we know this may not be a great help, but you're after the Goldilocks portfolio: not too long, not too short, but just right. One way to achieve this is to ruthlessly cut out duplicate projects. If you've done three-card sorting studies and two-paper prototyping exercises, it's tempting to include all of them. But don't. Instead, show just one case study of each type. Aim for one to two pages per project and keep it visual. As a rule of thumb, if you feel the need to include a table of contents, your portfolio is too long.

Focus on the Details

This one seems obvious—we all know it's rule number one when you're putting your CV together.

But hold on: There is an interesting twist when you're applying for a job in user experience. Both user research and design are inherently detail-oriented professions.

Of course your spelling and grammar will be ruthlessly examined. But it goes beyond this.

- What font will you use? (Hint: it won't be Comic Sans.)
- What kind of layout grid will you use for your case studies?
- Where is your call to action?

Once again: the medium is the message.

Related to detail is the way you order the case studies in your portfolio. Consider ordering your case studies to show your expertise in all parts of the user centered design process: for example, a case study on fleshing out the research problem; then a case study on creating personas; then one on developing a user journey map; then one on setting usability metrics; then an information architecture study; then a case study on usability testing; finishing off with analytics (such as a multivariate testing case study). It may take a few years to get your portfolio that complete, but it gives you a road map.

"How Can I Compensate for a Lack of Experience Without Lying?"

A variation on this question is: "How can I show more breadth when my day-to-day job is recruiting users or running card sorts or acting as an assistant to someone more senior?"

This paradox has more than one resolution—here are two.

One approach is to set yourself assignments. Let's say you've never run a usability test, and this is the glaring hole in your portfolio. In that case, be your ideal client and run a test. Pretend that you've been commissioned by a major media broadcaster to run a usability test of their catch-up television player's installation process. How did you plan and execute the test? How did you recruit users? How did you analyze the data?

In many ways, carrying out self-assignments shows more dedication than simply turning up for work to deliver on a real project—and it also shows it's all your own work, not someone else's that you've hijacked. If you need some ideas for self-assignments, take an online user experience training course where you get the opportunity to carry out user research and design activities on real life projects.

If the idea of a self-assignment doesn't motivate you, a second approach is to volunteer. There are no end of charities and non-profits who could boost donations with the kinds of insight you could provide with a usability test.

The History of Your Working Life

One final point. Your user experience portfolio also acts as a scrapbook of your working life. When you update it (and you should be updating it every six months or so), make sure you keep the earlier versions. This is a powerful way of showing you just how far you've traveled.

THINK LIKE A UX RESEARCHER

- Start a research journal to reflect on your practice. After each major user research activity, note down the user research activity you carried out; why you chose that specific user research activity rather than something else; what went well or badly; and what you will do differently next time. Consider asking your team (and even your research participants) for additional feedback on your strengths and weaknesses. Turn to this journal when you want to create a new portfolio entry.

(Continued)

THINK LIKE A UX RESEARCHER (Continued)

- Create a case study template in your favorite word processor. This should have four sections: the business problem you were trying to solve; your approach; the results; and the impact of your work (with reflections on how it could be better). Then populate it with a case study. Create a new case study once a month. Start now: make this your new routine.
- Create a portfolio template and begin to add the case studies to it. Design the first page of your portfolio with a photograph of you to draw the reader in. Also add your contact details, such as email, phone, and relevant social media contacts. The second page should be your biography; don't make the mistake of putting this as the last page of the portfolio. At the end of the portfolio, include a list of the training courses or conferences you've attended or presented at. That's also a good place to put some testimonials from happy clients and work colleagues.
- The very best UX researchers, like the very best people in any field, tend to move from job to job based on a personal recommendation or a referral. They may not have a portfolio because they have never needed one to get a job. Is there a risk that companies that insist on a portfolio will fail to hire the very best UX researchers? Considering where you are in your career, does this mean that you, personally, can ignore creating a portfolio? What proof, other than a portfolio, could you offer to show that you are a competent UX researcher?
- Imagine you've been hired to usability test a UX research portfolio. How would you do it? Who are the "users" of the portfolio? What are the tasks or goals? What criteria would you set to distinguish success from failure?

A Week-by-Week Guide to Your First Month in a UX Research Role

When you start a new job as a UX researcher, you need to both charm your work colleagues (so they take action on your future research findings) and challenge them (so they become more user centered). How can you best achieve this in your first four weeks in a new job?

In an earlier essay we referred to a quotation from UX researcher Harry Brignull: "A researcher who is keen to please the design team is useless."

One reason we like this quotation is that it makes the point that as a UX researcher you are like the grit in the oyster. In the same way that the grit irritates the oyster into growing a pearl, the UX researcher is continually finding problems. These might be problems with the initial design concept, problems with later designs or even problems with the fundamental purpose of the product. Your role is not to please the development team but to push them to do better work by understanding users.

There's an obvious risk with this however—the irritation can be taken too far. When you start a new job, it's important not to appear like a know-it-all smarty pants and be overly critical of what has gone before. After all, you are not yet aware of the constraints the development team is under. Perhaps some of those "bad" decisions were in fact the "least worst" decisions that could be made in the circumstances.

So you've started a new job. How can you irritate your colleagues and still stay friends with them after work?

Week 1: Map the Territory

As a UX researcher you will interact with everyone on the development team and many people beyond. Part of your job is to connect these people and create a shared understanding of users and their goals. Think of yourself as the glue that makes a good user experience happen. A good way to achieve this is to get all of your colleagues involved in UX research by planning and observing UX research sessions. And if you've just started the job, this means spending time getting to know people and allowing them to get to know you.

So an effective way to spend your first week is by mapping the territory. What is the product about? Where does it sit in relation to other products? Who makes decisions and whose opinions matter?

You can get this information through informal interviews and meetings. You may need to schedule some of these, especially with the busier members of your development team. But not all of these meetings need to be formal: conversations over coffee or lunch, water cooler conversations, or corridor meetings will all work.

Your aims in this week are to:

- Understand the constraints the team is under. What can and can't be done with the technology? What's driving the timeline?
- Get to know your team members. What is their understanding of user experience and usability? Have they met users in the past or observed any UX research activities? How do they rate the importance of user experience to the product? What is their definition of success—both for the product and in terms of what they think UX is about?
- Identify the stakeholders. Go beyond the development team and identify people in the organization who can make your project succeed or fail.
- Uncover the important business metrics. Hint: "Important business metrics" usually include a currency sign, whether it's about making more money or reducing costs.
- Take lunch and coffee with your colleagues but try not to do this with the same people every day. You need to avoid becoming part of an internal clique.
- Warn people that you need two hours of their time for a workshop next week (more of that later). Get it in their diary.
- If you can't prototype, find someone on the development team who can. They are soon to become your best friend.
- Based on what you've learned, estimate the team's user experience maturity.

Week 2: Help Your Team Understand Their Users

Your most important responsibility as a UX researcher is to help your team better understand their users. The team needs to appreciate that there are different groups of users, that some of these groups are more important than others and that one, or maybe two, of these groups will be the design target. Then you need to help the team gain an in-depth understanding of their users' goals, motivations and abilities.

Your aims in this week are to:

- Start compiling the research that has been done with users in the past (see the essay "How to approach desk research" in Chapter 2). This could be research done by the team or organization or by external researchers, such as universities.
- Run a workshop with the team and get them to create assumption personas. It doesn't matter if these are totally wrong. This exercise is a gentle way of helping the development team realize they are not the user (as well as helping you discover things about your users that you may not know about).
- Use this workshop to gain some understanding of the users' environments too: for example, which devices do they most commonly use?
- Build a research wall. Claim a whiteboard and start to make your work visible. Put the assumption personas on this wall.
- If there's time and budget, spend one or two days this week visiting a handful of users in context.
- If there's little time or a tiny budget, spend a day doing guerrilla research.
- If there's no time or budget for UX research, read over existing research and analyze any user data that's available (like web analytics or call center data).

Week 3: Help Your Team Understand Their Users' Tasks

Tasks are the activities that users do with a product in order to achieve their goals. Helping the team think in terms of users' tasks, rather than system functions, is an important step in getting the team to see the big picture. This is because users' tasks almost always require the use of several functions to complete, so it prevents siloed thinking.

Your overall goal this week is to identify the key tasks that users carry out with your product. This prevents the team from treating every function as equally important and helps prioritize development.

Your aims in this week are to:

- Speak to team members and create a list of all possible tasks. Then get team members to identify what they think are users' top 10 tasks.
- Take this same list of tasks and show it to users. Ask users to prioritize these tasks. You could do this either as part of a field visit to users or by distributing a top tasks survey to a subset of your audience.
- Compare and contrast the task importance rankings made by the development team with the rankings made by users. The more similar the rankings, the better your team understand their users.
- Turn the top handful of tasks (as rated by users) into usability test scenarios.

Week 4: Run a Usability Test

Running a usability test is always a good early activity to do when you join a new development team because it will help you flush out the influential stakeholders and gauge their attitude to involving users in your work (see the essay, "Deciding on your first research activity with users" in Chapter 2). It will also give you an idea of the budget that's available: Is there a usability lab, or are you allowed to hire one? If not, can you do remote, moderated usability testing? Or are you restricted to guerrilla, pop-up usability tests in coffee shops?

In terms of what you should usability test:

- Test the current product or prototype—or if there's no product yet, test the top competitor with around five users.
- If the budget is small, do one remote, moderated session and then do a handful of remote, unmoderated tests.
- If there's no budget, run a usability test with friends and family.

Your aims in this week are to:

- Get the team to observe at least one session, preferably live. If that's not possible, get each team member to review one of the session videos. And if that's not possible, create a highlights reel illustrating the main findings and present this in a show and tell.
- Involve the team in the analysis of the usability problems. First, get each team member to identify problems from the session they observed. Then, as a group, carry out an affinity sort to combine similar observations and decide which problems to fix first.
- Plan the next quarter: If there are gaps around understanding users and tasks, then consider a field visit. If you need a prototype, plan that (this is where your new best friend comes in handy). And if your organization doesn't want you to involve users at all... consider looking for another job.

Parting Thoughts

When starting a new job, people tend to ask themselves (often implicitly), "How are things done around here?" Then most people, over time, fall into step, or adjust their working practices to fit in, thereby negating the whole point of their being hired in the first place (since you are generally hired for what you can bring to the party—not because you can replicate what the organization is already doing).

On the other hand, to charge in and try to change things too quickly is a sure fire way to annoy your team. You need to walk a fine line between irritating your new colleagues and challenging them to become more user centered. Some of the ideas in this essay may just help you get the development team to create a few pearls.

THINK LIKE A UX RESEARCHER

- Implementing some of the ideas in this essay will require you to be assertive with your new work colleagues. This is fine if it fits your normal personality but what if you are less assertive by nature? How can you balance behaving authentically with trying new ways to help the team be successful?

- When you start work in a new organization, it's tempting to make many changes at once. But in his work on user experience maturity, Jakob Nielsen argues that a development team must progress through each user experience maturity level stage by stage. He writes: "A good metaphor is emerging from a deep dive: You can't go directly to the surface without getting the bends."[6] How would you assess the user experience maturity of a development team or organization? And how would you know when the team or organization is ready to move to the next level?

- Our approach is fine if you have autonomy in your job. But assume you have started a new job and your manager tells you that the team has lots of ideas for focus groups and surveys—and you are expected to carry them out. Could you still implement some of the ideas in this essay (albeit over a longer timescale)?

- The chances are that you're not in a new job but have been in your current role for some time. Could you wipe the slate clean and introduce some of the ideas in this essay? We find that blaming a book (like this) is often a good excuse: "I've just read this book on user experience where they suggested…"

- Imagine a situation where you are a new hire and are expected to work alongside another UX researcher. He has been in the company for many years and is very cynical about changing the organization. As you mention each of the ideas in this essay, he responds, "Yeah, I tried that a few years ago and it didn't work," or "That might work in another company, but it's just not practical here." How would you counter objections like these?

The Reflective UX Researcher

Hands-on practice, although important, does not necessarily lead to expertise. The best UX researchers analyze their work, deliberately and consciously. By reflecting on a UX research activity, they are able to increase the learning from a situation, identify their personal and professional strengths and find areas for improvement and training.

UX research is an interesting blend of both theory and practice. Practitioners need to be aware of *theory* to avoid making fundamental mistakes, such as biased protocols, that make it impossible to interpret the results of research. And practitioners also need *experience* to decide on a research approach that is good enough to meet the research objectives. Absence of practical experience can result in a UX researcher proposing activities that don't fit the project's budget or the organization's business goals.

So it's no surprise that most practitioners believe that the route to getting better at their job is to combine day-to-day experience ("learning on the job") with skills-based training courses to fill the gaps in their theoretical knowledge.

As people who train and coach UX researchers, we obviously have some sympathy with this approach. But we are also aware of its limitations. Although some of the people we work with go on to great success, both as accomplished UX researchers and as leaders of development teams, many others have a middling career in UX research or swap to a different career path. When we look at the differences between the groups, there is one behavior that tends to stand out. The most successful UX researchers don't just attend training courses and do the work day-to-day. They consciously and deliberately reflect on their work.

What Does It Mean to be a Reflective UX Researcher?

It's common for UX researchers to log the activities that they carry out either in a notebook or using electronic tools. For example, some UX researchers maintain a spreadsheet that lists details such as the date, the type of research and a short description of the activity. Every UX researcher should be doing this, but this isn't the same as being a reflective UX researcher.

And simply saying that a UX research activity went well or poorly is not being a reflective UX researcher either.

Being a reflective UX researcher means that you think critically about the work you have carried out. This is different from being *critical* of what you have done: it's about *analyzing* your performance. Why did you do it that way? What theory underpins your approach? What organizational constraints did you need to work within? Are there alternative methods you could have used?

The reason reflection is so powerful is because experience alone does not always lead to learning. To really learn from an experience we need to analyze it, deliberately and consciously.

When asking the more successful UX researchers why they engage in reflection, we hear different reasons from different people. Some of the reasons are:

- To improve my practice.
- To identify training gaps.
- To create a portfolio entry.
- To decide what I should do and what I shouldn't do next time in the same situation.
- To see if there are general research patterns I can apply to situations like this in the future.
- To create talks for conferences.
- To create articles for websites.
- To run what-if... scenarios. (For example, you may have wanted to do a field visit but been prevented from doing so because of budget constraints. On reflection, how would this have helped or hindered the final impact of the research?)

What Form Does Reflection Take?

Reflection can take many forms, and it's important to choose a method that suits your way of working. For example, if you spend an hour commuting every day, you could reflect in your head: It's not critical to have it written down. The *form* of reflection is less important than the *way* you reflect. Superficial reflection, or doing it because you feel you have to, won't get you very far. In the best kind of reflection, the UX researcher analyses what they have done, using evidence to decide how the activity could have been improved.

Nevertheless, a written record does have some benefits: The act of revisiting your journal on a periodic basis reminds you about what you thought was important. Think of the way some social media applications repost an event from your past. It immediately reminds you of something that you deemed important at an earlier point in your life. As you become more experienced, revisiting the event gives you the opportunity to think of advice you would give to your earlier self.

Here are some ways to make reflection part of your routine:

- Keep a Moleskine log book.
- Create an electronic notebook.
- Build a template in a word processor.
- Create a video or audio diary.
- Discuss the research activity with other UX researchers in your organization.
- Seek feedback from people on the project team whose opinion you respect.
- Ask for feedback from your research participants.
- Review participant videos (if you have them) to identify good and poor practice in the way you moderate usability tests or run user interviews.
- Talk with a mentor or a colleague outside the team or organization where you work.

It's true that you could hold a project post-mortem or a sprint retrospective. But, although this is good practice at the project level, this method isn't an ideal way to improve the UX research you carry out. This is because the attendees will want to discuss issues other than UX research, so you may find the UX research component is discussed for only a few minutes. Also, the team may not be that interested in UX research or be able to provide the quality of critical insight that you need.

When Should You Reflect?

This is something you should be doing continuously: not necessarily at the end of a project, but after each stage of a project. For example, you might do it after you've scoped the research plan with stakeholders, after you've recruited participants, after running a particularly good (or bad) user session, or after a show and tell with the development team. As a rule of thumb, whenever you find yourself worrying over a phase of the work, or feeling good about how something went, that's probably a good time to reflect. Initially, to make it part of your routine, try reflecting at the end of each sprint.

A Format for Reflection

If you're struggling for more specifics, here's a format you could use. But remember, it's important to do this in a way that will work for you, even if that's simply having a "meeting with yourself" in a coffee shop.

- What UX research activity did you carry out? Include the date, the type of research, a short description of the activity, the sample size, the session length and the total time spent.
- Why did you do that specific UX research activity rather than something else?
- What, specifically, went well? Try to identify two or three aspects.
- What, specifically, went badly? Try to identify two or three aspects.
- Analyze. For each of the aspects you have identified as good or bad, ask "Why?" Be careful to avoid superficial reflection and aim for a deeper level of understanding. Consider using the 5 Whys[7] technique to get a fuller understanding.
- Integrate into your practice. Thinking about what went well, how can you apply it to other situations? Under what situations might this approach *not* be effective?
- Ask, "What if?" Thinking about what went badly, how can you prevent this from happening in the future? What would you do differently in this type of situation next time?

THINK LIKE A UX RESEARCHER

- Use the format we've described to reflect on your most recent UX research activity. What would you have done differently?
- Sir Winston Churchill once said, "There is never a good time for a vacation so take one anyway." We might do worse than borrow his advice and apply it to our own work schedules when trying to find time to stop and think, to reflect on what we're doing. Take a look right now at your own daily work schedule. Allocate 15 minutes either at the very beginning or end of each working week and call those periods "Time for Reflection."
- Why is a team debrief not the same thing as reflecting on a project?
- At the risk of finding yourself "through the looking-glass," try reflecting on reflecting. In other words, think about how useful your reflecting method is and how you can improve it. Is the technique working for you? If not, what's getting in the way?
- How is reflecting on something different to other common techniques such as meditation or mindfulness? Specifically with respect to improving your UX research outcomes and your own user experience career, what other self-assessment techniques might be helpful?

Endnotes

Chapter 1

[1]Nisbett, R.E. & Wilson, T.D. (1977). "Telling more than we can know: Verbal reports on mental processes." *Psychological Review*, **84**(3): 231–259.

[2]Kahneman, D. & Tversky, A. (1979). "Prospect theory: An analysis of decision under risk." *Econometrica*, **47**(2): 263–291.

[3]Fitzpatrick, R. (2013). *The Mom Test: How to Talk to Customers and Learn If Your Business Is a Good Idea When Everyone Is Lying to You*. CreateSpace Independent Publishing Platform.

[4]Spool, J.M. (2011, March). "Fast path to a great UX–increased exposure hours." https://articles.uie.com/user_exposure_hours/.

[5]Both of us have PhDs in experimental psychology: David's is in vision and Philip's is in speech. We hope one day to team up with an expert in hearing so that we can form a consultancy band called The Three Monkeys.

[6]Conan Doyle, A. (1892). "A Scandal in Bohemia." In *The Adventures of Sherlock Holmes*. London, UK: George Newnes.

[7]Conan Doyle, A. (1892). "The Boscombe Valley Mystery." In *The Adventures of Sherlock Holmes*. London, UK: George Newnes.

[8]Conan Doyle, A. (1894). "The cardboard box." In *The Memoirs of Sherlock Holmes*. London, UK: George Newnes.

[9]Conan Doyle, A. (1894). "The red-headed league." In The Adventures of Sherlock Holmes. London, UK: George Newnes.

[10]Wikipedia. (2018, May). "Locard's exchange principle." https://en.wikipedia. org/ wiki/Locard%27s_exchange_principle.

[11]Ries, E. (2011). *The Lean Startup: How Constant Innovation Creates Radically Successful Businesses*. London, UK: Portfolio Penguin.

[12]One of our favorite examples is the "connected kitchen" concept. When we discuss this with people, most people agree that it would be cool to have your washing machine send you a text when it has completed its cycle, but "cool" doesn't necessarily mean useful.

[13]Tinbergen, N. (1963). "On aims and methods of ethology." *Zeitschrift für Tierpsychologie*, 20: 410–433.

[14]Martin, P. & Bateson, P. (1986). *Measuring Behavior: An Introductory Guide*. Cambridge, UK: Cambridge University Press.

[15]If you'd like to see this effect in practice, we urge you to view this video on YouTube: https://youtu.be/wRqyw-EwgTk. It demonstrates how compelling this phenomenon is.

[16]Lewin, K. (1936/2015). *Principles of Topological Psychology*. Translated by F. Heider. New York: Martino Fine Books.

[17]Design Council. (2005). "A study of the design process". https://www. designcouncil.org.uk/sites/default/files/asset/document/ElevenLessons_ Design_Council%20(2).pdf

[18]Godin, S. (2009, December). "First, organize 1,000." https://seths. blog/2009/12/first-organize-1000/.

[19]Allen, J., Reichheld, F.F., Hamilton, B. & Markey, R. (2005). "Closing the delivery gap: How to achieve true customer-led growth." Bain & Company, Inc. http://bain.com/bainweb/pdfs/cms/hotTopics/closingdeliverygap.pdf.

[20]Wikipedia. (2018, June). "Illusory superiority." https://en.wikipedia.org/wiki/Illusory_superiority.

[21]Svenson, O. (1981). "Are we all less risky and more skillful than our fellow drivers?" *Acta Psychologica*, **47**(2): 143–148.

Chapter 2

[1]Anderson, S. (2010, December). "$6.7 billion spent on marketing research each year." http://www.mdxresearch.com/6-7-billion-spent-on-marketingresearch-each-year/

[2]Deshpande, R. (2000). *Using Market Knowledge*. Thousand Oaks, CA: Sage Publications.

[3]Badke, W.B. (2011). *Research Strategies: Finding Your Way Through the Information Fog*. Bloomington, In: iUniverse.

[4]Defeo, J.A. & Juran, J.M. (2010). *Juran's Quality Handbook: The Complete Guide to Performance Excellence*, 6th ed. New York: Mcgraw-Hill Education.

[5]Pirsig, R. (1974). *Zen and the Art of Motorcycle Maintenance: An Inquiry into Values*. New York: William Morrow and Company.

[6]ISO 9241-11:2018 Ergonomics of human-system interaction—Part 11: Usability: Definitions and concepts.

[7]The Guardian. "How do I become…" https://www.theguardian.com/money/series/how-do-i-become-a

[8]The Guardian. "What I'm really thinking." https://www.theguardian.com/lifeandstyle/series/what-im-really-thinking

[9]Khalsa, M. (2008). *Let's Get Real or Let's Not Play: Transforming the Buyer/ Seller Relationship*, Expanded Edition. New York: Portfolio.

[10]Ries, E. (2011). *The Lean Startup: How Constant Innovation Creates Radically Successful Businesses*. London, UK: Portfolio Penguin.

[11]BBC News. (2016, May). "Guy Goma: 'greatest' case of mistaken identity on live TV ever?" https://www.youtube.com/watch?v=e6Y2uQn_wvc

[12]Wandke, H., Sengpiel, M. & Sönksen, M. (2012). "Myths about older people's use of information and communication technology." *Gerontology*, **58**(6): 564–570.

[13]Nielsen, J. (2000, March). "Why you only need to test with 5 users." https://www.nngroup.com/articles/why-you-only-need-to-test-with-5-users/

[14]Nielsen, J. & Landauer, T.K. (1993). "A mathematical model of the finding of usability problems." *CHI '93 Proceedings of the INTERACT '93 and CHI '93 Conference on Human Factors in Computing Systems*, pp. 206–213.

[15]Sauro, J. (2010, March). "Why you only need to test with five users (explained)." https://measuringu.com/five-users/

[16]Lindgaard, G. & Chattratichart, J. (2007). "Usability testing: What have we overlooked?" *CHI '07 Proceedings of the SIGCHI Conference on Human Factors in Computing Systems*, pp. 1415–1424.

[17]Hertzum, M., Jacobsen, N.E. & Molich, R. (2014). "What you get is what you see: Revisiting the evaluator effect in usability tests." *Behaviour & Information Technology*, **33**(2): 143–161.

Chapter 3

[1]GDPR places a number of requirements on how UX researchers should handle personal data. For a good review of the situation as it applies to UX researchers, see Troeth, S. & Kucharczyk, E. (2018, April). "General Data Protection Regulation (GDPR) and user research." https://medium.com/design-research-matters/general-data-protection-regulation-gdpr-and-user-research-e00a5b29338e.

[2]Malinowski, B. (1922). *Argonauts of the Western Pacific.* New York: E.P. Dutton & Co.

[3]Mead, M. (1928). *Coming of Age in Samoa.* New York: William Morrow and Company.

[4]Venkatesh, S. (2009). *Gang Leader for a Day. London,* UK: Penguin.

[5]Hughey, M. (2012). *White Bound: Nationalists, Antiracists, and the Shared Meanings of Race.* Stanford, CA: Stanford University Press.

[6]Corbett, S. (2008, April). "Can the cellphone help end global poverty?" https://www.nytimes.com/2008/04/13/magazine/13anthropology-t.html.

[7]Beyer, H. & Holtzblatt, K. (1997). *Contextual Design: Defining Customer-Centered Systems.* San Francisco, CA: Morgan Kaufmann.

[8]Lindgaard, G. & Chattratichart, J. (2007) "Usability testing: What have we overlooked?" *CHI '07 Proceedings of the SIGCHI Conference on Human Factors in Computing Systems,* pp. 1415–1424.

[9]Vicente, K.J. (2004). *The Human Factor: Revolutionizing the Way People Live with Technology.* New York: Routledge.

[10]Nielsen, J. & Landauer, T.K. (1993). "A mathematical model of the finding of usability problems." *Proceedings ACM/IFIP INTERCHI'93 Conference,* Amsterdam, the Netherlands, April 24–29, pp. 206–213.

[11]Nielsen, J. (1995). "10 usability heuristics for user interface design." https://www.nngroup.com/articles/ten-usability-heuristics/.

[12]ISO 9241-110. (2006). Ergonomics of human-system interaction—Part 110: Dialogue principles.

[13]Kandel, E.R. (2007). *In Search of Memory: The Emergence of a New Science of Mind.* New York: W. W. Norton & Company.

[14]Ries, E. (2011). *The Lean Startup: How Constant Innovation Creates Radically Successful Businesses.* London, UK: Portfolio Penguin.

[15]Kramer tries something similar in an episode of Seinfeld, with hilarious results: https://youtu.be/qM79_itR0Nc.

[16]Cordaro, L. & Ison, J.R. (1963). "Psychology of the scientist: X. Observer bias in classical conditioning of the planarian." *Psychological Reports,* **13**(3): 787–789.

[17]Rosenthal, R. (1966). *Experimenter Effects in Behavioral Research.* New York: Appleton-Century-Crofts.

[18]Goldacre, B. (2013). "Trial sans error: How pharma-funded research cherrypicks positive results." https://www.scientificamerican.com/article/trial-sanserror-how-pharma-funded-research-cherry-picks-positive-results/.

[19]Lexchin, J., Bero, L.A., Djulbegovic, B. & Clark, O. (2003). "Pharmaceutical industry sponsorship and research outcome and quality: Systematic review." https://www.ncbi.nlm.nih.gov/pmc/articles/PMC156458/.

[20]Rea, S. (2015, June). "Researchers find everyone has a bias blind spot." https://www.cmu.edu/news/stories/archives/2015/june/bias-blind-spot.html.

Chapter 4

[1]Ormerod, P. (2005). *Why Most Things Fail: Evolution, Extinction and Economics.* London, UK: Faber and Faber.

[2]Copernicus Marketing Consulting and Research. (2010, June). "Top 10 reasons for new product failure." https://www.greenbook.org/marketing-research/top-10-reasons-for-new-product-failure.

[3]Royer, I. (2003, February). "Why bad projects are so hard to kill." *Harvard Business Review*, **81**: 48–56.

[4]Sagan, C. (1997). *The Demon-Haunted World: Science as a Candle in the Dark.* Westminster, MD: Ballantine Books.

[5]A spread made from yeast extract that people either love or hate.

[6]Cooper, A. (1999). *The Inmates Are Running the Asylum: Why High-tech Products Drive Us Crazy and How to Restore the Sanity.* Indianapolis, IN: SAMS.

[7]Pruitt, J. & Adlin, T. (2006). *The Persona Lifecycle: Keeping People in Mind Throughout Product Design.* San Francisco, CA: Morgan Kaufmann.

[8]Marr, D. (1982). *Vision: A Computational Investigation into the Human Representation and Processing of Visual Information.* New York: Henry Holt and Co.

[9]Spool, J. (2008, January). "Personas are NOT a document." https://www.uie.com/brainsparks/2008/01/24/personas-are-not-a-document/.

[10]Brignull, H. (2016, July). "The thing that makes user research unique." https://www.90percentofeverything.com/2016/07/12/the-thing-that-makes-userresearch-unique/.

[11]This informal way of prioritizing works well with teams. If you need a more formal approach of prioritizing usability problems, follow the method in the previous essay.

[12]Krug, S. (2009). *Rocket Surgery Made Easy: The Do-It-Yourself Guide to Finding and Fixing Usability Problems.* Berkeley, CA: New Riders.

[13]Nielsen, J. (2001, January). "Usability metrics." https://www.nngroup.com/articles/usability-metrics/.

[14]Ramsay, A. (2011, July). "The UX of user stories, part 1." http://coderchronicles.org/2011/07/16/the-ux-of-user-stories-part-1/.

[15]Spool, J.M. (2009, January). "The $300 million button." https://articles.uie.com/three_hund_million_button/.

[16]Powell, D., Yu, J., DeWolf, M. & Holyoak, K.J. (2017). "The love of large numbers: A popularity bias in consumer choice." *Psychological Science*, 28(10): 1432–1442.

[17]Jarrett, C. (2016, April). "The survey octopus - getting valid data from surveys." https://www.slideshare.net/cjforms/the-survey-octopus-getting-valid-data-from-surveys-60948263.

[18]You can read more about sample sizes here: SurveyMonkey. "Sample size calculator." https://www.surveymonkey.co.uk/mp/sample-size-calculator/.

[19]Office for National Statistics. (2018, May). "Internet users in the UK: 2018." https://www.ons.gov.uk/businessindustryandtrade/itandinternetindustry/bulletins/internetusers/2018.

[20]Pew Research Center. (2018, March). "11% of Americans don't use the internet. Who are they?" http://www.pewresearch.org/fact-tank/2018/03/05/ some-americans-dont-use-the-internet-who-are-they/.

Chapter 5

[1]Spool, J.M. (2011, March). "Fast path to a great UX-increased exposure hours." https://articles.uie.com/user_exposure_hours/.

[2]Jarrett, C. (2014, July). https://twitter.com/cjforms/status/485001003226648577.

[3]These lean methods of reporting will not work in every situation. Some products, such as medical devices, do require a paper trail (known as "The Usability Engineering File") in order to comply with medical device standards, such as ISO/IEC 62366: Medical Devices—Part 1: Application of Usability Engineering to Medical Devices.

[4]Michalko, M. (2006). *Thinkertoys: A Handbook of Creative-Thinking Techniques*, 2nd ed. Berkeley, CA: Ten Speed Press.

[5]Scarc. (2008, October). "Clarifying three widespread quotes." https://paulingblog.wordpress.com/2008/10/28/clarifying-three-widespread-quotes/

[6]Say, M. (2013, July). "Creativity: How constraints drive genius." https://www.forbes.com/sites/groupthink/2013/07/12/creativity-how-constraints-drive-genius/

[7]Michalko, M. (2006). *Thinkertoys: A Handbook of Creative-Thinking Techniques*, 2nd ed. Berkeley, CA: Ten Speed Press.

[8]Sutton, B. (2009, February). "5127 failed prototypes: James Dyson and his vacuum cleaner." http://bobsutton.typepad.com/my_weblog/2009/02/5127-failed-prototypes-james-dyson-and-his-vacuum-cleaner.html.

[9]Moore, G.A. (1991). *Crossing the Chasm: Marketing and Selling Technology Products to Mainstream Customers*. New York: Harper Business Essentials.

[10]Wikipedia. (2018, June). "Dick Dale." https://en.wikipedia.org/wiki/Dick_Dale.

[11]Vlaskovits, P. (2011, August). "Henry Ford, innovation, and that 'faster horse' quote." https://hbr.org/2011/08/henry-ford-never-said-the-fast.

[12]Morris, B. (2008, March). "Steve Jobs speaks out." http://money.cnn.com/galleries/2008/fortune/0803/gallery.jobsqna.fortune/3.html.

[13]Prigg, M. (2012, March). "Sir Jonathan Ive: The iMan cometh." https://www.standard.co.uk/lifestyle/london-life/sir-jonathan-ive-the-imancometh-7562170.html

[14]Sheff, D. (1985, February). "Playboy interview: Steve Jobs." http://reprints.longform.org/playboy-interview-steve-jobs.

[15]Houde, S. & Hill, C. (1997). "What do prototypes prototype?" *In Handbook of Human-Computer Interaction* (2nd ed.), M. Helander, T. Landauer and P.Prabhu (Eds.). Amsterdam, the Netherlands: Elsevier Science.

[16]ISO 9241-11:2018 Ergonomics of human-system interaction—Part 11: Usability: Definitions and concepts.

[17]Feynman, R.P. & Leighton, R. (1985). "Cargo cult science." *In Surely You're Joking, Mr. Feynman! Adventures of a Curious Character*. New York: W.W.Norton.

[18]ISO 9241-210. (2010). Ergonomics of human-system interaction—Part 210: Human-centred design for interactive systems.

Chapter 6

[1]Peter, L.J. & Hull, R. (2011). *The Peter Principle: Why Things Always Go Wrong*, Reprint Edition. New York: Harper Business.

[2]Wikipedia. (2018, June). "Dunning–Kruger effect." https://en.wikipedia.org/wiki/Dunning–Kruger_effect.

[3]Merholz, P. & Skinner, K. (2016). *Org Design for Design Orgs: Building and Managing In-House Design Teams*. Sebastopol, CA: O'Reilly Media.

[4]BCS. (2018). "User experience foundation certificate." https://certifications.bcs.org/category/18446.

[5]Krug, S. (2009). *Rocket Surgery Made Easy: The Do-It-Yourself Guide to Finding and Fixing Usability Problems*. Thousand Oaks, CA: New Riders.

[6]Nielsen, J. (2006, May). "Corporate UX maturity: Stages 5-8." https://www.nngroup.com/articles/ux-maturity-stages-5-8/.

[7]Wikipedia. "5 whys." https://en.wikipedia.org/wiki/5_Whys.

Index

Note: Page numbers in italic and bold refer to figures and tables respectively.

Printed in the United States
by Baker & Taylor Publisher Services

Printed in the United States
by Baker & Taylor Publisher Services